D0863615

FROM ORPHAN TO ADOPTEE

DISCARDED

UNIVERSITY OF WINNIPEG (LIBRARY), 515 Portage Avenue, Winnipeg, MB R3B 2E9 Canada

DIFFERENCE INCORPORATED

Roderick A. Ferguson and Grace Kyungwon Hong,
Series Editors

HV
875
.58
K6.
P38
2014

FROM ORPHAN
TO ADOPTEE

U.S. Empire and Genealogies of
Korean Adoption

SOOJIN PATE

Difference Incorporated

University of Minnesota Press
Minneapolis
London

Copyright 2014 by the Regents of the University of Minnesota

All rights reserved. No part of this publication may be reproduced, stored in a retrieval system, or transmitted, in any form or by any means, electronic, mechanical, photocopying, recording, or otherwise, without the prior written permission of the publisher.

Published by the University of Minnesota Press
111 Third Avenue South, Suite 290
Minneapolis, MN 55401-2520
http://www.upress.umn.edu

Library of Congress Cataloging-in-Publication Data

Pate, SooJin.
    From orphan to adoptee : U.S. empire and genealogies of Korean adoption / SooJin Pate.
    (Difference incorporated)
    Includes bibliographical references and index.
    ISBN 978-0-8166-8305-5 (hc : alk. paper)
    ISBN 978-0-8166-8307-9 (pb : alk. paper)
1. Intercountry adoption—Korea (South). 2. Intercountry adoption—United States.
3. Interracial adoption—United States. 4. Orphans—Korea (South). 5. Adopted children—United States. 6. Korean American children—Cultural assimilation. I. Title.
    HV875.58.K6P38 2013
    362.734089'957073—dc23
                                    2013028365

Printed in the United States of America on acid-free paper

The University of Minnesota is an equal-opportunity educator and employer.

20 19 18 17 16 15 14   10 9 8 7 6 5 4 3 2 1

To my daughter Sxela
and to Korean adoptees around the world

CONTENTS

Figure 1. "GIs and the Orphans." People rarely associate images such as this with Korean adoption. Still image. "Christmas Party for Korean Orphans, IX Corps, Kinsal, Korea." National Archives at College Park.

FAMILY PORTRAIT shows Holt in Seoul sitting on floor of mission house clutching Paul, 10 months (left), and Betty, 8 months. On floor (left to right) are Joseph, 3½, Helen, 1, Christine, 2½, Nathaniel, 1½, Mary, 3, and Robert, 3.

Figure 2. "Holt Family Portrait." Considered the birth of Korean adoption, this picture encapsulates the dominant narrative of Korean adoption. Photograph by the Harry Holt Family. Used with permission from the Harry Holt Family and Holt International Children's Services.

INTRODUCTION

Challenging the Official Story of Korean Adoption

CONSIDER THESE TWO IMAGES. Both pictures were taken in South Korea. Figure 1 is a still image from a film produced by the Department of Defense on Christmas Eve in 1953, five months after the Korean War ended in a cease-fire agreement along the thirty-eighth parallel, or the demilitarized zone.[1] It features three orphans held in the arms of servicemen from IX Corps who organized a Christmas party for them. The second image was featured in a 1955 *Life* magazine article to document the inauguration of Harry Holt as the founding father of Korean adoption via the unprecedented adoption of these eight mixed-race Korean children. This single event has been considered the birth of Korean adoption as we now know it.[2] Indeed, historical accounts of Korean adoption almost always begin with Holt's adoption of these children. The story goes something like this. At the end of the Korean War, thousands of Korean children were orphaned. Harry Holt saw a need and decided to do something about it. Not only did he adopt eight Korean orphans (despite having six biological children of his own), but he also started his own adoption agency so that other American couples could adopt. Projected as a humanitarian rescue, in which kind and generous Americans opened their hearts and homes to needy orphans, this image has become the dominant face of Korean adoption.

What happens if we situate the emergence of Korean adoption in Figure 1 rather than Figure 2? When paired alongside the first image, "Holt Family Portrait" becomes entwined in a complex set of historical and geopolitical conditions. Figure 1 makes visible the militarized, gendered, racialized, sexualized, and imperialist dimensions of Korean adoption that the second photo elides through the depiction of Korean adoption as both a rescue project and a reproduction of white heteronormative kinship building. What Figure 1 makes explicit that Figure 2 conceals is the direct relationship between U.S. military occupation and Korean adoption. This is precisely what is wrong with the "Holt Family Portrait" becoming the face of Korean adoption: it eschews the role that the U.S. military played in creating the conditions in which Korean children could be made available for adoption. Beginning the story of Korean adoption with the act of rescue elides everything that came before that rescue.

From Orphan to Adoptee challenges this story of Korean adoption by situating it in Figure 1 in order to provide alternative genealogies of Korean adoption and the children involved: the orphan and the adoptee. By investigating the material conditions that made these two images possible, I locate Korean adoption within the context of U.S. militarization and empire-building projects during the Cold War era in order to illuminate the role that Korean children—both orphans and adoptees—played in facilitating neocolonial relations between the United States and Korea. More to the point, I reveal that the "Holt Family Portrait" is no less implicated in U.S. militarism; rather, I contend that these images are simply two versions of the same thing: American empire. In so doing, my project bridges the emergent field of critical adoption studies with transnational American studies by framing Korean adoption as a sine qua non of U.S. neocolonialism in Korea.

Taking into consideration these two images is particularly significant because a genealogical investigation of Korean adoption cannot take place without a rigorous accounting of the children involved. Without the figures of the Korean orphan and adoptee, Korean adoption could not exist. The arrival of the Korean orphan and adoptee signals the arrival of Korean adoption. Thus, a central objective of this book is to mine alternative histories of Korean adoption while at the same time investigating the subject formation of the orphan and the adoptee. Because the same forces that produced Korean adoption also produced the figures of the Korean orphan and adoptee, a genealogical investigation of Korean adoption is also a genealogical investigation of these two images.

In this book, I call for a reorientation of how we understand the history and persistence of Korean adoption by taking into consideration the geopolitical, socioeconomic, and cultural conditions of the Cold War era. Specifically, I situate Korean adoption and the subject formations of the Korean orphan and Korean adoptee within the following contexts: U.S. militarism, Cold War Orientalism, and white heteronormative kinship formation. On the basis of my archival research, I locate the emergence of Korean adoption neither in the Korean War (1950–53) nor in the postwar recovery efforts of the United States, but rather within the context of U.S. military occupation of the southern portion of Korea that began in 1945—five years before the Korean War and ten years before the official beginning of Korean adoption. This is a bold departure from historical studies of Korean adoption. Indeed, while a handful of scholars in the field of critical adoption studies are attending to the role that the U.S. military has played in creating the conditions of Korean adoption, they usually do so in the context of U.S. soldiers fathering mixed-race babies—the first population of Korean orphans to be adopted formally. Thus, these studies revise the official story of Korean adoption by placing it within the Korean War. This is problematic because it takes for granted that Korean adoption emerged from the devastating conditions caused by the Korean War. If Korean adoption emerged as a natural consequence of war, then why does it still persist sixty years later? If it was a by-product of postwar conditions, then it should have ceased, considering that South Korea is no longer a developing country.[3] Instead, the adoption of Korean children by Americans continues long after the warlike conditions have subsided. Thus, I suggest that rather than a natural consequence of war, Korean adoption emerged from the neocolonial relations between the United States and South Korea.[4] This relationship did not begin in 1950 with the start of the Korean War but in 1945.

Taking into consideration the interminable nature of U.S. imperialist and geopolitical investments regarding South Korea not only alters our understanding of Korean adoption but also our understanding of the children who are central to this story: the Korean orphan and the Korean adoptee. When we locate the emergence of Korean adoption with Holt, another problem arises: the Korean orphan becomes conflated with the Korean adoptee. Indeed, the terms *orphan* and *adoptee* were used interchangeably in the stories that swirled around the eight children he adopted, suggesting that they are the same. In addition, the dominant narrative of Korean adoption figures the orphan and adoptee as ahistorical, transparent categories of identity, thereby naturalizing the processes and conditions in which a child becomes categorized as surplus and available for adoption. The popular focus on the adoption triad (birth parent, adoptive parent, and adoptive child) that has organized much of Korean adoption scholarship does precisely this. In this formulation, the orphan is disavowed altogether, and the adoptee is seen as self-evident and as always already existing. I suggest otherwise. The Korean orphan and adoptee are actually two distinct entities, each shaped by different political, economic, and social conditions, and each serving the purposes of American and South Korean national interests in different ways. By revealing the marked difference in the production of these two figures, my work departs from current scholarship that oftentimes conflates the orphan and adoptee by presuming that being an orphan is the only prerequisite to being adopted. Just because a child is an orphan does not mean that he or she will become an adoptee. On the contrary, it takes innumerable resources and institutional support to make an orphan adoptable. Thus, this book also attends to the process in which orphans become adoptees, providing yet another genealogy of Korean adoption.

I also locate Korean adoption in the racially integrative project of what historian Christina Klein calls Cold War Orientalism, an ideology of global interdependence and racial tolerance that the United States created in order to justify its global power and expansion in Asia during the Cold War.[5] Under Cold War Orientalism, the family became the prime metaphor for U.S.–Asian relations. Casting foreign relations as sentimental familial relations allowed Americans, for the first time, to imagine familial bonds between white Americans and nonwhite Asians. The family could be mixed race; it no longer had to be defined through blood ties and biology.[6] However, the familial bond imagined between the American and the Asian was not one of siblings or cousins; rather, it was one of parent and child. For postwar Korean orphans, recasting the family in this way helped white Americans to envision the Korean child as a son or daughter while securing the neocolonial relationship between the United States and South Korea. In other words, naturalizing the parent–child relationship between white Americans and Korean children through the practice of Korean adoption worked to naturalize and normalize the neocolonial relations between the United States and South Korea.

Finally, I situate Korean adoption within the project of white heteronormativity, not to perpetuate the idea that adoptive families are normal but rather to expose the limits and failures of this project. Cold War Orientalism made possible a more expansive definition of family that surpassed both biological ties and racial categories; however, this expansion was contingent on the integration of the nonwhite Asian body as white. Current discussions of Korean adoption as a queer formation work to celebrate and illuminate the radical possibilities of this alternative formation of kinship. Indeed, the "Holt Family Portrait" (Figure 2) could be read as a queer formation of family—a family that is chosen rather than one that is born into, a family that eschews heterobiological ties, and a family that is not bound by a single race or nationality. However, the Holt family, like other American families with adopted Korean members, has tried to pass itself off as a normal white American family. In this way, I work to historicize this alternative formation of kinship by pointing out how the industry of Korean adoption, rather than embracing its queer dimensions, instead worked to elide them by assimilating the Korean child as white American. Rather than seeing a mixed-race family in our midst, the editors of *Life* magazine worked hard to construct Holt's new family as a typical (white) American family in their photo essay, "'The Lord is their sponsor': Korean Octet Gets a U.S. Home."

In this one-page photo spread, the "Holt Family Portrait" is accompanied by two additional photographs. One is of Bertha Holt, Harry's wife, rocking Betty and Nathaniel to sleep. It is a typical scene of a visibly sleep-deprived mother trying to get her babies to fall asleep in the nursery. Fatigue from being a new mother exudes from this photograph, as Bertha sits slumped over with a baby cradled in each arm. The maternal energy that radiates from the way the two children rest on her bosom suggests that they have already bonded and attached. The other photograph, which takes up nearly two-thirds of the page, is a picture of Joseph standing triumphantly, modeling his brand-new Davy Crockett jacket, which he received for his birthday, as his two younger siblings look on. Joseph looks absolutely thrilled with his gift, lighting up the entire page with his grin. The journalist acknowledges that the "children were nervous at first" when they arrived; however, as this short photo essay reveals, the children are "now happily ensconced in Crewell [Oregon]," bonding with their new parents and enjoying American life.[7] Apparently, their assimilation into the family has been seemingly just as painless and instant as renaming them with American-sounding names: Paul, Betty, Joseph, Helen, Christine, Nathaniel, Mary, and Robert.

The ideology of Cold War Orientalism constructed Korean adoption as a project of normativity and assimilation, working to integrate Korean children as no different from their white American family members. This project, however, was limited. The nonwhite body of the adoptee, no matter how assimilated he or she may be to white American norms, not only exposes the contradictions of white normativity but also its failure. Although Cold War Orientalism enabled the formation of mixed-race families, it disavowed the mixed-race family at the moment of recognition through assimilative practices and policies. By pointing out the failure of transforming Korean adoptees into white Americans, I offer another genealogy that signals the limits of U.S. neocolonialism. If naturalizing the parent–child relationship between white Americans and Korean children worked to naturalize the neocolonial relationship between the United States and South Korea, illuminating how this process breaks down through the very figure of the nonwhite Korean adoptee reveals the contradictions and limits of Cold War Orientalism as a neocolonial project.

To date, no study exists that proposes the 1945 U.S. military occupation of southern Korea as one possible beginning of Korean adoption. Nor is there a detailed study on the subject formation of both the Korean orphan and adoptee. Since Holt's adoption in 1955, much has been written about what happens to the Korean child after he or she has been adopted. Today, the overwhelming majority of the scholarship on Korean adoption continues to revolve around the adoptee. Furthermore, a thorough investigation of the mechanisms that made orphans adoptable remains absent in the field of critical adoption studies. Here I fill in these gaps by attending to the genealogies of the Korean orphan and the Korean adoptee; I also address the process in which an unwanted Korean orphan transforms into a desirable adoptee. It is in these specific ways that I broaden the field and expand the scope of current discussions taking place that consider the history, legacy, and persistence of Korean adoption.

"Speaking For" versus "Talking Back": Shifts in Korean Adoption Studies

Since Letitia DiVirgilio, a caseworker for Children's Aid Association, published her study "Adjustment of Foreign Children in Their Adoptive Homes" in the November 1955 issue of *Child Welfare,* much has been written about what happens to the adoptee after he or she has been adopted.[8] The primary methods used to study this figure have been predominantly quantitative methodologies of social science, which focus on issues of identity and adjustment. DiVirgilio observed the adjustments of twenty-four children (twelve from Greece, seven from South Korea, and one each from Austria, Germany, Japan, Lebanon, and Turkey) in their new American homes, sixteen of whom were placed through the American Branch of International Social Services (ISS-USA).[9] She concluded that all of the children made smooth transitions into their homes: "None of these children have displayed overt signs of emotional disorder. . . . All of them seemed to show evidence of being glad to be here."[10] Two years later, Margaret A. Valk made similar conclusions in her paper for the National Conference on Social Welfare, "Adjustment of Korean-American Children in American Adoptive

Homes." Drawing from a sample of ninety-three Korean children whose ages ranged from infant to ten years old,[11] Valk concluded that the majority of the children "have been able to adjust to their adoptive homes with such comparative ease" despite the period of struggle and conflict during the initial period of adjustment.[12]

Nearly twenty years later, Dong Soo Kim completed the first nationwide longitudinal study concerning the adjustment of Korean adoptees in the United States. Between 1975 and 1976, Kim collected data through the use of mailed questionnaires. Unlike the two earlier studies, which based their findings on participant observation, interviews with adoptive parents, and reports written by social workers, his subjects included 406 Korean adoptees—a group that consisted of nearly the entire pool of adolescent adoptees placed through the Holt Adoption Program, which later became Holt International Children's Services—and their adoptive parents. The adoptees ranged from twelve to seventeen years of age and were divided into two groups: the early group (those who were adopted at a year old or earlier) and the later group (those who were adopted at six years of age or older).[13] His major findings were as follows:

> As a whole, their self-concept was remarkably similar to that of other American people as represented by the norm group. Their self-esteem and certainty about self were virtually the same. . . . In short, the Korean adoptive children were like other American teenagers in many respects, and they were doing as well as or better than others, although they seemed to have some initial adjustment difficulties.[14]

He also concluded that the adoptee's racial background had little or no impact on the adoptee's concept of self.[15] For Kim, these findings proved that the practice of placing Korean children in American homes was successful in terms of producing happy, well-adjusted, well-developed adolescents. As a result, he recommended that "intercountry adoptions" such as Korean adoption "be continued and or even expanded elsewhere."[16] Nearly twenty-five years after Kim's study, Rita Simon and Howard Alstein conducted their own study of 168 adult Korean adoptees (again from Holt Adoption Program) who were adopted by 124 white American families between the late 1960s to 1970s and came up with similar findings. On the basis of phone interviews with Korean adoptees (ranging from high school age to middle-aged adults), they concluded that "Korean transracial adoptees are aware of their backgrounds but are not particularly interested in making them the center of their lives. They feel good about growing up with the families they did. They are committed to maintaining close ties with their adopted families and are supportive of policies that promote transracial adoptions."[17]

On the basis of the empirical studies of Korean adoptee identity formation by social workers, case consultants, and social scientists, a dominant discourse concerning Korean adoptee identity has emerged: a narrative that posits that race is not a significant factor in their formation of identity, and that the process of assimilation and adjustment is smooth and easy as long as there is an abundance of color-blind love. However, in the past twenty years, Korean adoptees have spoken out against such neat and tidy conclusions about adoptee identity and experience. Through their literature, film, and visual art, adult Korean adoptee artists are providing more complicated and complex narratives of Korean adoption than the one told by social scientists.

Since the 1990s, a body of cultural work produced by Korean adoptees themselves—including literary and cinematic personal narratives, visual art, performance art, poetry, plays, and mixed-genre artwork—has flourished. This flowering of Korean adoptee cultural production, as explained by adoptee filmmaker Nathan Adolfson in 2000, can be attributed to the fact that "a lot of those children who came in the early '70s are in their mid-20s or early 30s, and they're coming of that age where they're starting to question who they are and where they come from and [they're] old enough to articulate that."[18] This blossoming of artistic expression by Korean adoptees is significant considering that for much of the history concerning Korean adoption studies, adoptees have been spoken for by nonadoptees. Indeed, as the editors of *Outsiders Within: Writing on Transracial Adoption* point out, "Over the past fifty years, white adoptive parents, academics, psychiatrists, and social workers have dominated the literature on transracial [and transnational] adoption. These 'experts' have been the one to tell the public —including adoptees—'what it is like' and 'how we turn out.'"[19] Having reached a critical mass, adult Korean adoptees—most of whom are college educated—are talking back, speaking for themselves through their literary and cinematic productions. In *Seeds from a Silent Tree: An Anthology by Korean Adoptees* (1997), the first published anthology of Korean adoptee writing, editor Tonya Bishoff explains the purpose of this pathbreaking volume:

> With this anthology, we seek to break a certain silence—silence from our land of origin, silence from the lands we now inhabit—tongues tied by racism, some external, some painfully internal; tongues tied by social mores, codes, and contradictions; tongues tied by colonialist myths of rescue missions and smooth assimilations.

We hope to shatter these illusions, sowing new seeds for future generations
not to be silent—to seek out themselves and each other, to define, re-define,
explore, and question.[20]

Since the publication of *Seeds from a Silent Tree,* a wave of personal narratives by Korean adoptees in both literary and cinematic form have been
produced, providing an alternative epistemology of Korean adoption that
is rooted in their own experiences and perspectives.[21] Some of the most popular and critically acclaimed works include Korean adoptee memoirs such
as *The Language of Blood* (2003) by Jane Jeong Trenka; documentary films
such as *Passing Through* (1998) by Nathan Adolfson and *First Person Plural*
(2000) by Deann Borshay Liem; and the anthology *Outsiders Within* (2006),
a collection of academic essays, poetry, visual art, and personal narratives
edited by Jane Jeong Trenka, Julia Chinyere Oparah, and Sun Yung Shin.[22]
What these works reveal that past quantitative studies on Korean adoptee
identity do not address are the complex ways in which racial, cultural, and
national difference affect adoptee identity. Rather than depicting the experience of Korean adoption as smooth, peaceful, and progressive, the literary
and cinematic narratives by Korean adoptees present a much more complicated, fraught, painful, and melancholy picture of adoption and identity
formation. By highlighting the contradictions of Korean adoption, these
artists produce personal narratives that act as counterhegemonic narratives.

It is for these reasons that I juxtapose the historical pieces of my project with these contemporary enunciations of Korean adoption. The literary and cinematic narratives of Korean adoptees, as noted by Eleana Kim,
offer an unofficial history of Korean adoption, "one in which histories of
dislocation and displacement reveal the possibilities for counterhegemonic
reimaginings of social relations."[23] These adoptee narratives—because they
address histories of imperialism, immigration, racialized exploitation, and
gendered commodification—are a rich source to confront the contradictions of transnational adoption and to examine alternative understandings
of Korean adoptee subjectivity.

In putting contemporary Korean adoptee cultural production in conver-
sation with archival documents, I also want to illustrate how the geopolitical
and neocolonial conditions that produced Korean adoption also informed
the subject formations of Korean adoptees themselves. It is through these
contemporary enunciations by Korean adoptee artists that we see how certain neocolonialist and geopolitical activities have affected the adoptee. If
the figure of the orphan enables us to get at the historical dimensions of

Korean adoption, then the figure of the adoptee allows us to get at how history informs the present. I am not suggesting that the orphan is a historical subject and the adoptee is a contemporary one. But given my research questions, I use archival materials to investigate the formation of the orphan. Because I believe that any study on Korean adoptee identity formation should include these current works by adult adoptee artists, my examination of the adoptee draws from these contemporary writings. Thus, the time it takes for adoptees to come of age, for adult adoptee voices to reach critical mass, and for the publishing world to take notice and validate their work all contribute to the historical gap between my primary sources.

Theory and Methods

Because this book is a genealogical study of Korean adoption, orphans, and adoptees, I want to explain what I mean by genealogy and describe my approach to history. I engage with history neither to locate a single origin nor to tell a singular tale; rather, taking my cue from Michel Foucault, I interact with history in order to trace the "numberless beginnings" of Korean adoption.[24] According to Foucault, each concept has a genealogy— a history—and it is the task of the genealogist to examine its numberless beginnings rather than to search for truth via the identification of a singular origin.[25] Thus, rather than working to find the origins of Korean adoption, I seek to locate the emergences of Korean adoption and the various moments in which the figures of the Korean orphan and the Korean adoptee arrive. Borrowing again from Foucault, emergence is not the same as origins; rather, "emergence is always produced through a particular stage of forces . . . [It is produced by] the struggle these forces wage against each other or against adverse circumstances, and the attempt to avoid degeneration and regain strength by dividing these forces against themselves."[26] Thus, emergences are produced through conflict, tension, and contradiction, and the attempt to resolve those modes of crises.

Within this context, I investigate how particular moments of crisis, conflict, and contradiction constituted the emergence of Korean adoption and the figures of the orphan and adoptee. Specifically, I examine how they emerged as possible solutions to certain geopolitical and social problems such as expanding U.S. empire during an era of decolonization (chapters 1 and 2), incorporating Asian bodies into the national landscape during an era of Asian exclusion (chapter 3), transforming children considered the "discards of society" into viable American citizens (chapter 4), and assimilating nonwhite children into white families in order to resemble normal American families (chapter 5). Attending to the emergences of Korean adoption rather than the origins of Korean adoption enables me to locate beginnings other than Holt and his rescue mission and to tease out the various discursive terrains that have shaped Korean adoption and its orphans and adoptees.

My engagement with history is neither to produce a singular history of Korean adoption nor to construct a unified picture of Korean adoptee subjectivity. Rather, I juxtapose historical events (such as military occupation and war) with cultural production, including films, magazines, and memoirs, in order to theorize the discursive and material conditions in which the figures of the Korean orphan and adoptee were produced and to highlight the moments of dissonance, tension, and contradictions that shaped their production. It is in these moments that we can observe the shifting investments, particularly on the part of the U.S. government, concerning the production of these two figures and the continuation of Korean adoption.

Tracing the genealogies of the orphan and adoptee is a complicated affair because their formations are implicated in a vast web of historical, geopolitical, economic, and cultural processes that change over time. Their genealogies cannot be contained by a single story; nor can the nuances be fleshed out with a single disciplinary approach or theoretical framework. Therefore, retelling the story of Korean adoption through these two figures requires multiple methodologies and methods. As a historical materialist study of Korean adoption, this project combines archival methods with cultural studies methods.[27] The archival research I conducted at the National Archives, College Park, Maryland, and the Social Welfare History Archives, Minneapolis, Minnesota, has resulted in a collection of primary sources that includes U.S. congressional reports and military documents from 1945 to 1950, film reels produced by the U.S. Department of Defense during the 1950s (which to date have been unanalyzed in scholarly writings), newsreels from the 1950s, newspaper and magazine articles from the 1950s and 1960s, and administrative files and newsletters of adoption agencies from the 1950s to 1970s. My reliance on these particular archival collections—particularly those related to the Department of Defense—signals my attempt to not only rehistoricize Korean adoption but also to reorient the analysis of Asian transnational adoption toward militarism and empire-building projects. Furthermore, it signals my attempt to recuperate the figure of the orphan as a significant category of analysis. And as I noted previously, I also engage with the cultural production of Korean adoptees to shift the generate an "unsettling hermeneutic."[30] Reading the phenomenon of Korean adoption through the lens of postcolonial, feminist, and queer critique unsettles nearly half a century's work that has concluded that Korean adoptees have successfully assimilated and that they are "supportive of policies that promote transracial adoptions."[31] Reading Korean adoption through the lens of Asian American critique unsettles the dominant narrative of Korean adoption as a humanitarian rescue mission. It also unsettles Korean adoption as a pathway to creating "normal" white American families. From this analytic turbulence emerge the contradictions, tensions, and violence—both physical and epistemic—that have been ignored and disavowed by the nation-state and by adoption practitioners. Although I am interested in analyzing the material conditions of production and reception, I am also invested in locating those dangerous moments when imperialist and white heteronormative practices break down and produce Korean orphans and adoptees as contradictions, both incorporable into a U.S. neocolonial narrative while signaling its contradictions and failures.[32] Thus, the ability to locate alternative genealogies is possible through a rigorous accounting of the Korean orphan and the adoptee precisely because they embody the contradictions and limitations of U.S. neocolonial power.

Critical Adoption Studies

My project is situated within the emergent field of critical adoption studies. Historically, the majority of Korean adoption scholarship utilized social scientific methods and fell into three categories: issues related to adjustment (assimilation, acculturation), identity formation (self-esteem issues, racialization), and legislative policies. These studies promoted a celebratory approach to transnational adoption, as they focused on the gains (economic opportunities, familial and national identity, citizenship) accumulated by the adoptee via adoption. In the past decade, however, adoption research has experienced a paradigm shift as scholars examine the structural causes and inequities of Asian transnational adoption.[33] Unlike the adoption scholarship of the past that focused primarily on empirical studies of adoptee adjustment and identity issues, these works take into account the losses that come from being adopted, as well as privilege the perspective of the adoptee rather than the social worker, psychologist, adoptive agent, or adoptive parent.

Despite the proliferation of scholarship in critical adoption studies, there are few scholarly monographs that focus solely on Korean adoption. Tobias

Hübinette's *Comforting an Orphaned Nation: Representations of International Adoption and Adopted Koreans in Korean Popular Culture* (2006) and Eleana Kim's *Adopted Territory: Transnational Korean Adoptees and the Politics of Belonging* (2010) are two noteworthy exceptions. Both monographs are pathbreaking in their own right, but *From Orphan to Adoptee* departs from these books in three significant ways.[34] First, I frame Korean adoption within the context of U.S. militarism in South Korea. Second, I examine the preadoption stage by attending to the subject formation of the Korean orphan. As a result—and this leads me to the third way in which I depart from Hübinette and Kim—I take seriously the role that the orphanage played in facilitating Korean adoption. Indeed, my project is the first to examine the U.S. armed forces' role in the planning, constructing, and financing of the more than three hundred Korean orphanages that were erected between 1953 and 1954—the very orphanages that eventually supplied Holt and other adoption agencies with Korean children for transnational adoption. I would contend that the reason why these orphanages have been overlooked by scholars is because so much of Korean adoption scholarship, both old and new, centers on the adoptee and what happens to the child after he or she has been adopted. However, if we reorient our examination on the preadoption side, the significance of the orphanage and its role in producing not only orphans but also adoptees becomes clear. Thus, my work departs from current scholarship on Korean adoption by being the first book-length study that considers the role the U.S. military played in shaping the Korean social welfare system, that analyzes Korean orphanages, and that takes seriously the figure of the Korean orphan.

From Orphan to Adoptee attempts to bridge the emergent field of critical adoption studies with the postcolonial study of U.S. empire building in Asia. Despite the proliferation of critical analyses of race, nation, and culture in critical adoption studies, the militarized terrain of Asian transnational adoption—specifically Korean adoption—continues to be, for the most part, largely ignored. Whereas the legacies of U.S. militarism in South Korea have been poignantly addressed in studies that examine South Korean nationalism, military prostitution, and comfort women, this kind of analysis is virtually absent in the study of Korean adoption.[35] There is a substantial and exciting body of scholarship that considers how South Korean military prostitutes nurtured neocolonial relations between the United States and South Korea through the services they provided American serviceman. The groundbreaking work of Katharine Moon and scholars such as Ji-Yeon Yuh, Grace Cho, and Chunghee Sarah Soh who have built on Moon's thesis

have cogently articulated how U.S.–South Korea relations have been organized around the figure of the military prostitute.[36] Unfortunately, there is
a lack of scholarship that considers the figure of the Korean orphan within
this same context. I would contend, however, that neocolonial relations
between the United States and South Korea have also been dependent
on the figure of the Korean orphan. As military occupation gave birth to
figures such as the *gijichon* (camptown) woman and the *yanggongju* ("Yankee whore" or "Western princess"), so too did it give birth to the Korean
orphan and eventually the adoptee. There are a few articles and chapter-
length pieces that make the connection between U.S. militarism and Korean
adoption; however, they do so primarily within the context of mixed-race
Korean orphans who were fathered by American soldiers.[37] *From Orphan
to Adoptee* suggests that the impact of U.S. militarism goes much deeper.
Indeed, my archival research reveals that the U.S. military occupation and
intervention in South Korea during the 1940s and 1950s not only militarized its political economy but also its social welfare system. As such,
U.S. military activity in South Korea provided the conditions that set up
transnational adoption as the best solution to the Korean War orphan problem. These conditions were set up years before Holt entered South Korean
borders.

Given the popularity of transnational adoption in the public sphere and
the expansion of U.S. military power in Africa, Asia, and the Pacific, the
field of critical adoption studies must engage with the imperial and militarized dimensions that provide the context and oftentimes the impetus of
rerouting children into homes and families outside their birth country. My
hope is that *From Orphan to Adoptee* offers one model of how we can think
about U.S. militarism and neocolonial power in the context of transnational
adoption.

Summary of Chapters

This introduction opened with a consideration of two images: the "GIs and
the Orphans" and the "Holt Family Portrait." The first two chapters of this
book investigate the material conditions of possibility for the "GIs and the
Orphans." The third chapter examines the conditions that enabled the image
of "GIs and the Orphans" to transition into the "Holt Family Portrait." The
final two chapters examine the conditions that made the "Holt Family Portrait" possible. In tracing the material conditions that led to the emergences
of the Korean orphan and adoptee, I locate alternative genealogies of Korean

adoption. Specifically, I cull the genealogies of the Korean adoptee, whose subject formation begins with the production of the Korean orphan during the U.S. military occupation of the southern half of Korea and ends in the contemporary moment, where adult adoptees are redefining the terms of Korean adoptee subjectivity. Therefore, an effective way to analyze the larger geopolitical, economic, and cultural forces that have shaped Korean adoption is by scrutinizing the production, evolution, and shifting roles played by the Korean orphan and the Korean adoptee in nurturing neocolonial relations between the United States and South Korea. Thus, my chapters are organized to reflect this.

Chapter 1, "Militarized Humanitarianism: Rethinking the Emergence of Korean Adoption," reroutes the genealogy of Korean adoption and the arrival of the Korean orphan away from the Holt narrative and toward the U.S. military occupation of southern Korea after World War II. By using U.S. congressional reports and military documents from 1945 to 1950, film reels produced by the U.S. Department of Defense during the 1950s, and newspaper and magazine articles from the 1950s, I link the development of U.S. neocolonialism in South Korea to the neocolonial practice of Korean adoption by demonstrating how U.S. militarism and its projects of militarized humanitarianism became the precursors to this form of child welfare. If the postwar orphan was proof of the consequences of American military domination, then this figure also became the remedy to that image. Soldiers participated in projects such as constructing and financing orphanages and rescuing Korean children in an attempt to recuperate the eroding image of the United States as an anti-imperialist force. In rehabilitating the South Korean nation by taking care of its children, the U.S. government tried to rehabilitate its image of itself by fostering an image of benevolent helper rather than neocolonial occupier. As a result, these acts of militarized humanitarianism not only militarized South Korea's social welfare system but also fortified American neocolonial power by enabling U.S. military occupation in South Korea to persist under the guise of humanitarian relief and rescue. Thus, I argue that taking care of South Korea's children during and immediately after the war strengthened neocolonial relations between the United States and South Korea.

The orphanages in South Korea that were engineered, financed, and constructed by U.S. armed forces become a key site in not only proposing an alternative genealogy of Korean adoption but also locating the arrival of the Korean orphan as a militarized subject. In chapter 2, "Gender and the Militaristic Gaze," I consider Korean War orphans as the figurative offspring of U.S. militarism by revealing how the codes of militarized prostitution constructed male orphans as American soldiers and female orphans as *gijichon* women. Although projects of militarized humanitarianism worked to disavow the economies of race, gender, sexuality, and empire, militarized prostitution highlighted these economies. Analyzing Armed Forces Assistance to Korea (AFAK) film reels, articles from the military publication *Pacific Stars and Stripes,* and U.S. print media from the 1950s, I locate Korean adoption within the context of militarized prostitution in order to recuperate the racialized, gendered, sexualized, and imperial processes that have made Korean adoption possible. Furthermore, linking the genealogy of Korean adoption to militarized prostitution illuminates the role that Korean children have played in serving the imperial interests of the United States. As militarized subjects, Korean orphans have been used to secure American neocolonialism in South Korea.

Chapter 3, "Marketing the Social Orphan," examines the transformation of the Korean orphan from a militarized subject to a potential American citizen and family member. It ponders the question of how average American citizens could conceive of welcoming Korean children into their homes, given the history of Asian exclusion. What compelled average white Americans to adopt Korean children, given this history? Relying on 1950s newspaper articles, newsreels, and AFAK film reels, I argue that Orientalist fantasies, global capitalism, and the rise of a consumer commodity culture coalesced with the racially integrative politics of Cold War Orientalism to create a discourse of yellow desire that motivated Americans to imagine and welcome Korean children as a part of their national and private family. Informed by the 1950s Cold War Orientalist policies of racial integration, yellow desire runs on the logic that differences can be absorbed through assimilation. I contend that yellow desire facilitated the entrance of Korean children into American homes—making them exceptional state subjects— in an era of Asian exclusion.

Whereas the first three chapters are concerned primarily with the subject formation of the orphan, the last two chapters are focused primarily on the subject formation of the adoptee. Chapter 4, "Normalizing the Adopted Child," centers on answering this simple yet profound question: How does an orphan become an adoptee? Drawing on Holt Adoption Program newsletters, along with administrative files and letters from other adoption agencies (all from the 1950s and 1960s), I argue that the orphanage became a site of Foucauldian discipline that worked to normalize Korean children in order to make them adoptable via techniques of normalization and

Americanization.[38] No longer a site of militarization, the orphanages during the postwar period shifted into "processing stations for children being adopted by foreign families," as efforts to recruit prospective adoptive parents abroad became increasingly prioritized.[39] I use Holt Adoption Program's Il San orphanage as a case study to investigate the ways in which making Korean orphans normal, and therefore adoptable, attempted to ease the very visible disruption that the adoptee's nonwhite body would cause in his or her new American home. Indeed, the orphanage served as a processing station that prepared not only the legal entrance of the child into U.S. borders but also the child's social and cultural entrance into the white American middle-class home. It became the site where South Korea's social outcasts were shaped into useful subjects for the state: economically profitable for South Korea and politically beneficial for the United States by working to assure their successful assimilation into the white American home. Therefore, I argue that it is here, in the processing stations of the orphanage, that the subject formation of the adoptee is forged; it is here where the undesirable orphan transforms into a desirable adoptee.

Chapter 5, "'I Wanted My Head to Be Removed': The Limits of Normativity" serves as a response to the normative project of Korean adoption as explicated in chapter 4. By juxtaposing Holt Adoption Program's newsletter adoption updates (from the 1960s and 1970s) that portray Korean adoptees as model minorities par excellence with Jane Jeong Trenka's memoir *The Language of Blood,* I argue that the figure of the Korean adoptee—upon entrance into his or her new American family—documents the excesses, limits, and contradictions of Korean adoption as a project of white normativity. Even though the adoptee is disciplined in the orphanage to seamlessly assimilate into her new adoptive family, the very presence of the adoptee's body within the adoptive family disrupts the semblance of the all-American (read white) nuclear family. Whereas the newsletters work to promote Korean adoption as a white normative kinship formation—a structure of family that relies on making assimilation compulsory—Trenka's memoir exposes not only the violence and trauma that accompanies such a project but also the impossibility of such a project through the figures of the Korean birth mother and the Korean adoptee. In so doing, she reveals the nonnormative dimensions of Korean adoption. Thus, Trenka's memoir highlights the white heteronormative investments in Korean adoption not to promote it as a seamless project of assimilation and normativity, but rather to dismantle it in order to elicit the potential for Korean adoption to be a radical queer kinship formation.

The genealogies of Korean adoption are multiple and varied. By intro-ducing new primary sources and reading against the grain of conventional notions of Korean adoption, I provide other sites of emergence and other points of entry that may be used to analyze the significance and persistence of Korean adoption. Understanding the figures of the orphan and adoptee as geopolitical and socioeconomic constructions is significant because it not only denaturalizes Korean adoption but also illuminates the pivotal roles they played in building and preserving neocolonial relations between the United States and South Korea. The dominant narrative of Korean adop-tion that depicts it as a humanitarian project or rescue mission or a normal American family, however, makes illegible the material conditions that produced it. By reorienting Korean adoption as a project of empire, I make legible the violent conditions of U.S. militarism, war, neocolonialism, Cold War Orientalism, and compulsory assimilation—the very conditions that enabled the emergence and persistence of Korean adoption, as well as the subject formations of the orphan and adoptee.

1 MILITARIZED HUMANITARIANISM

Rethinking the Emergence of Korean Adoption

TAKING THE FIGURE OF THE "GIs and the Orphans" as the entry point for my investigation into the genealogies of Korean adoption, I use this chapter and the next to explore the material conditions of possibility for such a celluloid composition. What factors made possible the presence of displaced Korean children in the arms of American soldiers? What conditions transformed these casualties of war into trophies to be admired and celebrated? What circumstances brought these disparate groups—American GIs and Korean orphans—together so that by the end of the Korean War, their interaction with each other increases rather than decreases? And why did Korean children hold such importance to the U.S. military? In other words, what factors drove the U.S. armed forces to care so much about Korean children displaced by military combat? The answers to these questions may seem to be located in the Korean War. After all, the still image was taken in 1953, five months after the conflict ended in a cease-fire agreement. Situating Korean adoption within the Korean War, however, elides certain geopolitical and ideological factors that explain why the adoption of Korean children emerged as what was considered the best solution to the postwar orphan crisis. Thus, the answers to these questions do not reside in the Korean War; rather, they can be traced back to 1945, when the U.S. military began its occupation of the southern half of Korea.

Rather than a natural consequence of the Korean War, I claim that Korean adoption emerged from the neocolonial relationship that the United States forged with the southern portion of Korea in 1945 when it set up the United States Army Military Government (USAMG).[1] This neocolonial relationship created the material conditions of possibility of not only the still image but also Korean adoption in general. This chapter and the next thus examine the material conditions that made the image of the "GIs and the Orphans" and Korean adoption possible. It does so by relying on U.S. congressional reports and military documents from 1945 to 1950, film reels produced by the U.S. Department of Defense during the 1950s, and newspaper and magazine articles from the 1950s.

In this chapter, I begin by tracking the emergence of Korean adoption to U.S. military occupation, providing an abbreviated history of the five years (1945 to 1950) that led up to the Korean War. I do this in order to illustrate how certain geopolitical and economic policies that were implemented by the USAMG provided the conditions that made Korean adoption the primary solution to the postwar orphan crisis. I explain that this five-year period implemented a modus operandi of dependency between the two countries so that South Korea's political and social problems would be solved by American money in exchange for South Korea's allegiance to democratic ideals. As a result, I argue that the neocolonial relationship that was set up during this time was an absolute precondition for Korean adoption.

After the cease-fire agreement, the South Korean people and the American military encountered a new problem: the exponential rise in the number of displaced Korean children. Rather than naturalizing the logic that more orphans simply required more orphanages, I link the rise of Korean orphanages in the south to the emerging neocolonial relationship between the United States and South Korea. In the second section, I examine how U.S. military forces, along with American missionaries, came to be on the front lines of battling the orphan crisis at the end of the Korean War. They did so by building and sponsoring Korean orphanages. In this way, U.S. militarism militarized not only the geographical landscape and political economy of South Korea but also its social welfare services.

Constructing and financing orphanages were acts of militarized humanitarianism that worked to solve not only the war orphan problem but also the eroding image of the United States as anti-imperialist. I conclude this chapter by discussing how the rescue of Korean orphans attempted to rescue the image of the U.S. government by presenting the American soldier as a humanitarian. If the postwar orphan was proof of the consequences of American military domination, then this figure also became the remedy to that image. Indeed, the U.S. military projected images of the U.S. armed forces rescuing, aiding, and taking care of Korean orphans to recover and restore the national fantasy of American exceptionalism. In rehabilitating the South Korean nation by taking care of its children through these humanitarian initiatives, the U.S. government tried to rehabilitate its image of itself and its military by fostering an image of benevolent helper rather than neocolonial occupier. However, these humanitarian projects, despite their attempts to alleviate the image of the United States as an imperial force, actually fortified American neocolonialism in South Korea.

By taking care of displaced children after the Korean War, American soldiers and missionaries set up transnational adoption as South Korea's primary method of child welfare and social services. In so doing, the neocolonial relations between the United States and South Korea became preserved through this practice. This chapter works to link U.S. neocolonialism in the southern half of Korea to the neocolonial practice of Korean adoption by demonstrating how U.S. militarism and its policies of militarized humanitarianism provided the conditions of possibility for this particular form of child welfare and for the image of the "GIs and the Orphans."

Laying the Foundation for Militarized Humanitarianism, 1945–50

Toward the end of World War II, the Soviet Union and the United States worked together to fight off the Japanese in Korea. Because the United States did not have enough forces to defeat the Japanese troops, they solicited their Russian allies to help push out the Japanese colonizers in Korea. As a way to evenly distribute the work, Korea was divided arbitrarily at the 38th parallel by two U.S. colonels using a National Geographic map. It was decided that the Russians would be responsible for the northern half, while the United States would concentrate on the southern half. Working together, the Soviet Union and the United States defeated Japan in 1945 and brought independence from Japanese colonization to Korea for the first time in forty years. However, Korea's independence was short lived. Neither of the superpowers left; rather, each occupied their half of the divided peninsula.

The postwar politics of World War II quickly shifted into Cold War politics. Cold War ideology transformed these once allied powers into bitter rivals. What was initially a temporary division became more and more permanent as the Soviets and Americans during the Joint Commission proceedings failed to agree on the terms for establishing a sovereign and independent Korean government. Until an agreement was reached, the Soviets continued to set up a communist nation in the northern half, while Americans modeled the southern part after Western democracy. Installing these political systems under the sponsorship of these two foreign powers turned this Asian nation into a battleground between the Soviets and the Americans. Thus, as Korean social historian Dong Choon Kim argues, the initial splitting up of Korea among these two nations became the "de facto begin-ning of the Korean War. In this respect, the Korean War might be inter-preted as the logical extension of the U.S. and Soviet occupation policy."[2]

For geopolitical and ideological reasons, the United States remained invested in Korea at the end of World War II. At first glance, Korea does not seem like a country that would be in the middle of a fight between the two superpowers of the time. Korea, a country slightly larger than the state of Minnesota, is a mountainous peninsula with seemingly few resources to offer the United States. However, its location—its close proximity to the Soviet Union—made Korea extremely important to the United States. According to the Interdepartmental Committee on Korea (ICK),[3] a com-mittee that made policy recommendations to the Truman administration, Korea was too close to the Soviet Union, making it "vulnerable to Soviet influence."[4] Korea was also important because it was the only place in the world where the United States and the USSR "stand face to face alone. It is a testing ground for the effectiveness of the American concept of democ-racy as compared to Soviet ideology." Therefore, the committee believed that if democracy was not established in Korea, "other peoples and countries throughout the world will instinctively question both the effectiveness and virility of the United States and its form of government." They believed that if U.S. forces left the southern portion of Korea, it would strengthen com-munist ideology around the world, while a firm "holding the line in Korea" would strengthen democracy.[5] For these reasons, South Korea became the "first place in the postwar world where the Americans set up a dictatorial anticommunist government."[6]

The American government also justified their military occupation of southern Korea through the rhetoric of independence. According to ICK, the United States "has long been interested in the progressive development toward independence of dependent and suppressed peoples in the Far East."[7] As such, the committee believed that fighting for Korean independence (ironically via American military occupation) would not only demonstrate this commitment but also increase the confidence of dependent peoples in the United States and "enhance our position in the Pacific. Failure fully to live up to our Korean responsibilities would result in immediate damage to our position in dependent areas and those regions immediately subject to Soviet pressure, a development which would seriously affect our interests throughout the world."[8] Here, the committee sets up Korea as a metonym for democracy, so that winning in Korea means defeating communism not only there, but also around the world. As Donald Pease notes, "The construction of this national enemy in the image of an Evil Empire enabled the U.S. state to represent its imperial practices as preemptive measures that it was obliged to take to prevent the Soviet Empire from incorporating U.S. citizens [and 'those regions immediately subject to Soviet pressure'] within its imperial domain." U.S. imperialism becomes recoded as a national security issue, as a "nation-preserving measure," to justify its military occupation.[9] But perhaps even more significant than this is the recoding of U.S. imperialism as an anticolonial project. In this special report to the president, ICK articulates a version of American exceptionalism that justifies imperial expansion through the rhetoric of decolonization. In so doing, the committee revises the history of U.S. involvement in the Far East. By staging their commitment to decolonization efforts, the committee elides the history of U.S. imperialism in Asia and the Pacific. Korea becomes the newest site where the United States establishes its role as a democratic superpower under the guise of anti-imperialism.

However, being "caught in the grinder of the United States–USSR political ideological war," as the USAMG military governor, General John R. Hodge, so vividly wrote in a memo, left the Korean people to suffer physically.[10] Louise Yim, the first Korean delegate for the United Nations (from 1945 to 1948), reported in 1947 that the negotiations between the Soviet Union and the United States over the "unification for Korea" or the "Democratization of Korea" were, ironically, stalling Korea's process of becoming democratic or independent. In their attempt to reach an agreement, "Koreans starve as their economic life disintegrates" and are "frustrated because they cannot govern their own land."[11] South Korea was undergoing a severe economic crisis at this time. Because the USAMG was under the responsibility of the War Department, it was the War Department that took over the affairs of the state, including southern Korea's national economy. Therefore, the industrial economy became militarized as the War Department funded and oversaw efforts to rejuvenate the southern Korean economy. The U.S. military's hand was in all the various parts that made up a nation's economy: agriculture, energy, raw materials, consumer products, food, imports, exports, and employment. The military government worked to increase food production, rebuild industries in agriculture and fishing, raise employment, bring up the operational capacity of industrial plants (which were operating at only 10 percent to 20 percent capacity), improve the accessibility and distribution of materials and goods, and train qualified southern Koreans to replace the supervisory and technical roles that were first held by the Japanese and now by Americans.[12] Despite these attempts, however, inflation had caused prices to balloon: food cost ten times as much as it did in 1944, textiles fifteen times as much, and building materials up to thirty times as much.[13] The cost of rice, a staple of the Korean diet along with being the main crop and chief source of income, probably had the most damaging impact on Koreans. After less than a month in the southern half of Korea, the USAMG inaugurated a new rice policy in October 1945 that established a free market on rice, abolishing the former Japanese food control system that prohibited private ownership over rice.[14] Making rice a neo-colonial and market-regulated commodity led to food shortages, inflated prices, and widespread hunger. According to South Korean–U.S. diplomatic relations historian Jinwung Kim, after rice was made private, hoarding became so extreme that one could not even buy rice on the black market. Before the infiltration of the USAMG, rice cost 9.4 yen per bushel. After the establishment of the USAMG, rice cost 2,800 yen per bushel. It is for this reason that Jinwung Kim claims that one of the greatest failures of the American military occupation was its rice policy.[15] Indeed, Bertram Sarafan, an attorney for the USAMG, stated that "as a result of its handling of the rice problem, the Koreans arrived at a complete loss of faith in the Military Government."[16]

The tedious Joint Commission proceedings also created an atmosphere of distrust among southern Korean civilians and government officials toward the American government.[17] Disagreement between the two superpowers meant that Korea would have to wait even longer to act upon the independence they gained. In December 1945, the Soviet Union and the United States made an announcement that a five-year trusteeship would be set up for Korea under the guardianship of the United States, the USSR, Great Britain, and China. This announcement sparked immediate anger and rioting among the southern Koreans because their plan for trusteeship resembled the protectorate relationship that the Japanese had set up in 1905.[18] To the newly independent Korean nation, trusteeship was simply another manifestation of foreign rule rather than independence. Political conflict was fueled further by the fact that the U.S. military government kept in place Japanese-trained military leaders and police rather than removing them after the demise of Japanese colonialism in Korea.[19] This decision, along with plans for trusteeship, caused many Koreans to doubt the United States' commitment to Korea's postcolonial independence from Japan.

By 1947, many Korean civilians were distrustful and fed up with the American government and its promises for Korean self-government. General Hodge exclaimed in July 18, 1947, "The Korean people [are] rapidly

losing faith in American promises either implied or actual and we are near-
ing the point of complete distrust of and hostility to the United States."[20] An
American sergeant, Harry Savage, also questioned how helpful the American presence had been in Korea when he wrote, "I for myself cannot see
that the American army has done too much to help those people." In a letter written to President Harry Truman, Sergeant Savage informed the president of the mistreatment suffered by the Korean people. He described
how restoring law and order during riots involves "keep[ing] our machine
guns blazing" and seeing "dead bodies lying all over the streets." In addition, he explained how the Korean police (or military police) tortured and
killed civilians on suspicion of communism.[21] This mistreatment, which was
under the direction of the American military, led to an atmosphere of fear
and mistrust toward the American government. As General Hodge stated
in a memo to the Joint Chiefs of Staff, "I feel that the situation here is reach-
ing . . . the point of explosion."[22] The American military government was
quickly losing its status as liberator and bringer of democracy among the
Korean people in southern Korea. Congress knew it had to do something
to quell the situation and regain the support of southern Koreans. They
thus increased their economic aid program, seeking to solve political problems with money.

   Although the United States established an economic assistance program
after occupying the southern half of Korea in 1945, it was primarily done
in the spirit of providing war relief after the devastation caused from fighting the Japanese in World War II.[23] Through the Government Appropriation
for Relief in Occupied Areas (GARIOA), the United States assisted southern Korea with nearly $5 million in 1945 and $50 million in 1946.[24] However, with political and economic unrest increasing, the U.S. government
realized that more aid needed to be sent to Korea. In an attempt to stop the
Korean situation from becoming worse, ICK made some specific recommendations in February 1947 to both Congress and President Truman on
how to solve the Korean problem. By March, the recommendations they
made in February were drafted into a document called "Justification for a
Grant-in-Aid Program for the Rehabilitation of South Korea Covering Fiscal Years 1948 through 1950."

   In this document, members from the War and State departments offered
three different foreign policy strategies in an effort to squelch the explosive
atmosphere in southern Korea. The first was to withdraw completely from
Korea, including the troops and all financial and political assistance. The
second was to maintain the military occupation as is. The third was to carry

out a "positive political and economic program in our zone."[25] This political and economic program was the grant-in-aid program, which was conceived to "promote the establishment of a stable economy and a free and independent government for Korea." Here we see that political and economic interests merge for the first time in the United States' dealings with Korea. Indeed, the underlying belief behind this program was that building up the Korean economy would lead to political cooperation from the Korean people: "If sufficient funds can be made available it is believed it will be possible to halt this present trend toward economic disintegration which is causing the Korean people to become daily more antagonistic toward military government, toward U.S. objectives in Korea and even toward the United States itself. There have already been riots and loss of life."[26] Solving southern Korea's bankrupt economy, argued members from the War and State departments, would "create the basis for a friendly and democratic Korea" and help the U.S. military government "obtain the cooperation of the Korean people."[27] Under this program, the president would have available $540 million to spend over a three-year period (1948 to 1950) to help jumpstart the economy. "It is confidently believed," according to the members pushing the bill, that this money would "transform Southern Korea from a food deficit to a food surplus area," restart local industries, increase production, increase the number of trained technicians, and eradicate illiteracy.[28]

Although this program was supported by the "top echelons of the army" and promoted by the American news media, this bill was never passed by Congress because it was simply too expensive; however, the logic behind the justifications for increasing economic assistance were adopted by GARIOA.[29] Indeed, 1947 and 1948 were the years in which the U.S. government provided the most financial assistance to southern Korea: $175 million and $180 million, respectively.[30] This was a significant increase, considering that a total of $55 million was spent in the two previous years. In addition, in December 1948—four months after Syngman Rhee became president of the Republic of Korea—the first "government-to-government pact" was signed between the two nations. Entitled the ROK–US Agreement on Aid, this document outlined the stipulations under which South Korea would receive funds from the United States. Although these stipulations were cited as safeguards to prevent funds from being mishandled, the terms of the agreement worked to secure American influence in Korean political and economic affairs. As an aid agreement with strings attached, it set up a contentious donor–recipient relationship between the United States and South Korea, as it required the South Korean government to follow certain economic policies and capitalist practices set up by the U.S. government.[31] Consequently, despite winning independence from the United States in 1948, U.S. economic aid to South Korea kept intact U.S. neocolonial power over the newly formed South Korean nation. The five years leading up to the Korean War were significant for a variety of reasons. U.S. military occupation in the southern portion of Korea threaded American militarism into the national fabric of South Korean politics, economics, and society. Furthermore, the implementation of the economic assistance programs created a modus operandi that would be utilized after the Korean War: political and social problems would be solved with money and rehabilitation efforts by the U.S. military. This style of solving problems worked to secure a relationship of dependency between the United States and South Korea. As the United States depended on South Korea to hold allegiance to democracy and vilify communism, South Korea depended on the United States for military, political, and economic support. The southern portion of Korea received a total of $585 million in aid from the United States from 1945 to 1950. An additional $456 million was sent during the war, so that U.S. economic assistance to South Korea totaled $1.2 billion between 1945 and 1953.[32] From 1953 to 1962, the United States spent nearly $2 billion in economic aid and $1 billion in military aid, making South Korea one of the largest recipients of foreign aid.[33]

At the conclusion of the Korean War, when the crisis of war orphans arose, past solutions were used to solve this new problem. Programs like Armed Forces Assistance to Korea (AFAK) and Korea Civil Assistance Command (KCAC), which were created shortly after the conflict ended, provided money and rehabilitation services to alleviate the orphan crisis. In addition, as the industrial economy became militarized under the USAMG, social welfare would also become militarized through AFAK and KCAC as American servicemen would take center stage in the engineering, constructing, and funding of Korean orphanages. Unlike the economic assistance programs, however, the activities of the AFAK and KCAC were framed as humanitarian projects, which ultimately wedded militarism with humanitarianism.

Militarized Humanitarianism and the Erection of the Orphanage

Before World War II, fewer than 2,000 orphans resided in Korean orphanages. These orphans were primarily the products of Japanese colonization.[34]

During the period after Korea gained its independence from Japan, however, the number of orphaned children steadily increased as a result of armed combat (from 1945 and 1950) and the refugee movement from North Korea. By 1950, at the beginning of the Korean War, 7,000 orphans lived in South Korean orphanages. Three years of combat, grenade throwing, and napalm and bomb dropping destroyed entire cities and villages and killed over one million civilians. The destruction left in its path two million refugees, 300,000 widows, and 15,000 amputees.[35] In addition, 100,000 children were left without homes and separated from their families so that by the end of the war, over 40,000 orphans resided in orphanages. Less than a hundred orphanages existed in South Korea before the Korean War. However, by 1954—just one year after the war ended—there were over 400 registered orphanages in South Korea housing 50,936 children.[36]

What accounted for this exponential rise in the construction of orphanages? The simple logic of supply and demand is one possible answer—that is, more homeless children require more orphanages. However, this logic naturalizes adoption as the only possible solution to the war orphan problem. There are other factors at work. According to Korean adoption scholar Tobias Hübinette, the settlement of American missionaries in Korea during the late nineteenth century was "an absolute precondition for the following mass migration of Korean children."[37] Before American missionary settlement, an evolving system of policies and laws were developed during the Joseon dynasty (1392–1910) regarding orphaned children. During this 600-year period, various methods were created to take care of displaced children during times of war, famine, and social unrest. These methods included kinship care (children taken in by relatives), foster care, domestic adoption, and taking in the child as a slave or servant.[38] In addition, community compacts were set up where members of an entire village would pool their resources to take care of young orphans or destitute families unable to support themselves.[39]

This all changed, however, with the entrance of Western missionaries. According to social welfare scholars Jung-Woo Kim and Terry Henderson, American missionary activity in Korea at the turn of the twentieth century modernized the system of child welfare: "The foundations of the modern child welfare system in Korea were introduced by Western missionaries. Both the Catholic and Protestant missionaries and their non-profit sector activities in social care exerted a significant influence on the formation and maintenance of systems that, to this date, form the response to the care of displaced children." The primary system of care they established was "congregate care" (that is, orphanages), or the mobilization of orphans into facilities where they could be managed more easily through standardized care.[40] The first Western-style orphanage in Korea was set up by missionaries during the 1890s.[41] Thus, the practice of assembling parentless or homeless children into orphanages can be seen as a Western import that was introduced by American missionaries. Because this form of child welfare was already established, it seemed fitting that the crisis concerning orphans at the conclusion of the Korean War would be solved through the building of more orphanages. In this way, the Westernization and modernization of Korean child welfare laid the groundwork for Korean adoption.

In addition to the importation of a Western child welfare system, the neocolonial relationship that was forged between these two countries is another reason why the South Korean government relied on American intervention to solve the orphan problem at the war's conclusion. The South Korean government had no infrastructure in place to handle a crisis of this magnitude after the devastation of the war.[42] In addition, because the development of the modern child welfare system was undertaken by foreign missionaries, it significantly hindered the South Korean government from developing an indigenous response to this postwar dilemma.[43] There was a lack of trained Koreans who could work in the area of social services precisely because social welfare work in Korea had been predominantly handled by American missionaries. Furthermore, by the conflict's end, the South Korean government was much more concerned about building its military than providing social services. In 1954, 75 percent of the South Korean national budget went toward building and maintaining the army. That left only 25 percent for Welfare, Health, Reconstruction, Agriculture, Forestry, and other federal departments.[44] These factors not only resulted in South Korea's dependence on foreign aid and relief efforts after the war—a reliance that was established between 1945 and 1950—but also led to its dependence on the U.S. government to come up with a solution to the war orphan problem. The American government's solution was this: to set up programs that focused on rehabilitation—specifically the building of orphanages and the taking care of orphaned children.

Initiated in October 1953 (three months after the armistice was signed), the Department of Defense organized a response unit called Armed Forces Assistance to Korea (AFAK). The primary objective of the AFAK program was to help rehabilitate South Korea's infrastructure in order to provide public benefit and community good to the Korean people. AFAK "provide[s] assistance to the people of Korea in rehabilitating their country. This assistance is in the form of construction or reconstruction of community-type projects by units of the armed forces stationed in Korea, utilizing immediately available U.S. materials diverted to this program from other less urgent requirements."[45] In 1954 alone, the Department of Defense allotted $15 million to AFAK.[46] With this money, churches, schools, and roads were rebuilt; however, the building of orphanages held special importance to U.S. servicemen. In 1954 alone, AFAK built 115 orphanages to house the thousands of orphans left behind.[47] Under the purview of the U.S. military, the orphanages became militarized. In fact, not only did the military help build orphanages, but almost every U.S. military unit "adopted" an orphanage, allotting large portions of their pay to support the maintenance of orphanages and the care of orphans.[48] Some military units even founded orphanages, naming them after their own units; the 10th Brigade Orphanage, the 1st Marine Air Wing Orphanage, and the 5th Air Force Orphanage are a few examples. By the 1960s, more than 400 Korean orphanages had been built or repaired by American servicemen.[49]

It has also been estimated that soldiers contributed an additional $2 million in the form of cash and materials toward the support of orphanages.[50] Orphanage administrators reported that over 90 percent of their aid came directly from American servicemen, which kept their orphanages running.[51] In this way, the soldier became a pseudomissionary. Missionaries and military men, according to General Roy Parker, the U.S. chief of chaplains, were not incongruous.[52] Rather, Parker claimed that the "best missionary" is the "good soldier." In an article entitled "Military Help to Korean Orphanages," William Asbury of Christian Children's Fund detailed the contributions of the "good soldier" in helping to take care of the orphan population. He argued that the Korea Civil Assistance Command (KCAC), a military agency designed to "preven[t] unrest as a necessary function of war," had been the single largest source of help to orphaned children in South Korea.[53] Their military operation was to prevent disease, starvation, and unrest. One way they accomplished these things was by providing food, milk, clothing, blankets, and building materials to orphanages. The second greatest source of support, according to Asbury, came from American soldiers themselves.[54] They not only donated money to support orphanages and sponsor orphans, but they also engineered, built, and repaired orphanages. Through programs such as KCAC and AFAK, the U.S. military became entwined with South Korean social welfare services and humanitarian projects. In effect, these programs of militarized humanitarianism enabled U.S. military intervention and occupation in South Korea to persist under the guise of humanitarian relief and rescue projects.

The term *humanitarianism* has traditionally evoked civilian personnel and nongovernmental agencies. According to political scientist Michael Barnett, humanitarianism has denoted life-saving aid and relief measures based on the principles of impartiality, neutrality, and independence. It was originally conceived as an apolitical enterprise, free of state interests. Before World War I, humanitarian efforts followed this mission, working to maintain a distinct separation between state interests and humanitarian action. However, during World War II, as Barnett explains, the lines between humanitarianism and state interests began to blur because the U.S. government in particular began to see a connection between providing foreign aid and national security.[55] Therefore, during World War II, the U.S. government increasingly funded the activities of humanitarian organizations and aid programs, infusing state interests into humanitarian action.

Nowhere do we see this more clearly than in the creation of the War Relief Control Board (WRCB) and the Advisory Committee on Voluntary Foreign Aid, which replaced WRCB after World War II. Established by executive order in 1942, WRCB was deemed an independent agency; however, it was controlled by the State Department in order to regulate the activities of humanitarian aid organizations in such a way as to promote the agenda and aims of the United States during the war. As such, all humanitarian aid and relief agencies had to register with WRCB in order to gain access to those in need on the ground. Once they registered, the board approved their budgets, determined the methods for delivering and coordinating aid, oversaw their appeal campaigns, and handed out licenses. But most importantly, as Barnett points out, the board had the power to "command organizations to publicize their American funding in order to enhance U.S. prestige."[56] Thus, having regulatory and budgetary control over these organizations enabled the State Department to further their political interests through humanitarian agencies.

Despite the U.S. government's increased regulatory control over humanitarian aid organizations during World War II, there was still a distinction between the actions of the humanitarians on the ground and the actions of the military. After the combat years of the Korean War, however, this distinction erodes. To be clear, there were many humanitarian aid organizations that took part in helping with relief and aid efforts in postwar South Korea. For example, the American Red Cross, Catholic Relief Services, CARE (Cooperative for American Remittances to Europe), World Vision, the American-Korean Foundation, and Korean American Voluntary Associations all provided some kind of aid such as medical care, food, clothing, and money to support rehabilitation efforts. However, unlike in the previous wars, the GIs on the ground in South Korea were increasingly seen as humanitarians, as they replicated the same activities of these volunteer relief organizations. Militarism and humanitarianism became conflated through programs such as AFAK and KCAC, which produced what I call militarized humanitarianism.

Militarized humanitarianism is similar to military humanitarianism in terms of revealing the intertwined relationship between militarism and humanitarianism, or the wedding of military action and humanitarian aid. The term *military humanitarianism* appears most frequently in the context of post–Cold War United Nations peacekeeping missions. It is used to signal the ways in which humanitarian aid has been used to justify military intervention. For example, Inderpal Grewel uses military humanitarianism to illustrate how the military appropriates the language of human rights discourse to justify military intervention. Similarly, Slavoj Žižek explains how military humanitarianism is informed by the logic of militaristic humanism: "Under this doctrine, military intervention is dressed up as humanitarian salvation, justified according to depoliticised, universal human rights, so that anyone who opposes it is not only taking the enemy's side in an armed conflict but betraying the international community of civilised nations."[57]

Despite being informed by the same ideology of militaristic humanism, I prefer *militarized* over *military* to accompany the word *humanitarianism*. Rather than a new form of humanitarianism (military humanitarianism), I use *militarized humanitarianism* to signal the process in which humanitarianism has become militarized, to indicate the ways in which humanitarianism has been appropriated and used by the military to serve its own purposes. Furthermore, I use it to describe the process in which military personnel become seen as humanitarians. As a process, militarized humanitarianism connotes a past and a history that goes beyond the more contemporary manifestations of post–Cold War peacekeeping missions; rather, it evokes a history that can be traced back to the beginning of the Cold War. This is significant because within the post–Cold War context, military humanitarianism signals the ways in which the military uses the discourse and rhetoric of human rights and humanitarian aid to justify military intervention. This does not explain the situation between the United States and South Korea during the mid-1950s because the discourse of humanitarianism arose after military occupation. In the case of South Korea, military occupation and intervention provided the occasion for humanitarian initiatives to emerge and not the other way around. Militarized humanitarianism gets at this, whereas military humanitarianism—because it has been attributed to the post–Cold War era—does not. Therefore, militarized humanitarianism signals the ways in which military activity and intervention paved the way for gestures of humanitarianism on the part of the U.S. military. Military occupation and the acts of humanitarianism that accompanied them are the twin axis upon which Korean adoption is forged. Militarized humanitarianism, through the activities of the AFAK and KCAC, militarized South Korea's social welfare services by taking care of the war orphans by means of the building, financing, and supporting of orphanages. As militarized humanitarianism worked to solve the orphan crisis at the conclusion of the Korean War, it also worked to solve the American government's image problem. As Barnett reminds us, the primary reason why the U.S. government became invested in the humanitarian sector was because "they believed that humanitarian action would advance their foreign policy interests."[58] Militarized humanitarianism became the primary tool in which to assuage the image of the United States as colonizer and occupier, advancing the Cold War version of American exceptionalism. The phenomenon of GIs as humanitarians became the strategy in which to do so, and the means to accomplish this was through mass media marketing techniques.

Militarized Humanitarianism and the Recovery of American Exceptionalism

Participating in the efforts to rebuild the country by taking care of the children displaced by war became a crucial way for the U.S. military to rehabilitate its image of itself in the eyes of Koreans and the rest of the world. Indeed, the AFAK program director stated that AFAK's effectiveness depended as much on the "realization by the Koreans and other free peoples of the nature of our intentions as on the beneficial physical result produced."[59] What greater way to show the benevolent nature of the U.S. military's intention then to focus on the welfare of South Korea's most vulnerable and innocent population: its displaced children. In an effort to communicate these intentions with the rest of world, the U.S. Department of Defense engaged in marketing strategies. Specifically, AFAK units utilized motion pictures—along with posters and photographs—to publicize the military's benevolent intentions and effectiveness in rehabilitating the war-devastated country. Their footage became the raw materials for U.S. news outlets such as *Paramount News, Movietone News,* and even the *Bob Hope Show* (his Christmas specials). Their motion picture footage also appeared in *The Big Picture,* "a weekly television report to the nation on the activities of the Army at home and overseas" that aired on more than 320 television stations in the United States.[60] Through this army syndicated show, civilians not only learned about specific battles, units, and soldiers but also were informed about the good work of the U.S. military. That is where the AFAK film crew came in: they recorded soldiers lending a helping hand in postwar South Korea. As such, in these AFAK film reels, we see U.S. soldiers engaged in activities such as building orphanages, rescuing displaced children off the roadside, providing medical attention, and sorting through donated toys and clothing.[61] Constructing orphanages and meeting the basic needs of these children sent a powerful message to Koreans and "other free peoples" of the generosity and goodwill of the American military and government. In this way, the building of orphanages remedied not only the war orphan problem but also the American government's image problem. During World War II, the U.S. government publicized their funding of humanitarian organizations to enhance U.S. prestige. Here we see a similar strategy being used. This time, rather than using humanitarian agencies to publicize the goodwill of the U.S. government, it did so by using its own military.

Interestingly, the overwhelming majority of the AFAK film reels record soldiers throwing Christmas parties for orphans (in 1953 alone, 481 parties were given by army personnel) and handing out candy and cookies.[62] Grace Cho points out that the distribution of food, clothes, candy, and Christmas gifts "rests on a mutually lived-out rescue fantasy constructed not just through ideological impositions but also through sensory experiences that register at the level of affect."[63] These relief goods—especially the sugary kind—were not only used to help relieve (if only for a moment) the desperate conditions in which the orphans lived but also to help relieve the image of a ruthless American military.[64] These charitable acts of humanitarianism worked to rehabilitate the image of an imposing U.S. imperial power by not only erasing state violence but also by propping up American soldiers as rescuer rather than colonizer, relief worker rather than occupier.

The image of the GI as relief worker, however, has its limits. Despite the desire to create the conditions in which a fantasy of rescue can be lived out, there are moments in the AFAK film reels where we see orphaned children shatter this fantasy via their refusal to see the GI as a humanitarian. For example, although most of the AFAK film reels are silent, a segment of the

Christmas party in Do Bong has sound. In this scene, we are given a rare glimpse into the verbal interaction that took place between American soldiers and Korean orphans. As we see GIs passing out candy to the orphaned children, we hear a soldier say, "Huh? Number 1, huh?"[65] We cannot hear the children's voices; however, his question implies that he is most likely responding to the orphans calling out, "Number 1!" According to Paul Dickson in his study of American war slang, "Number 1," which is listed in the chapter "The Code of the Korean Conflict," means "the best."[66] It was a common phrase used by American soldiers during the Korean War to assert themselves as a new world power and leader after emerging from World War II victorious.

Of all the English phrases they could have learned, it is this one that emerges from the lips of these Korean children—or rather, to be more precise, it is this phrase that is repeated by the soldier. Silencing the children's voices while making the soldier's voice audible could be read as another instance of the U.S. military enacting violence against these children; however, we could also read this as an instance where the excesses of neocolonial contradiction are dumped on the solider. As "the best," American military domination over the southern portion of Korea is the very reason why these Korean children are displaced and gathered into orphanages built by U.S. armed forces. In other words, being Number 1 has relegated these children to their orphaned status. Furthermore, it is this very domination that created the conditions for this show of charity and humanitarianism. Dominance provided the occasion for benevolence. Without dominance, acts of charity and other forms of benevolence would not be necessary.[67] But even more than this, this scene reveals that no amount of candy, cookies, parties, and orphanages can erase the violence perpetrated by the state against these children.

Thus, this scene illustrates just how inadequate acts of benevolence are when followed by acts of dominance. The bodies of these children prove the limits of benevolence when it has been paved by the road of state violence. The soldier wielding sugary sweets (rather than a gun) embodies the limits of charity work as the children—in calling out "Number 1"—see him for who he really is: military power even though he is trying to pass as a humanitarian. They refuse to enable the U.S. military to live out its fantasy of rescue after behaving like a colonial occupier. By calling him out for who he really is, they shatter the fantasy of the American soldier as a humanitarian.

Interestingly, the soldier in this footage seems to be somewhat aware of this. From his response, he seems uncomfortable being assigned this status by these children, as it is incongruous for these orphaned children to be hailing U.S. military power in the very moment that the soldier is trying to assuage that power. But it is also incongruous for a man dressed in military garb to pose as a humanitarian. So consciously or not, intentionally or not, these inconsistencies are precisely what the Korean orphans are exposing when they say "Number 1" rather than "Thank you." Taken aback from this unexpected response, the soldier asks, "Huh? Number 1, huh?" These questions are not so much for the children as they are for himself. And they are not so much questions as they are reminders. They remind him that the children can see through his act, that this strategy of covering up state violence via candy and parties is not fooling anybody—especially not these children who have become by-products of war. They remind him that masking military power via charitable acts of humanitarianism actually highlights it.

It is important to note that projects of armed relief have always been a part of the military's activities. In past wars, the U.S. military provided instances of armed relief, where the armed forces participated in rescue and relief projects targeted toward civilian populations; however, what makes these acts examples of militarized humanitarianism rather than merely armed relief is that the state is assigning the rhetoric of humanitarianism to these particular relief projects in order to promote its own national interests. In this case, the U.S. government utilized images of militarized humanitarianism to rescue the state fantasy of American exceptionalism.

Programs such as AFAK and KCAC collaborated with American news media in order to report back to civilians the good work U.S. soldiers were doing in South Korea. For example, in the *New York Times Magazine* article "The GI's Give a Hand to the Koreans," the journalist writes:

> The men who saved a nation on the battlefield are pouring out their energy and money to heal its wounds of war. . . . The G.I.'s affection and respect for the Korean people have been reflected in an astonishing display of generosity. The men of the U.S. first core . . . have spontaneously donated nearly half a million dollars toward the building of hospitals, orphanages, schools, churches and institutions in the devastated hills and valleys of former battle area.[68]

Stories like this appeared in popular magazines and newspapers shortly after the war and worked to rehabilitate the image of the United States.[69] Conflating the solider as humanitarian worked to project an image of the U.S. military as a benevolent force in South Korea. If Koreans and the rest of the so-called free world were misinterpreting the presence of the U.S. military in South Korea, then these stories of generosity attempted to convey their altruistic intentions. By taking care of South Korea's most vulnerable population, the U.S. military advertised itself as a force of goodwill and humanitarianism that fostered an image of benevolence rather than imperialism, assistance rather than occupation. Thus, the U.S. news media tried to depict American presence and occupation in South Korea as beneficial rather than harmful to Koreans. Healing the wounds of war apparently took place on both physical and ideological levels.

Through these performances of militarized humanitarianism and charitable kindness, the state fantasy of American exceptionalism could be kept intact. As a concept that promotes the belief that the United States is anti-imperial, American exceptionalism depends on the active disavowal and denial of the existence of American empire and its participation in imperial activities. One way to do this is through recovery. Recovering the state fantasy of American exceptionalism through the literal recovery of the South Korean nation and its people worked to disavow the imperialist activities that led to their initial destruction. The acts of recovery performed by the U.S. military worked to cover over the acts of state violence that necessitated the need for recovery in the first place. In this way, disavowal arises at the moment of recovery.

American exceptionalism is also recovered when acts of empire are reconfigured as acts of altruism and humanitarianism. The activities of AFAK, KCAC, and the stories they passed along to American news media worked to reframe the military occupation of southern Korea as not only a rescue mission from communism but also a relief mission that saved the very lives of the Korean people. These activities humanized the military and reconfigured the military operation in South Korea as a humanitarian one, which not only worked to revive the fantasy of American exceptionalism but also eventually set the foundation for Korean adoption to be read as a humanitarian rescue mission, as well (which will be further discussed in chapter 3).

Ultimately, the settlement of Western missionaries during the late nineteenth century, the formation of neocolonial relations between the United States and South Korea during the mid-twentieth century, and the U.S. government's desire to rehabilitate its image in the service of American exceptionalism after the Korean War culminated to create the material conditions that made possible the image of the "GIs and the Orphans." This complex web of political, economic, religious, and geopolitical investments made the erection of orphanages the prescription and remedy to the war orphan problem. This mission of militarized humanitarianism—which was made possible by U.S. military occupation and intervention—not only enabled the United States to preserve the myth of American exceptionalism while establishing its imperial presence in South Korea but also served to solidify neocolonial relations by creating the conditions in which transnational adoption would become the fundamental form of child welfare in South Korea. The adoption of Korean orphans by foreigners, as a form of child welfare, was virtually nonexistent in South Korea before U.S. military occupation.[70] Without their military presence, Korean adoption would most likely never have existed. Indeed, while it is commonly believed that Harry Holt started Korean adoption with the adoption of eight mixed-race war orphans, the first people to actually adopt Korean War orphans were military men.[71]

Militarized humanitarianism provided not only the material conditions of possibility of the "GIs and the Orphans" but also the conditions in which postwar Korean orphans became militarized subjects. Constructing and financing orphanages, taking care of orphaned children, and throwing Christmas parties not only militarized the social welfare scene of South Korea but also militarized the orphans themselves. In the next chapter, I discuss how the highly racialized, gendered, and sexualized process of U.S. militarization transformed these children into militarized subjects who ended up serving the geopolitical interests of the United States. Specifically, I describe how the culture of militarized prostitution created the militaristic gaze, which informed the ways in which displaced Korean children were read and interpreted by American soldiers. In so doing, I argue that transforming these children into militarized subjects through the militaristic gaze further facilitated the neocolonial relations between the United States and South Korea.

2 GENDER AND THE MILITARISTIC GAZE

THE KOREAN WAR CHILDREN'S MEMORIAL (2003), which sounds like a site honoring the displaced children of the Korean War, is actually a memorial that valorizes the American armed forces. Founded by Korean War veteran George Drake, the memorial and its accompanying website were created in celebration of the fiftieth anniversary of the Korean War as a way to "hono[r] the American servicemen and women who, during the Korean War and the years following, rendered compassionate humanitarian aid to the children of that war torn nation."[1] The website houses over 1,000 photos and over 1,000 stories to promulgate the men of the armed forces as saviors, who "saved the lives of over 10,000 children and helped sustain over 50,000" through donations and material aid.[2] Some of these pictures and stories were featured in a book entitled *GIs and the Kids—A Love Story: American Armed Forces and the Children of Korea, 1950–1954* (2005). There is even a traveling photo exhibit of the same title.

Written and compiled by Drake and Al Zimmerman, *GIs and the Kids— A Love Story* is a collection of photos, newspaper clippings, and stories devoted entirely to the love that GIs had for Korean children.[3] Even though these children were displaced by the actions of the American armed forces, this essential fact is glossed over with picture after picture and story after story about the "outpouring of love and life-saving gifts by American armed forces in Korea." As a celebration and artifact of militarized humanitarianism, this book—along with the entire project of the Korean War Children's Memorial—reframes the brutal and violent American armed forces into "an Army of Compassion" by recoding military violence as humanitarianism and refiguring the GI as a humanitarian. Indeed, in the foreword that introduces the mission and objective of the book, William Asbury expeditiously repackages the first "hot war" of the Cold War into a child rescue mission:

"The extraordinary photographs and stories in this booklet tell the story of the war within the Korean War that followed the Communist assault. *That internal war was the long battle to save the lives of Korean children*" (emphasis added). Asbury then goes on to naturalize the building of orphanages and the taking care of Korean children via "adoption" as the only viable solution to this internal war:

> An estimated 100,000 Korean kids were orphaned. Orphanages needed to be created. . . . The GI was up to those needs. He and she took responsibility for individual kids. Army, Navy, Air Force, Marine Corps and even Merchant Marine units 'adopted' entire orphanages. American armed forces became an army of compassion, perhaps as never before or since.[4]

As a story of the "compassionate and humanitarian aid rendered the children of Korea in the period 1950 to 1954 by American servicemen and women," *GIs and the Kids—A Love Story* is neither a story about the mutual love between these two groups nor a story about the love Korean children had for GIs. Rather, it is about the charitable acts of love that GIs displayed toward these children. According to Drake and Zimmerman, while U.S. soldiers had to be taught to kill other human beings, "They did not have to be taught to offer solace to a crying child, feed a hungry child, treat an injured child or seek shelter for a homeless child. That came with being American."[5] It is precisely these seemingly innate acts of patriotic, humanitarian love on which the book focuses. Sections entitled "Saving Lives," "Orphanages," "Money Helps," "'Peanuts': Stories of Humanitarian Aid, Compassion, and Love for the Children," "Christmas Parties," "Help from Home," and "Mascots and Adoption" are filled with newspaper clippings and captioned photographs that describe the various ways in which the U.S. armed forces either saved or made better the lives of Korean children. This is the love in this particular love story. "The goal," according to the authors, "is to make sure that these loving moments in the middle of a horrendous war are not forgotten."[6]

While these "loving moments," as framed by militarized humanitarianism, erect American soldiers as beneficent heroes, Mihee-Nathalie Lemoine provides an alternative love story regarding the GI–South Korean encounter in her artwork entitled "Suck Me-Ho's First English Lesson" (Figure 3).[7] In this piece, Lemoine, a multimedia artist and queer Korean adoptee activist from Belgium, exposes the ways in which Western encounters with Korean female bodies are highly racialized, gendered, and sexualized: the very processes that *GIs and the Kids—A Love Story* and other artifacts of militarized humanitarianism attempt to foreclose. In stark opposition to the narrative created in *GIs and the Kids—A Love Story,* Lemoine's grammar book lesson highlights the relationship between American servicemen and Korean women, not as one of charitable love but as one of racialized sexual exploitation. Through this piece, Lemoine illustrates what historian Bruce Cumings has observed: the uneven exchange between the United States and South Korea has led to the "social construction of every Korean female as a potential object of pleasure for Americans."[8]

The fact that this is an English lesson (and not a French lesson, because Lemoine is Belgian) and that the English language is used to name and enfigure the speaker as a Korean prostitute works to implicate the role that the American military has played in constructing Korean females as solely sexual objects in service of Western men. According to historian Ji-Yeon Yuh, "For many American soldiers, Korea is synonymous with the proverbial rock 'n' rolling good time, and Korean women—treated as playthings easily bought and easily discarded—are essential to that experience.

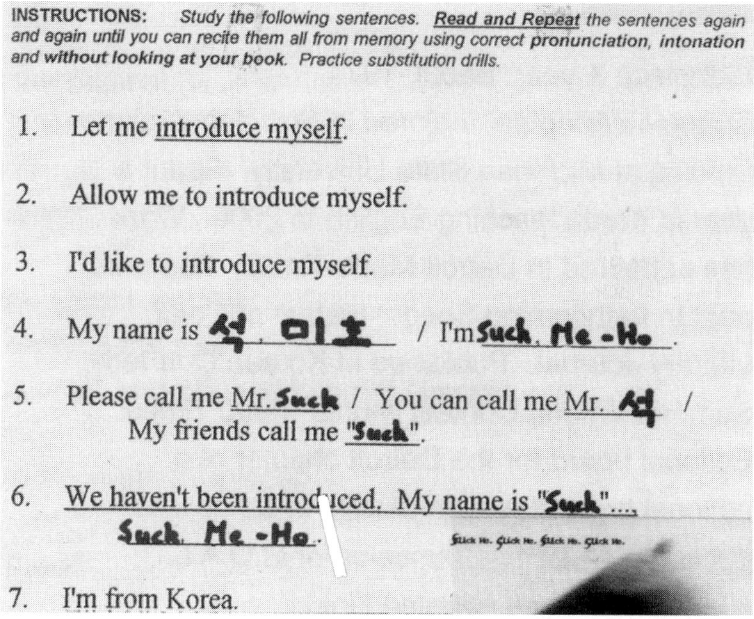

INSTRUCTIONS: *Study the following sentences.* <u>Read and Repeat</u> *the sentences again and again until you can recite them all from memory using correct **pronunciation, intonation** and **without looking at your book.** Practice substitution drills.*

1. Let me <u>introduce myself</u>.

2. Allow me to introduce myself.

3. I'd like to introduce myself.

4. My name is 석. 이호 / I'm Such. Me-Ho.

5. Please call me Mr. Such / You can call me Mr. 석 / My friends call me "Such".

6. We haven't been introduced. My name is "Such"....
   Such. Me-Ho.

7. I'm from Korea.

Figure 3. Visual artist Mihee-Nathalie Lemoine reinterprets the GI–Korean encounter as one of racialized, sexualized, and imperial exploitation in "Suck Me-Ho's First English Lesson." Collage on paper by Mihee-Nathalie Lemoine. Reproduced with permission from the artist.

The women are seen by the soldiers as innately sexual, even depraved, and doing what they do for fun and money."[9] This is precisely the political economy that Lemoine is exposing in her stereotypical reproduction of Asian women as exotic sex toys. Militarization has led to the racialized, gendered, and sexualized commodification of Asian female bodies, leading to the emergence of the *gijichon* (camptown) women and the *yanggongju* ("Yankee whore" or "Western princess").[10] In this particular case, militarized prostitution has not only constituted the subjectivity of Korean women as sexual playthings but also legitimized their exploitation. Suck Me-Ho's first lesson in English is a lesson that solicits her own objectification; her very name commands it: "Please call me *Mr. Suck* / You can call me *Mr 석*/ My friends call me '*Suck*.'"[11] The speaker—by introducing herself as Suck Me-Ho—invites her intended audience (the GI) to see, treat, and identify her in such a way that fulfills the soldier's fantasy. As a result, this English lesson has less to do with learning grammar than with inviting, and hence justifying, the U.S. military's exploitation of Korean female bodies. What Lemoine exposes that Drake and Zimmerman attempt to foreclose is that the Korean subject in both stories is constructed in the image of the U.S. military's fantasy. In the case of Drake and Zimmerman, the soldier's fantasy of rescue animates the children depicted in the pages of their book; militarized humanitarianism constructs the Korean children in such a way as to valorize the soldiers as heroes. In Lemoine's case, the soldier's fantasy of willing, exotic women who are eager to please his sexual appetites is what produces the speaker's identity; militarized prostitution enables her exploitation and hence constitutes her subject formation.

This English lesson has a double meaning: it could also be read as the production of not only the Korean military prostitute but also the Korean adoptee. The "Ho" in "Suck Me-Ho" could be read as "whore" or "whole." As "Suck Me-Whole," this work of art becomes a critique of Korean adoption in the sense that it has historically engaged in a process that swallows the Korean child whole through forced assimilation. The adoptee body is figuratively "sucked whole" upon entrance into his or her new family and country, as Korean culture, identity, and nationality are replaced by an American one. (I discuss this further in chapter 5.) As Suck Me-Whole, the speaker signifies the process in which the receiver of this exchange (in this case, the adoptive parent or family) envelops her in order to assimilate the Korean body as completely as possible. In this way, Lemoine exposes the ways in which the subject formation of the military prostitute and the adoptee are linked by tracing both their subjectivities back to U.S. military occupation.

Grace Cho argues that the "making of the yanggongju" begins in 1945, the year that "signaled the transition between the system of sexual slavery set up for the Japanese Imperial Army (the comfort stations) and the system of camptown prostitution set up for the U.S. military *(gijichon)*."[12] The year 1945 is also the year that produced Korean orphans who were the direct consequences of U.S. military occupation. Thus, the making of the *yanggongju* and the making of the Korean adoptee—which relies on the existence of the Korean orphan—both have a genealogy that links back to the beginning of U.S. military occupation in southern Korea. Lemoine signifies this through the conflation of the *yanggongju* (Suck Me-Whore) and the adoptee (Suck Me-Whole) via the double entendre of the subject's name "Suck Me-Ho."

I begin this chapter with Drake and Zimmerman's *GIs and the Kids—A Love Story* and Lemoine's "Suck Me-Ho's First English Lesson" to set the stage for the kind of interventions I will be making in this chapter. If chapter 1 identified militarized humanitarianism as a condition of possibility for the image of the "GIs and the Orphans," then this chapter centers militarized prostitution as another material condition that makes this image possible. Citing militarized prostitution as a key material condition of possibility is significant because it makes legible a particular set of conditions that militarized humanitarianism disavows. As this introduction has demonstrated, juxtaposing Lemoine's critique of militarized prostitution next to Drake and Zimmerman's record of militarized humanitarianism makes visible the gendered, racialized, sexualized, and colonial processes that shape the relationship between GIs and Korean children. "Suck Me-Ho's First English Lesson" rearticulates the interaction between the GIs and Korean women not as charitable acts of love but as acts of exploitation, which are implicated in the larger imperial, racialized, gendered, and sexual economies of occupation, militarism, and war. I attempt to make a similar move as I examine Armed Forces Assistance to Korea (AFAK) film reels, articles from the military publication *Pacific Stars and Stripes,* and U.S. print media from the 1950s to illuminate how Korean children became constructed in the fantasies and desires of the U.S. military and how Korean adoption was constituted by militarized prostitution.

Militarized Prostitution and Critical Adoption Studies

According to Cumings, the system of militarized prostitution is "the most important aspect of the whole relationship [between the United States and South Korea] and the primary memory of Korea for generations of young Americans who have served there."[13] Although this aspect of U.S.–South Korea relations has been studied in respect to the figure of the *giji-chon* woman and *yanggongju,* more work needs to be done on the explicit and implicit ways in which militarized prostitution enfigures the Korean orphan.[14] The handful of articles that do situate Asian transnational adoption within the context of militarized prostitution do so in light of GIs fathering mixed-race Korean orphans. For example, Patti Duncan argues that the continued presence of Amerasian children—who are by-products of military camptowns—and the subsequent practice of transnational adoption verifies the persistent effects of the Korean War. She states that Korean camptown prostitutes, military brides, and their Amerasian children are "living symbols of the devastation of the Korean War and partition." Jodi Kim also makes a similar observation when she writes: "Whether military brides, military sex workers, or . . . transnational adoptees, these are gendered racial bodies that emerge out of the Korean War." Like Duncan, Kim also explains how these mixed-race children—who are not only the literal offspring of U.S. militarism—are unwanted reminders of U.S. military domination and neoimperialism in South Korea. Consequently, they are stigmatized, shunned, and actively disavowed from national consciousness.[15]

Katharine Moon also reveals the direct links between military prostitution and Korean orphans when she explains that the earliest camptown prostitutes were girls who were orphaned during the ravages of war. Moon notes: "The earliest prostitutes were camp followers of troops during the Korean War; they did laundry, cooked, and tended to the soldiers' sexual demands. Some had been widowed by the war, others orphaned or lost during a family's flight from bombs and grenades." She goes on to say that the war, because it caused poverty, chaos, and the separation of families, "created a large supply of girls and women without homes and livelihoods," leading to a mass production of camptown prostitutes.[16]

I want to extend Duncan and Kim's analysis and Moon's observations by discussing how Korean orphans during and immediately after the Korean War were constituted by militarized prostitution—not as biological offspring (that is, Amerasian children) or camptown prostitutes but as the figurative, geopolitical offspring of U.S. militarism. American militarism, in choosing orphanages as the solution to manage the rising number of homeless Korean children after the war, inadvertently birthed a new subject: the militarized war orphan. In the discussion that follows, I explain how the culture of U.S. militarism materialized on the bodies of Korean orphans and turned them into militarized subjects. The military culture of camptown life seeped into the orphanage and shaped the ways in which these children were seen, interpreted, and ultimately treated by American soldiers. However, even more significantly, it bore the key players in facilitating and preserving U.S. neocolonial power in South Korea: the process of militarization refigured male orphans as American soldiers, while female orphans were recast as Korean military prostitutes. Moon, in her pathbreaking book *Sex among Allies: Military Prostitution in U.S.–Korea Relations,* has noted that camptown prostitutes have facilitated U.S. neocolonialism in South Korea by playing an instrumental role in preserving national security interests and fostering "the smooth operation of U.S. military organization in Korea."[17] Making war orphans into the image of the GI and camptown prostitute reinforces this relationship and as a result reifies U.S. neocolonial power. Thus, the militarization of war orphans—via the culture and discourse of militarized prostitution—reproduces the conditions in which to secure the neocolonial relationship between the United States and South Korea.

Furthermore, this chapter teases out what I refer to as the militaristic gaze that is produced by the spatial intimacy between Korean children and U.S. soldiers. I use this phrase to get at the racial, gendered, sexual, and colonial dimensions of U.S. militarism and occupation. This act of looking and desiring becomes another form of military invasion and intrusion. Interestingly, it too is informed by the logic of militarized humanitarianism as the militaristic gaze attempts to occupy the Korean bodies of children under the auspices of altruism.

I end this chapter by attending to the strategies of resistance that war orphans utilized to critique U.S. military occupation. Although the purpose of the AFAK film reels was to display the benevolent nature of their (U.S. military forces') intentions, the film footage also caught moments of resistance wherein orphans protested aspects of American military intervention. Identifying these instances of resistance is important because it not only disrupts the image of orphaned children as passive victims but also reveals how the project of militarized humanitarianism is never complete. No matter how much the U.S. government and its armed forces believed that they were providing beneficial services to these children, the actions on behalf of some children proved that these services were unwelcomed and inadequate. Thus, these moments of resistance and critique displayed by these war orphans can be read as a precursor to some of the contemporary artistic expressions in which Korean adoptees talk back.

Male Orphans as American Soldiers

Cynthia Enloe, in *Globalization and Militarism: Feminists Make the Link,* states that "anything is on its way to becoming militarized if it is increasingly coming under the control of a military—of a military's rules, its budget, its command structure."[18] To be militarized means having a direct relationship with the Department of Defense or to be in some way supported by the defense bureaucracy.[19] Under this definition, the Korean orphan emerged as a militarized subject because the majority of the orphanages that were built after the war were orchestrated and financed by the U.S. Department of Defense through programs such as the AFAK and KCAC (Korea Civil Assistance Command). In addition, as I cited earlier, many of the orphanages were supported by military units themselves. Reconfiguring the postwar orphan as a militarized subject is significant because it recuperates the history of U.S. military occupation and neocolonialism in South Korea—a history that is elided when we conceive the orphan as a priori. Furthermore, the actual phrase "orphan as militarized subject" suggests the close proximity of child and soldier. I use this semantic intimacy to get at the literal spatial intimacy between Korean children and American serviceman during and after the war.

Watching the AFAK film reels (the majority of which are silent), one witnesses the highly involved nature of the military in the lives of orphans. At every stage, the military is present: the initial identification of the orphanage site, the drawing of the blueprints, the groundbreaking, and the actual construction and dedication of the orphanage.[20] In other AFAK film reels, we see GIs evacuating war orphans,[21] picking up children off the roadside,[22] vaccinating and providing medical care,[23] loading and unloading building materials,[24] transporting orphans, supplies, and donations (such as food and clothes),[25] sorting through donations,[26] throwing Christmas parties,[27] and handing out candy and cookies.[28] These scenes not only portray the military as generous and kindhearted, but they also indicate the military's wide reach in terms of influencing and impacting the lives of displaced Korean children. Because most of the Korean orphanages were under the auspices of the U.S. Department of Defense, the orphans themselves became militarized.

As Cumings has noted, militarized prostitution and the culture of camptowns played an "integral part in Korea's subordination to . . . American interests."[29] This system has played a key role in shaping not only U.S.–South Korea relations but also the Korean orphan during and shortly after the Korean War. Although footage of camptown life and culture is absent in the AFAK film reels, the vestiges of militarized prostitution are present.

The cultural and social aspects of militarized prostitution become the organizing logic that shapes the ways in which the U.S. military sees, treats, and ultimately constructs the orphan.

As it relates to male orphans, the culture of militarized prostitution refigures them as minisoldiers. In the film footage taken at the Heimyung Children's Home and Orphanage, first lady Francesca Donner (South Korean president Syngman Rhee's wife), along with other important government and military personnel, inspects and passes out clothing and toys donated by the American first lady (Mamie Eisenhower) and American soldiers.[30] In one scene, orphan boys dressed in fatigues—surplus uniforms donated by the U.S. military—assemble themselves into military formation (Figure 4).[31] Organized into rows, Korean first lady Donner disperses the toys. What she hands them are toy rifles.

If we didn't know that this was an orphanage, we could easily mistake these orphans for a children's army. Indeed, in other film reels, male orphans dressed in fatigues march and move into military formation. Their attire, their stance, and their weapons (even if they are only for play) all suggest the military world (Figures 5 and 6).

After we see Donner pass out toy rifles to the boys, the camera zooms in on a chaplain (who is also a lieutenant) with a young boy (who looks to be about three or four years old) sitting on his knee (Figure 7). This tender vision is disrupted when we see the boy's chubby, dimpled hands grasping a toy rifle. He inspects it closely as the chaplain shows him how to pull the trigger. His hands are so tiny that it takes four fingers to grasp the trigger.

Seeing images of young boys play with donated toy rifles and guns or using them to shoot at pretend targets may be quite normal because boys are socialized to demonstrate their masculinity in these ways. However, given this particular situation, it becomes ironic. Through the act of imitation, these orphaned boys—as young as two or three years of age—are mimicking the very activities that caused them to become orphaned in the first place. The violence that American (and South Korean) soldiers enacted on Koreans during the war destroyed the families of the very children they are teaching to shoot, even if they are just playing. In another reel entitled "7th Division Christmas Celebration," we see a young boy form his hand into the shape of a gun, point straight at the camera, and shoot.[32] When his friends stand in his way, blocking him from his shot, he changes positions and realigns his gun (finger). Even though this footage is silent, you can imagine him saying, "Bang! Bang!" as he weaves around his friends, making sure to hit his intended target (the camera and/or cameraman). His

Figure 4. South Korean first lady Francesca Donner hands out toy rifles to the male orphans. The two girls squatting on the ground play with a blonde doll that crawls and a sewing machine. Although engaged in play, this scene reinforces the patriarchal notion that a boy's place is in the battlefield of war, while a girl's place is within the domestic sphere. Still image. "304th BN Orphanage in Seoul, Korea." National Archives at College Park.

Figure 5. Under the tenure of U.S. military occupation, the orphanage became a site of militarization as these Korean orphans were disciplined to resemble child soldiers. Still image. "Epidemic Control Unit (USN), Ulleung-do, Korea." National Archives at College Park.

Figure 6. *Young boys play with donated toy rifles. Through their play, these boys enact the very violence that orphaned them in the first place. Still image. "304th BN Orphanage in Seoul, Korea." National Archives at College Park.*

Figure 7. *A lieutenant chaplain teaches a young boy how to pull the trigger on this toy gun. Still image. "304th BN Orphanage in Seoul, Korea." National Archives at College Park.*

actions reveal how gun violence has become naturalized among male orphans because of what they've witnessed from the war and from soldiers interacting with them in such a way as to reinforce this kind of violent play. However, this boy's actions could also be read as a critique. He turns the table on the cameraman and his immediate audience (the Department of Defense) by making them the target of militarized violence. In so doing, he positions the U.S. military as an enemy rather than an ally. He treats them as a threatening rather than benevolent force. Similar to the orphans who called out "Number 1" rather than "Thank you," this boy sees the military for who they are (oppressors) rather than what they are posing to be (in this case, Santa's helpers who are delivering Christmas gifts).[33]

The grooming of young boys as soldiers extended beyond the walls of the orphanage as American servicemen adopted some of the boys. For example, a *Life* magazine article entitled "A New American Comes 'Home'" tells of Chief Petty Officer Vincent Paladino adopting Lee Kyung Soo, a young Korean orphan he had seen begging in the U.S. naval mess halls of Incheon, South Korea. Paladino had watched over him for a year when he was reassigned back to the States. Unwilling to leave the little boy, he decided to adopt him after finding out that Lee had no family. The pictures that accompany the story are revealing. On the cover page, Lee, who looks like the miniature version of Paladino, is dressed in full uniform. He has even adopted the swagger of a military man, as captured in the cover photo that shows him walking with his adoptive father around the Alameda naval base in California.[34]

Lee's story in some ways parallels the previous stories we have seen and heard concerning the helping hand that American GIs extended to postwar Korean orphans. Lee's transformation from a distraught postwar orphan into a confident minisoldier is offered as evidence of the positive impact that American forces are having in South Korea. Unlike the previous stories where the Korean children remain orphans, this *Life* magazine article takes America's power of influence a step further: American presence and occupation in South Korea can turn its youngest and most vulnerable charges into Americans. U.S. military presence turns unproductive surplus (orphans) into productive citizen-subjects (Americans). To be more precise, American intervention makes Korean boys into American men. As Michel Foucault's soldier par excellence, Lee serves as proof of the transformative powers of military discipline.[35]

But perhaps even more significant than becoming an American man is that the Korean boy becomes remade in the image of the American soldier.

In *American Tropics: Articulating Filipino America,* Allan Punzalan Isaac points out that the project of building American empire involved "turn[ing] the colonized brown youth into youthful versions of masculine violence that the occupying power symbolized." One of the first places to test out this method of empire building was in the Philippine archipelago, after it was incorporated as a U.S. territory in 1902 at the conclusion of the Philippine–American war. Isaac explains that the U.S. colonization of the Philippine archipelago began to recast its inhabitants in America's image. Thus, the colonized natives became the "offspring of benevolent assimilation."[36]

Almost fifty years later, South Korea becomes another stage where this imperial drama of molding brown youth into the image of the United States is enacted. Indeed, the before-and-after pictures that are included in the article are literally before and after assimilation. Once a shy, timid boy who was considered "the smallest, the loneliest, the one most easily pushed aside by others," the "after" pictures reveal a confident, self-assured, and commanding Lee. When he tries on a three-piece suit, he scolds the clerk by saying, "Whattsa matta with you? Too Big." After being asked the same question more than once, he admonishes the reporter: "Whattsa matta? You ask that before." To prove what a young man he is, Lee, as described by the journalist, "manfully downs" an ice cream cone despite his complaints that it is "too cold, too cold."[37] Despite being just four and a half years old, Lee commands authority and carries himself like the chief petty officer that his adoptive father is. Like his Filipino predecessors, he "proves himself the perfect colonized native—childish, loyal, and ready for American tutelage—the tamed offspring of benevolent assimilation."[38] Lee has been recast into the patriarchal image of his American sailor/father and thus made in the image of the United States, becoming the offspring of not only U.S. empire but also the U.S. armed forces.

The figure of the Korean male orphan turned American soldier comes to symbolize America's hopes and dreams for the Korean nation itself. Indeed, we could read this figure as a stand-in for the Korean nation. In the same way that this Korean orphan has been adopted by an American military man, South Korea—treated by the United States as if it too is an orphan—has also been adopted by the American military government. The U.S. nation becomes the adoptive father to South Korea. Reframing U.S.–South Korea relations in this way—as an adoption—works to displace not only the colonial and military origins of this relationship but also its genealogical ties to other territories (such as the Philippines) that have been occupied in the name of U.S. expansion in Asia and the Pacific, "wiping away all memories of conflict between the colonizer and the colonized."[39] Reframing U.S.–South Korea relations in this way also makes the United States the parent of South Korea, which works to legitimize U.S. authority. Consequently, Korean adoption both preserves and maintains American neocolonialism. Similar to Lee, it is believed that South Korea will become more modern and civilized—simply more American under the tutelage of the United States. The hope is that South Korea will be made into the image of the United States as smoothly and successfully as the process shown here through Lee's story. The fantasy is that South Korea will strive to imitate and mimic its parent nation with as much ferocity as Lee imitates his adoptive father.[40]

There is, however, an unintended critique that arises when portraying the Korean orphan as an American soldier. In Lee's imitation of this naval officer turned adoptive father, the Korean orphan becomes enfigured as a veteran of war, which is altogether different than being a by-product of war. To be a veteran denotes that one has served in the military. In this issue of *Life* magazine, there is not just one Korean War veteran appearing on the cover; there are two. Reading the orphan as war veteran recuperates the ways in which Korean orphans served in the Korean War in various capacities. It is unknown how many male orphans became unofficial members of the U.S. armed forces, but it is certain that Korean orphans—both boys and girls—served as mascots for the armed forces.[41] Being a mascot meant that the child was informally adopted by a unit.[42] Military units would end up developing relationships with the children they picked up along the roadside. Sometimes, these children were placed in an orphanage; other times, a unit would pay a "mama-san" to take care of the child.[43] Those who stayed with the unit (usually because they refused to remain at the orphanage) became "adopted" and served as the unit's mascot. They participated in the troop's daily activities, ran errands, and performed daily chores. Some even became fully fledged members of the U.S. Army. One mascot called Chocoletto worked his way up to become a sergeant in the U.S. Marines. He proved to be invaluable to the regiment by providing intelligence about the enemy.[44]

Perhaps the most famous mascot was Pon Son See, aka Jimmy Pusan (Figure 8). After his family was killed during the war, the military police took him to the refugee stockade in Pusan. On his way there, two American sailors who were drawn to him persuaded the military police to release the boy to them. He spent the day with them on the ship, until they dropped him off at S.O.S. Orphanage. Jimmy, who ran away from the orphanage, came to the ship the next day and "indicated that he was ready to 'turn to.'" From then on, the sailors of USS *Whitehurst* "adopted" him. Initially considered the mascot of the USS *Whitehurst,* Jimmy, as crew members called him, quickly became an honorary seaman. He engaged in all the activities that other sailors did; he performed all ship drills and exercises, swept decks and shined shoes, and even became a member of the gunnery department.[45] Excelling in his duties, he bypassed some his older crew members, receiving more stripes than they did. Like Chocoletto, Jimmy became valuable to the navy because he acted as a spy for the U.S. military.[46] There is suspicion that both female and male orphans were used as spies for the American government, providing intelligence about the whereabouts and strategies of communist Koreans. According to Korean War veteran and sailor Andy Bisaccia, "Several of these Korean orphans, boys as well as girls, were used for [spy work]. They could pass, unnoticed, as grimy little rug rats, to be pitied and ignored."[47]

Thinking about Korean orphans as veterans and not just by-products of war implicates the U.S. military in using child soldiers. The United Nations considers child soldiers as boys and girls under the age of eighteen who either engage in armed combat or serve as spies, informants, couriers, or sex slaves.[48] According to *Child Soldiers: Implications for U.S. Forces,* a seminar report written and published by the Center for Emerging Threats and Opportunities (CETO), a think tank for the U.S. Marine Corps, the phenomenon of the child solider is considered a post–Cold War epidemic.[49] Indeed, the majority of scholarship written about the child soldier centers on armed military conflicts post–Cold War era.[50] In writings from the perspective of the United States, such as the report by CETO, child soldiers are considered to be employed by nations and countries outside the United States.[51] In other words, it is considered to be a phenomenon in other countries, but not in the United States. The stories about Korean orphans turned mascots turned child soldiers, however, forces us to rethink the phenomenon of child soldiers as primarily a post–Cold War practice and as a practice engaged in by everyone except the United States. Thinking about the Korean orphan as an American veteran places the child soldier inside U.S. troops, at least since the first "hot war" of the Cold War. As a result, the Korean War veteran—refigured in the body of a young Korean boy—revives a history in which the U.S. military engaged in the production of child soldiers.[52] In this way, one could posit that the genealogy of the current child soldier crisis may be traced back to the Korean War (or earlier), where U.S. military forces employed Korean orphans as spies, informants, couriers, and sex slaves.

Figure 8. Like the rest of the male orphan population, Jimmy has his head shaved. Notice how the shaved head signifies the military. Cartoon. Permission granted by Max Crow. www.de634.org.

Female Orphans as Camptown Women

As Korean boys were fashioned into American soldiers, Korean girls were constructed in the image of the camptown sex worker. In "Visual Pleasure and Narrative Cinema," Laura Mulvey not only reveals how cinema replicates the male gaze by "highlighting the woman's to-be-looked-at-ness" but also, and more significantly, exposes how cinema becomes the male gaze by "build[ing] the way she is to be looked at." In other words, "cinematic codes create a gaze, a world, an object, thereby producing an illusion cut to the measure of desire."[53] I use Mulvey's insights on the relationship between cinema and the fetishization of women to tease out the relationship between American military culture and the objectification of Korean girls both during and after the Korean War. Specifically, I argue here that the code of militarized prostitution creates a gaze and culture that constructs female orphans in the image of the *gijichon* women, thereby turning the child into an object of pleasure and desire.

On the basis of the AFAK film reels, it is evident that orphan girls do most of the entertaining when American military personnel visit the orphanages. Scenes of girls dancing and singing for American troops far outnumber scenes where orphan boys sing and dance. In most of the performances, the girls dress in *hanbok* (Korean traditional dress) while singing and dancing traditional Korean folk songs (Figure 9).[54] Along with the image of little girls dancing and singing for GIs is the all too common sight of orphan girls presenting guests and other important military men with a bouquet of flowers, as they act as members of the welcoming or thank-you committee. It is unclear how the girls who served as part of the welcoming committee were chosen. Perhaps the most appealing girl of the group was picked. What is clear, however, is that extra effort is made to highlight, in the words of Mulvey, their "to-be-looked-at-ness." A viewer can almost always identify the designated hostess because she stands out from the rest of the orphan population. Extra care is taken to make her especially eye-catching: her hair is accessorized with a ribbon, bow, or barrette; she wears the more formal-looking *hanbok* reserved for special occasions; and sometimes her face is painted with some lipstick and blush. All this is done to attract her intended audience: the very important military man or men in attendance. Almost always, the little girl ends up in the arms of a GI, signaling her success at getting his attention. Although these children did not provide sexual services like the *gijichon* women, female orphans worked to lift the morale and spirits of American GIs by performing similar roles as entertainer and hostess. Indeed, *gijichon* women were euphemistically called "hostesses" and "special entertainers."[55] As hostess and entertainer, the female orphan's primary duty was to make the soldier feel honored, happy, and appreciated by ensuring that he was the focus of attention and that he had an enjoyable visit.

Presenting flowers and singing and dancing for white men can be seen as another extension of the kind of services that Korean sex workers provided at this time: giving pleasure and entertaining foreign servicemen. Moon

Figure 9. In their all-too-common role as entertainers for the U.S. military, these female Korean orphans sing and dance for sailors aboard the USS Mt. McKinley. Photograph. Pacific Stars and Stripes.

explains that *gijichon* women were viewed by both governments (Korean and American) as nurturing "friendly relations" between the two countries by keeping U.S. soldiers happy.[56] As America's comfort women, *gijichon* women became a fundamental aspect of American military culture in South Korea. Yuh, in her study of military camptowns in South Korea, explains that despite efforts to eliminate prostitution in military bases around Europe, the "United States adopted a 'boys will be boys' policy toward camptown prostitution in South Korea." They were able to justify this policy by linking military prostitution to issues of national security. Citing a 1965 study on troop–community relations conducted by the Eighth U.S. Army, Yuh explains that "'fraternization' [in the form of prostitution] endears Korea to the soldiers, making them more willing to fight."[57] Thus, *gijichon* women became a crucial aspect of not only military culture but also of national security issues in that the services they provided lifted the morale of American soldiers during times of war.

I want to take a moment here to further expand my discussion on the militarization of boys. Boys were not immune to the codes of militarized prostitution. On the contrary, we can see its impact through the figure of the mascot. Mascots—the majority of whom were male—were "adopted" into military units and participated in a troop's daily activities, performing domestic chores and running errands. And as I have already noted, some even became members of the U.S. armed forces. However, like the *gijichon* woman, their primary duty was to entertain and keep soldiers happy. According to Paul Shin, who served as a mascot when he was fifteen years old, a mascot's primary duty was to help GIs "find some comfort in what was an otherwise difficult situation." Another Korean boy puts it this way: a mascot is "somebody who plays and has fun with the GIs."[58] As historian Arissa Oh so cogently points out, "As a child, toy, or pet to be teased, played with, and cared for, [the mascot] offered a sense of everyday-ness, fun, and semblance of family for serviceman who were far from home, weary and very often miserable." In this way, Oh explains that mascots operated in the same kind of economy as camptown prostitutes by entering into informal contracts and providing emotional and physical services in exchange for material goods.[59]

The female orphan resembles the *gijichon* woman through her duties as hostess and entertainer as well as through her role as an ambassador. In her reading of the figure of the *yanggongju*, Cho points out that the camptown sex worker became a diplomat during postwar South Korea by "fulfilling her duties to the nation by keeping U.S. interests engaged." Cho goes on to say that as a symbol of South Korea's national security, her "body became a site of control as well as a playing field for negotiating international relations."[60] One could argue that female orphans also served to keep U.S. interests engaged by charming them through their dancing and singing.[61] As stated earlier, without the financial support provided by GIs themselves, many of the orphanages would have shut down. Singing, dancing, and making the soldiers feel special were not only gestures of gratitude but also strategies to keep the donations coming. In this way, the girls were presented as offerings to the soldiers in exchange for their financial support and national security.

The recasting of female orphans in the image of the *gijichon* woman becomes apparent in the stories that were woven around GI encounters with them. For example, the *Pacific Stars and Stripes* article "Redlegs Adopt Korean Pin-up" is about Chun Jea Lee, a four-year-old orphan who was brought to the 57th Field Artillery to be transported to a refugee camp.

However, "the men fell in love with her and decided to keep her with them until she could be nursed back to health." They bathed, fed, and dressed her. They even collected money to "buy her a complete feminine wardrobe." Under their care, this "battalion sweetheart" was named "Miss 57th Field Artillery," or "pin-up girl of 1951."[62] In another article by *Pacific Stars and Stripes* entitled "'Adopted' Korean Girl Loves Officer, Now Happy," the journalist writes, "The lieutenant . . . and Baby-san fell for each other the minute they met on a street in Suwon last April."[63] After several weeks together, however, the lieutenant reached the conclusion that "she had to go" because "Baby-san didn't fit into the military picture." As a result, the story that began with "love at first sight" ended with the lieutenant dropping off Baby-san at an orphanage. One could easily mistake this story to be about a *giji-chon* woman and a GI rather than a six-year-old girl and a lieutenant. Indeed, the setting and plot are the same: a street meeting leads to a period of infatuation that eventually leads to male abandonment. The abandonment scene is so dramatic that it is captured on film and shown across the world. The article continues: "But the time to leave finally came, and again Baby-san didn't like it. As she clung to [Lieutenant] Doernbach, crying and trying to stop his departure, newsmen's cameras caught the scene. For a few days she was the most popular Korean child in the United States." Even the gifts he gave her were items that were popular among *gijichon* women. When he visited Baby-san in the orphanage, he gave her "Stateside shoes, a dress and stockings."[64] Articles such as these illustrate the ways in which the racialized, gendered, and sexualized dimensions of militarized prostitution extended to the orphanages and disciplined the Korean female orphans. More significantly, however, these articles verify that militarized prostitution structured the way she was seen, interpreted, and consumed by the soldier's gaze, "cut to the measure of desire."

"GIs and the Orphans" and the Militaristic Gaze

Coming full circle, I return to the image that has been the cornerstone of the first two chapters. "GIs and the Orphans" vividly demonstrates how the code of militarized prostitution became encoded on the bodies of postwar female orphans. Here we see three white soldiers each holding a young girl, propped up in his arms (Figure 1). These girls are wearing special-occasion *hanbok* and have ribbons tied in their hair. Although they don't look older than five years of age, they have makeup on their faces. They look like porcelain Oriental dolls, with their painted faces and rosebud lips. Despite the sexual innocence that a doll conveys, their positioning, along with the highly charged political and historical context, eroticizes this doll-like image. The pairing of these exoticized Asian female bodies next to the white militaristic male body conjures up militarized prostitution. Indeed, these girls, despite their very young age, look like they could be sexual partners to these men. With grimaces on their faces, each white soldier proudly props up his girl, as if on display. The GIs hold them like they are accessories—trophies—and look upon them with desire.[65]

This look of desire is what I call the militaristic gaze. The militaristic gaze is an imperial male gaze that emerges from the close encounters between foreign servicemen and Korean orphans and the cultural codes of militarized prostitution.[66] It is fraught with contradictions. Shrouded in Orientalism and paternalism, it is a gaze mixed with the desire to possess and the desire to save.[67] It is a look that pities the child and at the same time wants to conquer the child; to care for the child and also to dominate the child; to be both father and lover. On the one hand, this gaze objectifies the orphan in order to bolster the identity of the soldier. On the other hand, the militaristic gaze works to assuage military might and imperial power by projecting the soldier as a humanitarian. The orphan—who is constructed as helpless, hungry, and innocent—becomes a conduit through which the masculinity and humanity of the GI is fortified. The orphan's mere existence provides the GI with the opportunity to demonstrate his patriotism, manhood, and virility—as well as his softer, sensitive side—by helping the little waifs. In short, the orphan becomes the vessel through which the GI becomes both a military hero and humanitarian.

Although one can gaze from afar, the militaristic gaze almost always engenders physical contact between the soldier and child. Gazing leads to touching, which is almost always done in the spirit of giving. The handing out of sweet treats, the trying on of donated clothes, the distribution of toys, the administering of medicine—these all provide the occasion for the soldier to be close and to touch the child. Charity becomes the stage in which the militaristic gaze is activated. This spatial intimacy—along with the pervasive culture of militarized prostitution—leads to the eroticism of innocence, which is another condition of the militaristic gaze. In *Erotic Innocence: The Culture of Child Molesting*, James Kincaid posits that the modern child was constructed in tandem with modern sexuality.[68] The modern child, whom he argues was formulated in the eighteenth century, was assigned the Romantic virtues of innocence, naturalness, and even divinity.[69] The child became antithetical to the adult, packaged as "free of adult corruptions: not yet burdened with the weight of responsibility, mortality, and sexuality." Constructing children as innocent and pure was not the problem. What became dangerous, as Kincaid points out, is that we also assigned the same qualities to what is sexually desirable: innocence, purity, and sweetness. Consequently, we came to see the child and the erotic as coincident, or similar in nature.[70] This is how innocence became erotic.

Figures 10 and 11 indicate the erotic dimensions of innocence and the militaristic gaze. According to Kincaid, the vacant, hollow look of the children makes them all the more appealing to the viewer because it signifies their innocence.[71] In addition, the way these orphans are intimately positioned against the soldier—propped up in the GI's arms, standing eye to eye, draped across the GI's neck and shoulders, and crouching between the GI's legs—along with the look of desire on the soldiers' faces infuses the partnership with eroticism. However, Kincaid's thesis can take us only so far in analyzing these children because he focuses predominately on images of white children. Although the bodies of the Korean War orphans are prepubescent bodies, in this instance, Orientalist viewing practices further infantilize the Asian body, making the orphan hyperinnocent.[72] Furthermore, because they are the victims of war, the sense of injustice that is enacted upon them is heightened precisely because they are children. The hyperinnocence, along with the heightened sense of injustice, made these children almost irresistible under the gaze of GIs because the fantasy of rescue activates the militaristic gaze. It is the combination of these two qualities that enables the militaristic gaze to embody both erotic desire and the heroic impulse to save.

Clothed in the rhetoric of democracy and freedom, American GIs invaded the homes, bodies, and minds of the Korean people. The militaristic gaze continues to do the same kind of violence, yet it comes across as less harmful and destructive because it is veiled in the desire to save, to care for, and most importantly to love the orphan. As a technology of American empire and an extension of the physical occupation of the U.S. military on foreign soil, the militaristic gaze invades the space and bodies of Korean children. One of the primary ways it does this is through the camera. This is dramatically captured in an AFAK film reel entitled "Epidemic Control Unit."

Resisting the Militaristic Gaze

This three-part series documents the activities of the epidemic control unit on the eastern island of Ulleung-do, July 7–13, 1952. Since the Korean War

Figure 10. The militaristic gaze is activated as the GI looks at the young girl with desire during a Christmas party and as Mr. United States (Colonel Dean Hess) admires an orphan from Hope Inc. Orphans' Home of Korea. Still images. "Christmas Party for Korean Orphans, IX Corps, Kinsal, Korea" and Paramount News. National Archives at College Park.

Figure 11. In the first photograph, Kim Kum Soun, called Dotty by members of the 7th Cavalry, is draped over a GI. She is the mascot of K Company. In the second photo, Korean orphan Rocky crouches between the legs of Lieutenant Robert W. Field, who solicited his parents to adopt the young boy. Photographs. Pacific Stars and Stripes. Permission granted by George F. Drake. www.koreanchildren.org.

broke out, a typhus epidemic was prevalent in 1951 and 1952 on both the northern and southern portions of the peninsula.[73] Having heard about a typhus outbreak on this island, the U.S. Navy transported a medical team to contain it. The six days they were on the island are captured on three separate reels. The first reel includes the following scenes: the USS *Unadilla* approaching Ulleung-do, medical supplies being unloaded onto the island, and the medical party walking through the village in order to take stock of the situation. A small group of children in the village have been affected. They are quarantined and their blood is drawn.[74] There is also a boys' orphanage on the island. The second reel focuses on these orphaned boys, who are getting rectal smears and blood drawn from their arms. This second reel also provides footage of the medical team testing the samples in their makeshift laboratory onboard the *Unadilla*.[75] The third and final reel shows the naval crew and medical team converting a pump into a compressor. Before they leave, they use this compressor to spray DDT along the homes of the villagers as well as the orphanage yard and buildings. This reel ends with a shot of the orphaned boys attending a prayer meeting in the yard.[76]

I am particularly interested in the second reel, where the focus is on the boys at the orphanage. The reel is about twelve minutes long. It opens with personnel from the medical team engaged in a volleyball game against the villagers. They are playing in the orphanage yard. In the next scene, the yard has been transformed into a huge waiting area, as male orphans walk in military formation, lining up to get examined. During this sequence, we see close-up shots of the boys who are waiting patiently in line. Some smile for the camera and some giggle; however, most either look deadpan into the camera or look shyly away. Later on, we see medics swabbing the boys' rectums and drawing their blood in order to test for infection. The other half of the reel shows the medical team on the aft of the *Unadilla*, where they have set up their laboratory. It shows them testing the samples they have collected.[77] These images and scenes are what one might expect from a reel entitled "Epidemic Control Unit (USN), Ullong-do, Korea." What is unexpected, however, is the one-minute scene that appears between these two sequences.

In this one-minute scene, we see both the invasion of the militaristic gaze and the resistance to this invasion at play. After filming the boys getting rectal smears and having their blood drawn, the next shot is of a naked little boy running into the East Sea, where there are other naked boys swimming and playing on an inner tube. It seems puzzling that film footage about containing sickness and disease on an island would include clips of naked boys frolicking in the sea, but that is precisely what we witness. Although there are just as many boys on the beach who are fully clothed (as we see in the background shots), the camera lingers on the nude bodies and foregrounds them in this scene. The cameraman zooms in on nude boys sitting and standing on the beach and running into the sea. Their small, lean bodies are tossed about in the crashing waves, which heightens the already homoerotic quality of the footage. Furthermore, as groups of young boys play, their bodies become entangled and wrapped around each other as the waves push them together.[78] In this scene, frontal nudity is also captured. Under the militaristic gaze, this scopophilic series of shots become eye candy for the gaping soldier. Their innocent play becomes eroticized for the sheer pleasure of the looking adult male. This footage of naked young male bodies tossed about the waves seems completely out of place in a film reel about epidemic control; however, as I mentioned earlier, the militaristic gaze can emerge whenever an orphan shares space with a serviceman.

Similar to the physical occupation of South Korea by U.S. forces, the intrusion of the gazing soldier and the eye of the camera holds the boys captive. The camera lens not only captures the image in terms of preserving a moment but also literally captures the child, seizing the child within its frame so that the viewer too can gaze. Thus, the camera acts as an instrument of the militaristic gaze. Objectified by the eye of the camera and cameraman, the young boys are subordinated to the whims and will of the imperial male gaze. The man behind the camera selects which orphans upon which to focus his attention. The camera serves as both eye and hand as it seizes the object held in its frame. Once the cameraman has had his fill, he moves onto the next child that catches his eye.

It would be erroneous, however, to assume the all-consuming power of the camera's gaze or of the man behind the camera. To be sure, the AFAK films are riddled with acts of resistance, both subtle and overt, by the children. There are many instances when children are encouraged to perform for the camera after receiving some kind of aid or donation from the military. Children are nudged by soldiers, orphanage directors, or their caretakers to smile, wave "hi" to the camera, or to show off the Christmas present, donated toy, or sweater they received. Although some children do as they are prodded to do, others blankly stare back and do nothing, ignoring the request of the adult to perform for the camera.[79] For example, in "GIs and the Orphans," we not only see the militaristic gaze in action but also the resistance to that gaze. The girls actively resist the militaristic gaze by refusing to perform—smile—for the camera. In stark contrast to the men proudly holding them, the girls stare solemnly at the camera. Not once do they smile. Later in the scene, the soldiers introduce General Hickey, General MacArthur's chief of staff, to them. In response, the girls actively stare away from the soldiers and the general and instead stare sadly into the camera.[80] In another reel, we see a young girl sitting on cement steps with her head facing away from the camera. A soldier begins to pat her back. She turns to see who is touching her. As she turns to look behind her, she notices the camera and realizes that she is being filmed. In response to the multiple invasions—the unsolicited touch of the GI and the roving eye of the camera—the young girl hides her face in her lap, curls up into a fetal position, and slowly rocks her body away from the GI who is rubbing her back and now her hair.[81] From the way she literally contorts her body away from the soldier and hides her face from the camera, it is obvious that such advances—including being filmed—were unwelcome. Because the camera is an uninvited guest, we see many children repel away from the machine. Some literally run away from the gazing eye of the camera. This is precisely what we witness toward the end of the minute-long scene that featured the naked boys in "Epidemic Control Unit (USN), Ullong-do, Korea."

There is a voyeuristic quality to this footage, as if capturing the children in a private moment. In this particular instance, a little boy is caught by surprise when he looks up and sees the camera lens staring straight at him. In the series of shots in Figure 12, we see that at the moment of recognition, the young boy attempts to scurry away from the camera's eye. The camera, however, continues to follow him. Unable to get away, the little boy surrenders and smiles shyly at the camera. Then, in a final act of defiance, he looks straight into the camera and points his finger, as if to say, "I see you. I can gaze back too" (Figure 13). At this moment, the cameraman quickly cuts back to a wide shot of the boys swimming in the water, which marks the end of the scene.

All the elements of the militaristic gaze come together in this one scene: invasion, captivity, objectification, and (pre)occupation. The militaristic gaze of the camera invades the boy's private, personal space. Like American military occupation, it holds the boy captive. However, what is unexpected in this scene is that the boy challenges the gaze—not only by running away but, more importantly, by gazing back. In *Colonial Harem*, Malek Alloula indicates that for the Algerian woman, the veil not only functions as a "closure of private space" (the woman's body becoming a no-trespassing zone to the colonial eye of the Western camera) but also becomes her own personal camera in which to gaze back at the colonial photographer:

Figure 12. The young boy attempts to run away from the militaristic gaze of the camera. Still images. "Epidemic Control Unit (USN), Ulleung-do, Korea." National Archives at College Park.

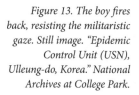

Figure 13. The boy fires back, resisting the militaristic gaze. Still image. "Epidemic Control Unit (USN), Ulleung-do, Korea." National Archives at College Park.

The feminine gaze that filters through the veil is a gaze of a particular kind: concentrated by the tiny orifice for the eye, this womanly gaze is a little like the eye of a camera, like the photographic lens that takes aim at everything.

The photographer makes no mistake about it: he knows the gaze well; it resembles his own. . . . Thrust in the presence of a veiled woman, the photographer feels photographed; having himself become an object-to-be-seen, he loses initiative: *he is dispossessed of his own gaze.*[82]

We can read the Korean boy's defiance in the same way: he dispossesses the militaristic gaze of the cameraman by returning the gaze. The cameraman feels "shot at" not only by the boy's focused stare—which mirrors the hard stare of the camera lens—but also by his pointed finger, which could be taken to symbolize a gun. As a tool of colonial domination, the camera, as Ella Shohat points out, was referred to as a gun "precisely because the camera has been used as a gun by colonial powers" and because of its "gun-like apparatus."[83] The child's response evokes this history by fighting back in kind. He—like the boy at the 7th Division Christmas party—defends himself with his "gun" (finger) in response to being "shot" by the GI's "gun" (camera). Having become the object to be seen, the cameraman not only "loses initiative" but also loses his possession of the little boy and moves onto less threatening territory (a wide shot of naked boys swimming) where he can reassume his role of gazer.

If we track the boy's movement from the first frame to the last frame, we discover that the boy returns the gaze only when he is in the company of fully dressed compatriots. In his attempt to escape the militaristic gaze, he moves the eye of the camera from nude male bodies to fully clothed orphans. The boys' clothing—like the Algerian women's veil—acts like a protective barrier against objectification and occupation. In this footage, fully dressed boys are of no interest here; the militaristic gaze is only interested in nude boys in this particular scene. So the enclosure created by the group of fully clothed boys acts like a safe zone, a "no trespassing" or "no gazing" zone, for the fleeing child. Once there, with the support and protection of his mates, the little boy is able to stand up to his intruders: the camera, the cameraman, and the militaristic gaze. In so doing, he not only protects himself but also offers reprieve from the objectifying eye of the camera for the other nude boys who were captured in the same frame with him just moments ago.[84]

What I want to suggest here with my twofold argument regarding the militaristic gaze and the orphan as militarized subject is this: military occupation, militarized humanitarianism, and militarized prostitution were the conditions that made "GIs and the Orphans" possible. In arguing that Korean orphans during and immediately after the war are constituted by militarized prostitution—that they are made in the image of the American soldier and the *gijichon* woman—I am not suggesting that they are the same. Although some male orphans did indeed become members of the U.S. military, and although some female orphans did indeed become camptown prostitutes, making the claim that Korean orphans are just like American soldiers or are just like *gijichon* women has not been my purpose here. There are clear differences among them. According to Moon, "kijich'on women are living symbols of the destruction, poverty, bloodshed, and separation from family of Korea's civil war. They are living testaments of Korea's geographical and political division into North and South and of the South's military insecurity and consequent dependence on the United States." It is precisely because they index the ugly side of war that *gijichon* women and the system of camptown prostitution have been neglected in much of Korean War scholarship: "Kijich'on prostitution surely is not a matter of heroism in war. . . . It is not a practice or story to be proud of."[85] Korean orphans, on the other hand, have been figured as living symbols of American exceptionalism. They have become constructed in the national imaginary and in dominant American culture as living testaments to the kindness, generosity, and benevolence of the American armed forces. They are the stuff on which stories of heroism have been built. Militarized humanitarianism, as explained in chapter 1 and archived in *GIs and the Kids—A Love Story,* reconfigures the destruction and devastation of war into acts of heroism. Concerning the Korean War orphan crisis, homelessness and the loss of family became the raw materials used to create narratives of charitable love and kindness that staged the GI as a benevolent hero. However, by invoking the system of militarized prostitution as a key material condition that made Korean adoption possible, I have used this chapter to dislodge postwar Korean orphans from being a "matter of heroism in war" by recuperating the imperial, racialized, gendered, and sexualized economies that have constituted the Korean orphan.

Revealing the overlaps and interconnections between the culture of militarized prostitution and the portrayal of Korean orphans in AFAK films and American print media exposes the fundamental ways in which militarized prostitution shaped the subjectivities of Korean orphans during and after the war. As militarized subjects, Korean orphans naturally appealed to other military subjects, such as GIs. As stated earlier, American servicemen were the first group of people to adopt Korean children orphaned by U.S. military activity.[86] However, given the withdrawal of troops after the signing of the cease-fire agreement, their appeal needed to be expanded to a broader base: the civilian population. Because these children were ultimately designated for transnational rather than domestic adoption, militarized orphans underwent some changes to make them even more appealing to foreigners, particularly white Americans. The material conditions that made "GIs and the Orphans" possible are not the same as the conditions that made the "Holt Family Portrait" possible. The next two chapters focus on the new set of circumstances that enabled these changes, along with the strategies that were used to inspire average Americans to act on behalf of Korean War orphans halfway across the world.

3 MARKETING THE SOCIAL ORPHAN

IF THE FIRST TWO CHAPTERS EXPLORED the material conditions of "GIs and the Orphans," then these next two chapters investigate the conditions that made possible the image that has become the dominant face of Korean adoption: the "Holt Family Portrait." For this particular chapter, I focus on the following questions: What factors enabled the transfer of Korean orphans from the arms of GIs into the arms of average American civilians? What motivated them to act? In other words, what inspired these civilians to care for and "save" the displaced children of South Korea through transnational adoption? What conditions allowed white American civilians to imagine an Asian child as a son or daughter during an era of Asian exclusion? By answering these questions, I explain the process in which "GIs and the Orphans" transforms into the "Holt Family Portrait."

This chapter attends to the various discursive strategies that constructed Korean orphans in such a way as to facilitate their inclusion into the domestic and national family of the United States. Whereas the previous chapter examined the production of Korean orphans in the fantasies of American soldiers, this chapter analyzes their construction in the fantasies of American civilians. I begin by providing the political and ideological setting of 1950s America. I rely on Christina Klein's theorization of Cold War Orientalism to help set the scene because it effectively explains the ideological shift toward Asians—from racial exclusion to racial tolerance and inclusion— that took place during this decade. The prime metaphor that was used to envision the incorporation of Asians into American politics and life was that of family. In other words, the integrationist policies that emerged from Cold War Orientalism refigured U.S.–Asia relations in terms of familial relations. In order to become a part of the American family, however, the Asian body had to be stripped of his or her national affiliation. We see this play out in the construction of the displaced Korean child as a social orphan—an orphan whose familial and national ties are severed in order to reincorporate him or her into the national and domestic American family.

I then discuss how the narratives of militarized humanitarianism and visual iconographies of rescue motivated ordinary Americans to act on behalf of Asian children halfway around the world. Relying on 1950s newspaper articles, newsreels, and film reels from the Department of Defense, I explain how the figure of the Korean social orphan—along with the narratives of rescue and compassion that accompanied this figure—inspired civilians to participate in the activities of militarized humanitarianism initiated by U.S. soldiers overseas. The stories and images of Korean social orphans that circulated in popular media served as pedagogical tools that helped ordinary civilians imagine new affiliations with Asian peoples. Pleas for help by U.S. soldiers, along with news stories about Korean children literally dying of hunger, spurred not only average Americans but also big corporations to donate food, clothing, and money to the postwar relief activities that targeted Korean children. These small acts of rescue eventually led to the permanent rescue of these children via Korean adoption.

The final part of this chapter explicates how Orientalism and commodity fetishism coalesced to make the Korean social orphan marketable and therefore consumable in order to facilitate his or her entrance into American homes. More specifically, an image of the Korean social orphan as Oriental doll was mass-produced to make the Asian body desirable and less threatening. Race and gender intersected to reduce the Korean child into an object, turning her into a target of yellow desire, which was integral to fostering a new vision of an American family—both national and domestic—that included Asians.

Cold War Orientalism and the Production of the Social Orphan

For most of American history, the United States' policy toward the presence of Asians in America has been one of exclusion. A series of immigration laws, such as the 1882 Chinese Exclusion Act and the 1924 Immigration Act, had, for the most part, barred the legal immigration of Asians into the United States; however, World War II became a watershed year in terms of the shifting and contradictory policies the U.S. government had concerning Asians.[1] By fighting the Nazis in Germany, the United States worked to position itself as a promoter of racial equality. As cultural historian

Robert G. Lee explains, despite the segregation between whites and blacks on the home front and in the military and the anti-Semitic policy of denying refugee status to European Jews, "the U.S. government condemned the Nazi's doctrine of racial superiority and identified the defeat of racism as one of the reasons 'Why We Fight.'"[2]

This new change in attitude greatly affected the government's policy toward Asians living inside and outside U.S. borders. For example, in 1943, the Magnuson Bill was signed, repealing the Chinese exclusion laws. According to historian Erika Lee, this repeal was "mostly a symbolic gesture of friendship to China (a wartime ally against Japan)" because the immigration quota only allowed 105 Chinese to enter per year. However, despite its symbolic nature, Robert G. Lee maintains that it still signaled a shift in policy from outright restriction to a gradual integration of Asian subjects into the U.S. citizenry. The Magnuson Bill allowed Chinese immigrants to become naturalized citizens. The War Brides acts of 1945 and 1947 enabled those alien subjects who fought for the U.S. military to bypass quotas and bring their foreign-born spouses and children into the United States.[3] Even the issuing of Executive Order 9066 in 1942, which evacuated persons of Japanese descent into internment camps, could be perceived as a project of integration within this context. Caroline Chung Simpson suggests precisely this when she argues that Japanese internment was not only about outright exclusion but also about incorporation and reintegration of the seemingly unassimilable Asian body. Simpson claims that the Japanese internment camps served as an experiment on American citizenship, testing the capabilities of Asians to assimilate into the U.S. national family and training them to be better citizen-subjects.[4] She writes, "The internment itself was conceived as the first step in a program to make Japanese Americans more 'American' and thus less alien to non–Asian Americans." The "experiment in racial integration" continued through the 1943 War Relocation Authority (WRA) Resettlement Project, which worked to ease the smooth integration of Japanese Americans into public society, primarily by reintroducing only the most loyal Japanese Americans.[5]

These racially integrative projects such as repeal, Japanese internment, and resettlement can be seen as preludes to another kind of racially integrative project: the inclusion of Korean orphans into predominantly white American families. Part of the reason why white Americans could perceive Korean children as potential family members via transnational adoption, despite the long history of Asian exclusion, is precisely because of these initial efforts to incorporate and integrate the racialized Asian body into the white American national landscape. These efforts were shaped by the changing geopolitical relationship between the United States and Asia within the Cold War era.

According to historian Christina Klein, the geopolitics of the Cold War provided an occasion for an ideological sea change in the way Asians were perceived at this time: from exclusion to integration. In *Cold War Orientalism: Asia in the Middlebrow Imagination, 1945–1961,* Klein investigates the expansion of U.S. power during an era of global decolonization by examining how the United States dealt with this key question: "How can we define our nation as a nonimperial world power in the age of decolonization?"[6] Klein argues that Cold War Orientalism—produced by middlebrow Americans and policy-making elites—worked to resolve this paradox. Specifically, she asserts that through Cold War Orientalism, the U.S. government constructed an ideology that justified its military and imperial expansion in Asia during the era of revolutionary decolonization via a politics of integration. If Orientalism, as theorized by Edward Said, was a discursive strategy that was used to legitimize Europe's coercive domination and colonial control of the Far East during the nineteenth century, then Cold War Orientalism employed tactics of affiliation and interdependence to justify its expansion in Asia during the Cold War.[7] As Klein eloquently explains:

> Different kinds of expansion demand and produce different legitimating discourses. Because U.S. expansion into Asia was predicated on the principle of international integration rather than on territorial imperialism, it demanded an ideology of global interdependence rather than one of racial difference. The Cold War Orientalism generated by middlebrow intellectuals articulated precisely such an ideology.[8]

This ideology of global interdependence and racial tolerance underwrote a variety of projects that the United States created in order to assert its global power and expansion in Asia under the guise of anti-imperialism. One of these projects was the U.S.-funded humanitarian aid and relief efforts to South Korea immediately after the Korean War. Other projects included child sponsorship programs and the actual adoption of postwar orphans.

Klein indicates that the 1950s became a decade where the family became inaugurated as the prime metaphor for U.S.–Asian relations. Casting foreign relations as sentimental familial relations allowed Americans—for the first time—to imagine familial bonds between white Americans and nonwhite

Asians. The family could be mixed race; it no longer had to be defined through blood ties and biology.[9] But the familial bond imagined between the American and the Asian was not one of siblings or cousins; rather it was one of parent and child, with the white American as the parent and the non-white Asian as the child. As it relates to postwar Korean orphans, recasting the family in this way helped white Americans to envision the Korean child as a son or daughter while securing the neocolonial relationship between the United States and South Korea.

Perceiving the postwar Korean child as both a member of the national and domestic American family required the child to be stripped of his or her previous national and kinship ties. Consequently, all displaced Korean children—whether or not their parents were living—were categorized as orphaned. During the Joseon dynasty (1392–1910), distinctions were made among children who were abandoned, lost, or orphaned. Orphans were described as "children who are left alone with no one to depend on after the death of a [family] member."[10] Not until after the Korean War did such distinctions become blurred. The distinction that marked a child who was abandoned (a child with a living parent) from a child who was orphaned (a child whose parents were deceased) quickly eroded during the chaos and confusion of war. Families ravaged by guerilla warfare and bombing left tens of thousands of children displaced. Many were indeed orphaned, as their families were killed. But many others were separated or lost during the chaos, unsure whether or not their parents were alive. The hectic circumstances, along with the sheer size of this new demographic of children, made it difficult to distinguish which children were indeed orphans and which were separated from their parents. The label *orphan,* as it was used after the war, was a misnomer because many of the war orphans had at least one parent living. In the case of mixed-race orphans, both parents were usually alive. Thus, the category of orphans included not only children who were orphaned but also those who were abandoned or lost.

This conflation of the abandoned or lost child with the orphaned child turned the displaced Korean child into a social orphan—an orphan in legal terms rather than in fact. According to Jodi Kim,

> The very production of the adoptee as a legal orphan, which severs the adoptee from any kinship ties and makes her an exceptional state subject, renders her the barest of social identities and strips her of her social personhood. This social death is paradoxically produced precisely so that the orphan can legally become an adoptee, a process that presumably negates her social death through a formal re-attachment to kinship and thus a restoration of social identity and personhood.[11]

Here, Kim explains that the precondition for the Korean child's adoption, precisely because he or she was not an orphan in the strictest sense of the word (that is, losing both biological parents), is social death. Similar to Giorgio Agamben's *homo sacer*, the Korean child's inclusion into the juridical order of the United States necessitates that an exclusion takes place—in this case, social death.[12]

Severing family ties to South Korea facilitates the child's ability to take on another alternative social and familial identity. However, I would add that given the close discursive relationship between family and nation, the severing of the Korean family also makes space for an alternative American nationality to be acquired. In this way, social death facilitates the Korean child's inclusion into the U.S. citizenry. Cutting national ties becomes necessary for the Korean orphan to be adoptable and to become an American citizen. In other words, killing off the Korean family (by conflating the lost or abandoned child with the orphaned child) inadvertently destabilizes the child's national affiliation to Korea, which is required for the Korean child to take on an alternative American national identity. Norwegian scholar Signe Howell puts it another way: she argues that adoption across national borders is possible for the Korean child because the child is "socially naked." Howell explains: "The child is denuded of all kinship; denuded of meaningful relatedness. . . . By being abandoned by relatives . . . and left for strangers to look after, the children are at the same time 'de-kinned' by them, removed from kinned sociality." Here, Howell uses clothing as a metaphor for family and nation. By stripping the child of his or her family, and thus of his or her national affiliation, the child becomes naked. This allows the child to clothe him- or herself with new raiment: "The nakedness enables the state to relinquish a citizen, and the new state to accept one, because she will not be naked in her new country. She enters it fully clothed in new relatives."[13]

Mobilizing Ideologies of Rescue

The construction of the Korean social orphan was crucial to inspiring average American civilians to act on behalf of the children displaced by the Korean War. After all, the purpose of turning the displaced Korean child into a social orphan was to facilitate adoption. The figure of the Korean social orphan appeared in popular media outlets during the 1950s, including radio programs, telecasts, newspapers, magazines, and newsreels. Referred to as "waif," "urchin" or "moppet" in these various media outlets, the Korean social orphan took center stage in many human-interest stories pertaining to the Korean War.[14] If social death facilitated the legal adoption of Korean children, then the prospect of literal physical death compelled ordinary Americans to take the first step: to begin caring about the well-being of the children they saw in magazines, newspapers, and newsreels. The American news media was able to recruit Americans to care about Korean War orphans by weaving stories that capitalized on the possibility of their imminent death, if not for the intervention of Americans.

Stories that touted the tragic circumstances of Korean orphans began with American soldiers writing to their family and friends back home. On the front lines, American serviceman had firsthand accounts of the dire situation involving the Korean children, and they passed these stories onto their loved ones through the letters they wrote.

In the *Pacific Stars and Stripes* article, "Yank's Appeal Brings Flood of Donations," the following story is relayed (Figure 14):

> HQ., U.S. 7TH DIV., Korea—A soldier's letter to his mother on behalf of needy Korean children has resulted in a flood of donations from the citizens of Ludington, Mich.
>
> "I have seen kids about five years old die from hunger and cold," wrote PFC William Lange. "I have seen them begging for food like dogs" and "go to the dump and pick for food."
>
> The soldier, assigned to B Btry., 57th FA Bn., asked his mother to "please send CARE boxes to Korea—even if it's just a 10-cent can of soup or a pair of socks— but please give and the Lord will bless you for it."
>
> Lange's mother sent the letter to a newspaper in Ludington. When the letter appeared in the paper, Ludington citizens decided to do something about it.
>
> They formed an association, The Ludington Helping Hand for Korean Children. Housewives and businessmen made their homes and stores collecting points for clothing, food and toys.
>
> Soon after, Mrs. Gerald Heslipen, chairman of the association, wrote Capt. Wilfred C. Oelrich, Lange's battery commander, telling him of the town's response. She enclosed a photo of 22 boxes being mailed at the local post office. In addition to the boxes of needed items, the association ordered four large CARE food packages and 95 U.S. Food Surplus Holiday CARE packages.[15]

Here we witness how the militarized humanitarianism of American soldiers influenced the activities of civilians back home. Militarized humanitarianism served not only to promote the United States as a benevolent occupier (as discussed in chapter 1) but also to recruit civilians back home to participate in the cause. By utilizing the American news media to spread the word about the good work they were doing abroad, the U.S. military was able to

U.N., Reds to Debate Sabre-MIG Dogfight

S&S.Korea Bureau

PANMUNJOM, Korea—U.N. Command and Communist delegates to the Military Armistice Commission meet here again Thursday morning for the second consecutive day—this time to take up Red charges that UNC personnel violated the demarcation line.

These charges, originally slated to be discussed at Wednesday's meeting, were set aside when the Reds asserted that last Saturday's dog fight between U.S. Sabrejets and Communist MIGs was over North Korea.

Two U.S. Sabres of the 5th Air Force's 4th Fighter- Interceptor Wg. knocked down two Red MIGs Saturday while flying cover for a U.S. RB-45 reconnaissance plane over international waters of the Yellow Sea.

Ignore Lost MIGs

In Wednesday's MAC meeting, the Communists did not mention the loss of the two MIGs, but claimed that their planes chased eight U.S. Sabrejets, and an American bomber out of North Korea last Saturday.

They said the same number of U.S. planes entered North Korea again Tuesday.

Chief Communist delegate Lt. Gen Lee Sang Cho demanded the UNC "severely punish the instigators" of the incidents. But Maj. Gen. Leslie D. Carter, chief UNC delegate to the MAC, tore into the Communists with immediate countercharges which put the Reds on the defensive in the cold war of words.

Vigorous Reply

Carter told Lee that he knew only of "an unwarranted attack which forced our aircraft to defend themselves" over international waters last Saturday.

Carter pointed out to the Reds that "the fact "hat you now acknowledge ownership of the attacking aircraft confirms . . . that your side has committed a hostile act . . . in this unprovoked and unjustified attack."

The fact that the MIGs headed back to North Korea "offers convincing proof," said Carter, that the Communists have illegally introduced new combat aircraft into North Korea since the signing of the armistice.

Witness Says PWs Too Weak to Flee

FORT SILL, Okla. (UP)—U.S. prisoners of war in North Korean Camp 12 were too weak to escape if given a chance, a witness testified Wednesday at the court-martial of Army Maj. Ambrose Nugent.

The court-martial is hearing testimony on 13 charges of collaborating with North Korean Communists against Nugent.

The 19th witness in the third week of the trial, M/Sgt. Roy T. Gordon of Tacoma, Wash., said he was in Camp 12 where Nugent also was a prisoner.

Members of the court-martial board asked Gordon about the camp's physical setup. He said there was no barbed wire and the prisoners were allowed to wander into the woods.

AF Selects 10 For Staff School

TOKYO (S&S)—Ten FEAF officers have been chosen to enter the Armed Forces Staff College at Norfolk, Va. in August.

The group includes three officers from FEAF Hq., five from the Fifth Air Force and two from the Twentieth Air Force. The officers selected are: Col. Linus F. Upson Jr., Lt. Cols. James E. Lazenby and Glen A. Stoll of FEAF Hq.; Lt. Cols. Harold J. Cott, John M. Rett, Ralph E .Mo- Daniel, Richard M. Scott and Robert F. Todd of Fifth Air Force; and Col. Travis B. Hoover and Lt. Col. David B. Tudor of Twentieth Air Force.

NEW AERIAL WORK-HORSE—The Lockheed Hercules, the YC-130, a powerful new USAF transport designed for tough assignments, cruises over the California countryside during a test flight. The new turbo-prop cargo carrier can take off from short runways and fly higher and faster than existing military transports and has a 132-foot wingspan. (Lockheed Photo)

Lawton in Saigon After Report to Ike

SAIGON, Indochina (AP)—General J. Lawton Collins, President Dwight D. Eisenhower's special envoy to Indochina, arrived here Wednesday to resume his duties after reporting to the President in Washington.

Camp Nara Changes Administrative Hands

CAMP NARA, Japan (9thMarReg)—Sub-unit No. 1, Hq. and Svc. Co., 9th Marine Regt. has taken over Camp Nara, former home of the 4th Marine Regt.

The majority of the marines in the Nara detachment are former members of the 4th Marine Regt., who are scheduled for rotation in February and March.

Members of the detachment provide security and working details for the camp area. Portions of Camp Nara will be turned back to the Army when the Marines leave.

German, Japan Employees Lead

WASHINGTON (UP) —More Japanese and Germans work for the U.S. military abroad than any other foreign, nationals, a congressional report indicated Saturday.

The report on federal personnel and pay showed that nearly 159,000 foreign nationals work for the Army, Navy and Air Force in Japan and over 124,000, for those agencies in Germany.

SERVICE NEWS

Mishiri Bar Owners Plan War on Vice

CAMP WHITTINGTON, Japan (1stCavDiv) — Bar owners of Mishiri village near here have pledged to fight the sale of drugs and other illegal activities after a meeting with Col. Harry L. Seivers, 8th Cavalry Regt. and Camp Whittington commander.

Seivers had threatened to put the area adjacent to Whittington off limits unless it was cleaned up.

He emphasized, however, that "good places" would stay open to provide relaxation for the troops.

The owners have formed an organization to help check illicit activities.

Kumagaya Police Chief Chuichi Okutomi called on the owners of local businesses to get the cooperation of those not at the meeting.

The amusement area near Whittington sprang up "overnight" last year when the 8th Cav. Regt. was redeployed there.

Home Classes Graduate Nine

SENDAI, Japan (1stCavDiv) —The Red Cross Home Care of the Sick course has graduated nine students at Camp Younghans.

The course was the second half of a two-part class which began with mother and baby care. Mrs. Liebnow, a registered nurse, was the volunteer instructor.

Yank's Appeal Brings Flood of Donations

HQ., U.S. 7TH DIV., Korea—A soldier's letter to his mother on behalf of needy Korean children has resulted in a flood of donations from the citizens of Ludington, Mich.

"I have seen kids about five years old die from hunger and cold," wrote PFC William Lange. "I have seen them begging for food like dogs" and "go to the dump and pick for food."

The soldier, assigned to B Btry., 57th FA Bn., asked his mother to "please send CARE boxes to Korea—even if it's just a 10-cent can of soup or a pair of socks—but please give and the Lord will bless you for it."

Lange's mother sent the letter to a newspaper in Ludington. When the letter appeared in the paper, Ludington citizens decided to do something about it.

They formed an association, The Ludington Helping Hand for Korean Children. Housewives and businessmen made their homes and stores collecting points for clothing, food and soys.

Soon after, Mrs. Gerald Hea-

USA Photo
LANGE (CENTER) PRESENTS A JACKET FROM LUDINGTON

lpen, chairman of the association, wrote Capt. Wilfred C. Oelrich, Lange's battery commander, telling him of the town's response. She enclosed a photo of 22 boxes being mail-ed at the local post office.

In addition to the boxes of needed items, the association ordered four large CARE food packages and 90 U.S. Food Bar-plus Holiday CARE packages.

Howls, Hurrahs Greet Coming Revelation of Air Force Knees

WASHINGTON (UP) — Air Force men began worrying about exposing their knobbly knees to the public as word spread that shorts will become a part of their hot weather uniform.

"I have fairly attractive legs myself, but I don't know how some of the other boys are going to look," one Washington pilot said jokingly.

The Air Force made the newest note in military fashion to add to the comfort of its men in the summer ahead. The comfort angle appealed to the airmen, but the problem of appearance is a hot subject of barracks debate.

Some airmen said shorts in the service, but officials said military females will be kept in skirts except when they go to the gym.

T/Sgt. George A. Bishop of Lake Worth, Fla., stationed at Hensley AFB, Dallas, Tex., said he couldn't approve of shorts "for the best interests of the Air Force."

"I wore that kind of dress in the Johnston Islands, but under extenuating circumstances without the fearful consequence of public opinion."

A S/C Eugene Woods of Newport, Pa., stationed at Hamilton AFB, San Francisco, said, "I think shorts are a good idea for hot weather, but I wouldn't want to wear them around here."

STARS AND STRIPES
PACIFIC

Published daily in Tokyo, Japan, by Pacific Stars and Stripes Revenue-Producing Fund, APO 500, under the administrative jurisdiction of TI&E Hq, AFFE/8th Army, APO 343 by authorization of FEC Home or billet delivery $1.70 per month. Unit subscriptions in bulk $1.50 per month plus postage if paid delivery made. Subscriptions must be paid in advance (AR 210-60, AFR 176-1). AFPS materials are indicated. Editorial opinions expressed are not necessarily those of the Department of Defense.

Officer in Charge .... Lt. Col. James A. Kidd
• Executive Officer .... Maj. Herot E. Ewing (USAF)
Business Manager .... James A. Rose
Managing Editor .... Eugene R. Miller
Production Manager .... Gordon A. Sloan
Circulation Manager .... Gerald D. Lawson
News Editor, Edmund A. Richiazzi City Editor, M/Sgt. Herbert H. Scott; Feature Editor, Richard H. Lavelle Sports Editor, Sgt. Robert Schmidt; Service News Editor, Stephen K. Zimmerman; Korea Bureau Chief S&t, Robert L. Brown Okinawa Bureau Chief, PFC Robert L. Tousing Officer in Charge Korea Printing Plant, Maj. Richard T. Copeland.

Figure 14. Militarized humanitarianism is illustrated in this photograph accompanying the story "Yank's Appeal Brings Flood of Donations." Here we see soldiers providing donated items to a young Korean boy. Used with permission by Stars and Stripes. Copyright 1955, 2012 Stars and Stripes.

get civilians involved. For example, as the commander of the Korean Communication Zone in 1953, General William S. Lawton implemented Operation Good Will, a mission that culminated in the donation of money and materials to orphanages, schools, and hospitals shortly after the cease-fire agreement was signed, as a way to improve relations between the U.S. military and Korean civilians. He had his men write letters to families, friends, and civic organizations back home to contribute to the mission; he also solicited help from Arthur Godfrey, one of the most influential radio and television personalities of the time. The publicity of Operation Good Will on both Godfrey's television and radio shows led to generous contributions from the American public, leading to a successful mission that ended on Christmas Day.[16]

Not only did the accounts from soldiers inspire average American citizens to support projects of militarized humanitarianism, but also the stories themselves served as pedagogical tools, teaching the American civilian population how to interpret the postwar orphan crisis and how to gaze at the orphans themselves. Put another way, stories of militarized humanitarianism that proliferated in American news media shaped how these children were to be seen, interpreted, and received by the American audience. Highly dramatic stories about dead Korean children or starving children scavenging like animals for food taught readers that the orphans in South Korea were innocent victims of war who were at death's door, and only they—the readers—can save them. Although many of these stories came from GIs, Christian missionaries and social workers who were directly involved in providing postwar relief services for the children also circulated these stories. For example, Harry Holt informs readers of the *Oregonian* that hundreds of orphans are "doomed to a life of misery and early death unless they could be brought to this country." His message is clear: without the help of Americans, these orphans will die. Just in case his message gets overlooked, Holt's wife uses a more direct approach. One newspaper headline reads: "Mrs. Holt Says Korea Tots Dying."[17] The Holts were not the only ones to create a sense of emergency when it came to the plight of these children. Susan Pettiss, the director of International Social Services–United States of America Branch Inc. (ISS-USA), also reports in a San Francisco newspaper that the situation in South Korea is "extremely urgent" as a result of overcrowding.[18] It is precisely the frantic tone of urgency that was conveyed in these postwar accounts of the Korean social orphan that compelled many Americans to rescue these children in their state of emergency.[19] In so doing, these stories taught readers how to fulfill their new role as rescuers of postwar Korean children.

Images of waifs who were at death's door—and the stories that accompanied them—created what Laura Briggs calls a "visual iconography of rescue," where representations of needy children mobilized ideologies of rescue and compassion by drawing attention away from the structural factors that caused their plight in the first place.[20] In this particular case, the visual iconography of rescue propped up white Americans as rescuers to non-white children while eliding the material conditions of military occupation and military violence that caused the crisis in the first place. Furthermore, because the visual iconography of rescue produced the figure of the needy waif, then it also, according to Briggs, produced its counterpart: the "would-be rescuer."[21] Given this insight, we can see the GI's letter to his mother, the publicity around Operation Good Will, and the newspaper headings that cited dying Korean orphans as not only visual iconographies of rescue but also solicitations for a would-be rescuer, compelling readers to act.

News programs such as *Paramount News*—considered to be "The Eyes and Ears of the World"—were especially effective in mobilizing ideologies of rescue and compassion by featuring stories of successful rescue missions.[22] One news story, "Hand of Mercy . . . Canadian GIs Save Korean Orphanage," proclaims that "300 Korean youngsters at a Seoul orphanage can sing and smile now" because men from the Royal Canadian Medical Corps supplied them—"in the nick of time"—with food and medical supplies.[23] "Homeless, cold, and hungry," the voice-over continues, "the youngsters would be wanderers once more amidst the bitter backwash of war." After a dramatic pause in the music, the shot fades out of the classroom that the children are sitting in and fades into the dining hall. The narrator enthusiastically says the next line: "But now you'd never know there was suffering from sickness and malnutrition." Accompanied by these words is a shot of the children tightly packed into the dining hall. The camera zooms in on several boys eating from bowls overflowing with rice and vegetables (Figure 15). They open wide their mouths to take in the large spoonfuls of food. The news clip ends with the narrator reminding us that "a truly humane helping hand" is responsible for the temporary state of abundance we see here.[24]

It is no coincidence that so many of these stories concerning the social orphan center on food—either the lack of it (the starving child) or the abundance of it (via Western intervention). Indeed, Klein explains that the narrative of the hungry child was popular during this time, as Cold War geopolitics linked hunger to communism: "Hungry children are susceptible to communist promises of a better future; thus hungry children threaten the security of Americans."[25] The narrator in this newsreel alludes to this

Figure 15. Orphans fill their stomachs full of food, thanks to the donations and help brought in by Canadian soldiers. Still image. Paramount News. National Archives at College Park.

by creating a causal relationship between "homeless, cold, and hungry" to "wanderers once more amidst the bitter backwash of war." As wanderers amid the bitter backwash of war, these children become susceptible to communist influence. Linking hunger to communism also had the effect of producing a convenient way for average citizens to participate in the national fight against communism. As historian Arissa Oh observes about the media depiction of Korean War orphans at the time, "Implicit in these kinds of stories was the message that Americans could win the ideological battle with [communist] North Korea and its allies by helping these orphans."[26]

Amid tales of cold, starving, and dying orphans, accounts about a soldier's mother mobilizing an entire community to donate food, clothing, and toys, reports about a general who got an entire nation to participate in Operation Good Will, and news features like the Canadian GIs in *Paramount News* were particularly important because they provided evidence that small acts could make a big difference in the seemingly overwhelming war orphan crisis and fight against communism. These stories reassured those who were watching that ordinary people could effect extraordinary change. Witnessing others participate compelled readers and viewers alike to join in the relief efforts. Publicizing these acts of militarized humanitarianism became a powerful recruiting tool because it offered visual proof that small gestures of humanitarianism, such as donating clothes or money, can save lives. Winning the battle against communism could be as easy as donating a ten-cent can of food.

Images of militarized humanitarianism persuaded not only individual Americans to participate in the cause concerning Korean orphans but also big corporations. In a 1953 *Life* editorial, the editor solicits businesses to donate money to take care of South Korea's children. Leading by example, the author points out that Time Inc., which publishes *Life* magazine, made a "substantial corporate gift" to the American-Korean Foundation (AKF), a private agency that matches donors with certain rehabilitation projects in South Korea. As an added incentive, the editor informs the reader that businesses can give up to 5 percent of their net income to charities—tax-free. He explains why corporations should get involved: "The successful rehabilitation of Korea will be good for U.S. foreign policy, and therefore for American business." The editorial ends with this petition: "We urge corporate executives, as well as individuals, to get in touch with A.K.F. A hundred dollars will support one child in an orphanage for a year. A thousand will equip a 20-bed hospital ward."[27]

The *Life* magazine editor's invitation is not unlike the strategy used by the Christian Children's Fund (CCF) to get their readers to "adopt" a child. According to Klein, the CCF pamphlets and advertisements can be seen as an invitation to participate in Cold War international and domestic politics. For a mere $10 a month, Americans "can purchase a child, protection from communism, and relief from a sense of political powerlessness."[28] In effect, rescuing the child from starvation became a foreign relations strategy and an issue of national security. Likewise, through his editorial, the *Life* magazine editor recruited corporations to participate in the global politics of the Cold War. Neocolonialism, national security, and global capitalism coalesced in the rehabilitation of South Korea through the figure of the Korean social orphan.

These invitations for political participation via the rescue of the Korean child were rampant among American popular culture—so much so that in 1955, *Look* magazine (subtitled "America's Family Magazine") included a quiz, exhorting readers to "Test yourself! How many of these important messages have reached you?" The introduction states that "it isn't too surprising if your score on this quiz is pretty high. For the fact is that the public service projects shown on these pages are heavily advertised." These projects

Figure 16. Question #7 of "Test Yourself!" reveals the wide extent to which relief and rescue projects targeting Korean children permeated the public discourse in postwar America. Reproduced with permission from Martha Roby Stephens.

included the Red Cross, National Safety Council, and Ground Observer Corps. Interestingly, of the nine quiz questions, one is about the Korean social orphan (Figure 16). Question/Box 7 reads: "This little Korean girl has just received a package from America. Can you fill in the letters on the box?"[29]

The fact that this question is included attests to the high visibility of the Korean social orphan in American popular culture. Indeed, tens of thousands of Americans responded to these powerful stories by sending relief packages through CARE (Cooperative for Assistance and Relief Everywhere), an international humanitarian agency that was founded in 1945; donating money to organizations such as AKF; and sponsoring Korean orphans through CCF. In addition, being able to answer "yes" to this question gave the reader not only a sense of satisfaction in knowing the answer but also gave the reader who actually did send a CARE package a sense of accomplishment by having participated in a cause that "America's Family Magazine" recognized as important and worthwhile.

Ideologies of rescue and compassion were mobilized around activities such as donating food, clothing, and money to Korean orphans. It did not take long for these same ideologies to be transferred to the activity of transnational adoption. The ISS-USA records are filled with letters from prospective adoptive parents (PAPs) who became interested in adopting because of what they saw in the media and heard from organizations such as World Vision and Holt Adoption Program concerning Korean orphans. Indeed, ISS senior case consultant Margaret Valk lists the following reasons why Americans, who had never before been interested in overseas adoption, wanted to adopt a Korean child:

> They [prospective adoptive families] were asking specifically for a Korean child because of their humanitarian and religious concern. Many have strong religious affiliations and had learned of the miserable plight of the children through the missionary groups in Korea. Others had read articles and seen pictures in the press or had been aroused by the reports of American servicemen who had given firsthand accounts of the devastation of the Korean War and the appalling conditions under which these orphans live and die.[30]

Here we see the direct link between militarized humanitarianism and Korean adoption. The language and discourse used to reconfigure the military operation in South Korea as a humanitarian one provided the very framework that enabled civilians to see transnational adoption as a humanitarian act. This is how Korean adoption became conflated with humanitarian rescue. Furthermore, Valk's explanation about why Americans wanted to adopt proves just how influential the reports of militarized humanitarianism and the visual iconographies of rescue that proliferated American popular culture were in tugging the purse strings and heartstrings of the American people. Holt, like the prospective adoptive parents at ISS, became interested in adopting Korean orphans after hearing Reverend Bob Pierce of World Vision Inc. describe their plight. According to Oh, Christian organizations like World Vision "appealed to Christians' sense of responsibility . . . and put the onus directly on Americans" by making the survival of these children dependent on the charitable actions of Americans.[31] The desperate portrayal of the Korean War orphan, the success stories of relief and rescue, and a strong sense of Christian duty inspired Holt and other civilians to permanently rescue these children through adoption. Thus, in the same way that the needy waif produced the would-be rescuer, the construction of the Korean social orphan also produced its counterpart: the prospective adoptive parent. For ISS, adoptions increased by over 50 percent.[32] Holt Adoption Program had so many applicants from PAPs that they stopped processing new applications shortly after a year in the business.[33] Clearly, the visual iconographies of rescue and the accounts of militarized humanitarianism that were disseminated by the American media had a direct impact on fueling the adoption of Korean children.

Projects of rescue, however, are uneven—and even discriminatory—in that not all people are considered to be worthy of rescue. As Briggs points out, ideologies of rescue "position some people as legitimately within a circle of care and deserving of resources" and position some people outside this circle of care and resources.[34] As a result, I argue that there is another element at work that made Asian bodies—specifically the bodies of Korean social orphans—especially suitable targets of American rescue and salvation: their gendered racialization as Oriental dolls.

"Isn't she a doll?"

Social death may have displaced the orphan's national identity as Korean; however, the child's gendered racial identity as Oriental was preserved through a nexus of interweaving demands and desires. The geopolitics of the Cold War and the discourse of Cold War Orientalism created a particular set of conditions that made the bodies of Korean children highly desirable. These children were highly desirable because they were perceived as exotic and cute and because they were perhaps the least threatening group of Asians that the United States had ever encountered: they were children, many of them infants. In addition, undergoing social death severed their familial and national ties to Korea, which primed them to take on a new American identity, making them less threatening. The aura of not being a threat was also fed by conventional Orientalist stereotypes, as the discourses that circulated around these children in the U.S. media constructed them as docile, submissive, and compliant, thus assuring Americans of their successful assimilation. This was particularly important given the goals of Cold War Orientalism. Nonthreatening Korean War orphans in need of rescue provided a salve to the predominant Asian stereotype of the day: the yellow peril. Thus, Korean social orphans emerged as a prime group of candidates on which America's new policy of integrating Asians into America's national family during the Cold War could be tested.

The combination of traditional Orientalist stereotypes and Cold War politics of integration produced what I call yellow desire. Yellow desire is a discursive practice that exploits difference for the purpose of eradicating difference. It runs on the logic that differences can be tamed, managed, and controlled through assimilation. In other words, under yellow desire, the bodies of Korean children become desirable because of their potential to integrate successfully in American society and in their new American family. A significant by-product of yellow desire is that it positioned these children as being worthy of rescue. The belief that Asian bodies could be assimilable placed Korean children "legitimately within a circle of care and deserving of resources." As such, yellow desire catapulted Korean adoptees into exceptional state subjects, providing them with legal protection and rights that were given to a select few.

Because these children were entering U.S. borders during the period of anti-Asian immigration, certain laws were suspended while new legal provisions were created for adopted Koreans. Between the 1924 Immigration Act (which enacted quotas) and the 1965 Immigration Act (which abolished quotas), the immigration of peoples from Asian countries was highly restricted.[35] For Korean children assigned to U.S. homes, they needed a special law to help them bypass the anti-immigration acts in place. In 1953, Congress passed the Refugee Relief Act, which not only allowed American couples to adopt Korean children (only two children per couple) but also legalized the practice of proxy adoption, for which Holt Adoption Program was infamous.[36] Because the Refugee Relief Act was about to expire on December 31, 1956, new legislation had to be created to enable the immigration of Korean children into U.S. homes. As a result of Harry Holt's successful lobbying, Congress passed the Orphan Bill in 1957, which exempted Korean orphans from immigration quotas. In so doing, this bill, according to Tobias Hübinette, "secur[ed] the future for international adoption from Korea to the U.S."[37] Four years later, the Immigration and Nationality Act was amended to give transnational adoption from South Korea a permanent place in American law by codifying and making permanent the laws that admitted overseas adopted children.[38] In this way, the Korean adoptee became an exceptional state subject not only because she underwent social death, as Jodi Kim pointed out, but also because her personhood as an adoptee was produced via the suspension of laws.[39] Yellow desire and the burgeoning discourse of the Asian as a model minority during the 1950s was so powerful that it facilitated the Korean child's immigration in an era of Asian exclusion.[40]

An effective way to assure their compliance and docility was to fashion Korean social orphans into dolls. In *Orientals: Asian Americans in Popular*

Culture, Robert G. Lee identifies and examines the historical and political context in which the "six faces of the Oriental" emerged. They are "the pollutant, the coolie, the deviant, the yellow peril, the model minority, and the gook."[41] I suggest that another face of the Oriental became prevalent in American popular culture during the mid-twentieth century: the Oriental doll. Like the other faces of the Oriental, the Oriental doll was produced under specific political, social, and cultural conditions and functioned to perform specific ideological tasks. The Oriental doll also arose from certain "transformations of the structure of accumulation." Citing economic historians David M. Gordon and Michael Reich, Lee explains that "at each stage of capitalist development, new 'emergent' public spheres are constituted and new demands arise for participation in the dominant public sphere."[42] As such, economic shifts produce the emergence of new faces— new racialized, gendered, and sexualized constructions of the Asian. Given the economic shift toward consumer capitalism in the 1950s, this particular change in the structure of accumulation provided the conditions in which Korean children as Oriental dolls became mass-marketed commodities for consumption.

The first step in turning Korean social orphans into dolls was to erase individual markers of difference. With over 40,000 orphans in existence immediately after the war, the Korean government, under the guidance of American military personnel and Christian missionaries, organized this body into a manageable group. The government worked to control and regulate this diverse population through techniques that homogenized and erased difference. One way, as previously discussed, was through taxonomy: conflating displaced and lost children with orphaned children and categorizing them all as orphans. Another way was through physical appearance: making them appear indistinguishable from one another. With very few exceptions, all female orphans had blunt bobbed hair cut at or just below the ear, and all male orphans had shaved heads. Some people attribute the shaved head as a precaution toward the spread of lice, but only male orphans wore this hairstyle, which connoted masculinity, discipline, and order.[43] (After all, girls were also afflicted with lice, but their heads were not shaved.) The children's hairstyles were so similar that from the back, they all looked the same. For example, in the *Paramount News* story about Canadian GIs, a row of girls have their backs to the camera (Figure 17). They look exactly the same because all that can be seen is the back of their heads. Only the clothes they wear mark their difference.[44] Sometimes, however, even their clothes are the same, so it becomes harder to distinguish the children individually.

Figure 17. Korean orphans congregate to eat food that was donated by Canadian soldiers. At a closer look, the row of children with their backs to the camera all look alike. There is a semblance of sameness among both male orphans and female orphans, implying mass production. Still image. Paramount News. National Archives at College Park.

Erasing individual difference not only creates a semblance of order and management, but it also creates an aura of mass production. In *Children of Calamity,* John Caldwell recounts cables from CCF headquarters: "Rush me 500 orphans"; "Need 200 Korean, 10 Japanese mixed-blood, 50 Chinese, 10 Arabs." These requests sound like department store back orders, as Klein correctly describes. Indeed, Caldwell reports one "memorable occasion" where the request from Richmond, Virginia, was for a whopping 2,400 Korean orphans.[45] As surplus population, the individual subject is discarded, and in its place, the individual orphan takes on a collective subjectivity. In this case, being a part of the collective reduces the orphan into an object or product that can fill orders and be collected. In other words, the very language that is used to place these orders for orphaned children transfigures them from human beings into mass-produced products that can be dispersed when cabled and purchased by Westerners.[46]

As previously explicated in chapter 2, the militarized production of Korean orphans configured the male and female orphan into miniature replicas of the GI and the *gijichon* woman, respectively. The perceived doll-like visage of these children eventually reduced them to just that: dolls. Males became little toy soldiers, and girls came to resemble the Oriental dolls of the twentieth century (Figure 18). Next to the Geisha doll, this less erotic, less physically mature, and less sexualized version of the Asian female body was readily visible in American culture. To be sure, Naoko Shibusawa claims that the "Japan craze" movement of the late nineteenth and early twentieth centuries sparked Orientalist visions of Japan as a "toy-world" made up of people living in "doll-houses." In addition, she observes, "The product that Americans and Europeans most associated with the Japanese was probably the handcrafted Japanese doll." According to Shibusawa, the popularity of the "Jap doll" or "Jappie" (as it was "affectionately" called) "inspired westerners to objectify actual Japanese as 'dolls.'"[47]

The objectification of Asian girls as Oriental dolls was further fueled by the 1927 Doll Exchange between Japan and the United States. As a way to decrease the political tension that was created after the Immigration Act of 1924 prevented the Japanese from entering U.S. borders, Dr. Sidney Gluick, a former missionary in Japan, formed the Committee on World Friendship among Children.[48] Its first project had American children from every state send 11,000 blue-eyed dolls as ambassadors of goodwill and friendship

Figure 18. Prototypes of the Korean orphan: toy soldier and Oriental doll. Still image. "Construction of AFAK Orphanage, Seoul, Korea." National Archives at College Park.

to the annual Japanese Doll Festival. In response, Japanese schoolchildren contributed a yen each to purchase fifty-eight Japanese dolls to send to the United States in an effort to "let Americans know our true love and feeling" so that "there will be friendship between Japan and America."[49] The Japanese friendship dolls, as they were called, toured the United States, making appearances in museums and exhibits.

About two decades after this event, the Effanbee Doll Company, which made popular dolls, created a doll named Chinese Patsy, after the original Patsy became a best seller.[50] Here we see how Asian girls are packaged in such a way as to replicate the Oriental doll. Susie Skinner, a Chinese girl adopted in 1954 by Americans, looks exactly like Chinese Patsy when she arrives in the United States (Figure 19).[51] The Asian adoptee is dressed and positioned in such a way as to evoke the Oriental dolls of the past. Like a doll, Susie is put on display, as admiring eyes closely inspect and touch her. You can almost imagine the question, "Isn't she a doll?" emerging from the lips of her onlookers.[52]

The Japan craze, the Japanese friendship dolls, and Chinese Patsy all served as precursors to help Americans imagine the Korean social orphan as a literal doll. By the time that Korean adoption began, there was already a history of Americans perceiving Asian bodies as playthings, as curios, and as toys. Because Orientalism often conflated (and continues to conflate) Asian ethnicities, the Oriental doll became a universal Asian object: it often did not matter if the doll was Japanese, Chinese, or Korean. The only important feature was that the doll was racially marked as Asian. Therefore, while I suggest that the Korean orphan resembled the Oriental dolls of the first half of the twentieth century, the same can be said about other Asian orphans.

In noting the likeness between Oriental dolls and Asian orphans, I want to demonstrate the salient connection between the imagined and the real, the plastic and the human. The Japanese friendship dolls and the Effanbee doll invoked a popular image of Asian children in the minds of Americans. This plastic image was transferred onto the real bodies of Asian orphans, as we saw from the photo of Susie Skinner. Transforming the Korean child into a commodity simultaneously turned her into a fetish. According to Karl Marx, the production of a commodity automatically leads to the production of a fetish; they are inseparable. The fetishism of a commodity ends up disguising the product's relationship to its production, disguising the social relations between things, which ultimately gives the commodity a magical and hence desirable quality. Likening the Korean female orphan to a doll transfers all the connotations that "Oriental doll" has onto the child herself,

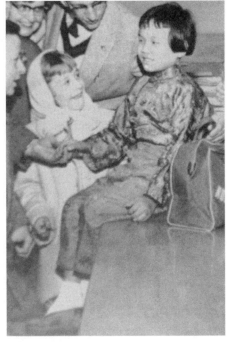

Figure 19. Effanbee Doll Company's Chinese Patsy (circa 1946) closely resembles Chinese adoptee Susie Skinner, who arrived in the United States in 1954 (from Children of Calamity). Photograph of "Chinese Patsy" was taken by Penny Zarneski. Courtesy of Penny Zarneski.

turning the Korean girl, to borrow Marx's words, into a "natural objec[t] with strange social properties."[53] Because the Oriental doll connotes femininity, exoticness, delicateness, silence, and docility, these very descriptions become assigned to the Korean female orphan. As a fetishized commodity, separated from the material conditions of production, these characteristics seem inherent and natural to the child rather than fabricated from racist, sexist, and imperialist notions about Asian female bodies. In short, the human child becomes confused with the plastic doll (Figure 20).

Given this conflation and the geopolitical context of U.S.–South Korea relations, the Korean social orphan as Oriental doll could be seen as the Korean version of the Japanese friendship doll. The Korean social orphan as Oriental doll performs similar labor as the Japanese friendship doll in that she serves to ease political tension and build friendly relations between the two countries. In this way, she continues the work of the *gijichon* women but in a more palatable, G-rated way. Her labor becomes more palatable precisely because of her fetishized commodification. The Korean orphan as Oriental doll is more successful at disguising her relationship to her production (namely U.S. military intervention and neocolonialism) than the *gijichon* women, who by definition and name denote American military occupation—not only because she is a doll (an object presumed to be ahistorical) but also because her consumption is framed within the context of humanitarian rescue, kinship building, and caretaking. Thus, the Korean social orphan as Oriental doll facilitates the expansion of U.S. empire through the guise of benevolent consumption/adoption by the American consumer/adoptive parent. In this context, the Korean female body—whether she be a military prostitute, orphan, or Oriental doll—becomes the site upon which neocolonial relations between the United States and South Korea are transacted and secured.

Militarized humanitarianism, the visual iconography of rescue, and the construction of the Korean social orphan as Oriental doll all share the logic of commodity fetishization in that they work to disguise the relationship between what is produced and the conditions that produced it. This is precisely what I am working against. I want to expose this relationship because the dominant narrative of Korean adoption has actively worked to elide the material conditions that have made it possible.

The doll-like attributes and aesthetics that were assigned to Korean social orphans facilitated their consumption via transnational adoption. After all, a significant reason why Korean children—and not all needy children— were (and still are) considered worthy of rescue was because they were

Figure 20. The doll and human become conflated, as this Korean doll standing on the floor of a concession stand on a U.S. military base in South Korea looks just like the thousands of orphan girls we see in the film reels. They have the same haircut, the same round face, and the same look of docility. Still images. "Opening of PX Concession for Korean War Widows, Main PX, Seoul, Korea" and "Brownson's Congressional Committee Investigation, Japan and Korea." National Archives at College Park.

depicted as highly assimilable, as potential model minorities. If the visual iconographies of rescue spurred average, predominantly white Americans to act on behalf of Korean War orphans, then the celluloid images of dancing, smiling, happy, cute orphans worked to reassure prospective adoptive families that their adopted child would be easy to parent. This became especially important in an era when the U.S. government was engaged in projects and programs that experimented with integrating Asian bodies into the national landscape of the United States. The adoption of Korean children into predominantly white American homes became another racially integrative project to test out the viability of Asian assimilation. Depicting Korean orphans as model minority material assured average white Americans of their success. This is clearly seen in the *Paramount News* feature entitled "Party for 2,000 . . . GI's Host to Korean Orphans."

This particular news segment works to recast the female Korean orphan as a potential American family member by highlighting her cuteness and resilience and by naturalizing her physical connection to white American bodies. If there is a thesis that is being articulated here in this newsreel, it resides in this proclamation made by the voice-over narrator: "The small fry in Korea is like the small fry anywhere" (Figure 21).[54] We see the children sing and dance, play ring-around-the-rosie, make funny faces, stand in line for sack lunches, eat picnic style, and, after a long day of activities, fall asleep in the arms of an adult. We even see a group of orphans dressed like American Girl Scouts (Figure 22).

These scenes resemble a typical summer party that any middle-class white American child might attend. (One major difference is the presence of GIs and the overwhelming number of children in attendance compared to adults.) Seeing these Korean orphans engaged in typical children's activities—even participating in Girl Scouts—makes them more relatable to the predominantly white American audience watching this newsreel. Images like these narrowed the distance that many Americans may have felt toward the children as a result of differences in race, nationality, and culture. Film coverage like this fueled yellow desire by making their incorporation less threatening, portraying them as cute little dolls and marketing them to be "like the small fry anywhere." This was especially significant considering that, as Klein noted, Americans were slowly starting to reimagine an American family that included Asians. Depicting these children as if they could be any child made it possible for wary Americans to imagine them as their own: if the child is like *any* child, she could potentially be *my* child.

Even though the narrator acknowledges the fact that these children are different—that they have experienced tremendous trauma at such a

Figure 21. The facial expression on this little girl not only entertains but also endears, like a cute little doll. Still image. Paramount News. National Archives at College Park.

Figure 22. Korean orphans dress in Girl Scout uniforms, making them relatable to the American audience viewing this newsreel. After receiving her bag lunch from a GI, the Girl Scout salutes him. Still image. Paramount News. National Archives at College Park.

young age—the focus is on the similarities that these children have to other (American) children. The voice-over narration is as follows: "Over 100,000 children lost both parents in a war that ravaged their country, but there's no sadness today because it's party day! . . . Now off to the dance. And what they lack in fancy footwork, they make up in facial expressions. Happiness and play for Korean orphans. Their past tragedies temporarily forgotten."[55] The children's tragic circumstances are only mentioned to highlight the joy and carefree spirit of the children filmed. However, even more significantly, they are mentioned to communicate to the viewer that these orphans are highly resilient. The message is clear: they are not permanently traumatized by the war; rather, their grieving time is short, and as a result, they can quickly move on with their lives. Thus, one can be assured that their adjustment period will be short and smooth as well.[56]

Because the type of help solicited was gradually evolving from emergency aid (food, clothing, and shelter) to finding permanent American homes for these children, it became important to portray these children in a palatable, relatable way to help average white Americans envision them as part of their family. Depicting them as cute little dolls and portraying them as a kind of everychild were effective strategies. Displaying their supposedly high level of resilience through images of dancing and smiling orphans was another; however, just in case Americans had trouble imagining Asian bodies in their homes, newsreels such as this one did the work for them by showing Korean children in intimate contact with white American bodies. The newsreel ends with the final image of a little girl sleeping in the arms of a colonel (Figure 23). The narrator remarks, "Little Miss, you've had a busy day."[57]

The nonnormative dimensions of this still image are quickly elided as this image works to normalize the physical, and most importantly parental, bond between Korean child and white American adult. Although the white American represented here is a soldier, male and female viewers can both identify with him because the heightened sentimental and paternal tone that their body composition evokes makes him less of a military man and more of a parent. Viewers are touched not only by his show of sensitivity and warmth but also by the image of the exhausted child seeking comfort and rest in his arms. The seeming ease with which she curls up and lays her head on his shoulder gives the impression that she belongs to him and he belongs to her. There are no walls—no racial, cultural, or national barriers—between them. No issues of attachment are evident here. They seem natural together, like father and daughter.

A newsreel that began by highlighting the Korean orphan as an Oriental doll ends with a scene that recasts the Korean orphan as a potential

American daughter. Her racial and cultural difference is suspended as she is held like a daughter. For a split second, the Oriental doll has become an American child via the figure of the white American patriarch. Her humanization is brought out by the parental energy of this American. The seemingly effortless quality of this union between the Korean child and the American adult (parent) signals to the viewer that Korean orphans would fit easily and naturally into their American homes. Thus, rather than a depiction of a queer kinship formation, the picture here suggests that Korean adoption could be made to resemble normal white American families.

For many Americans, Korea hardly existed in their consciousness. According to Harold Isaacs who conducted a study of American perceptions of Asia, "vagueness about Asia" had been the "natural condition even of the educated American."[58] Eliminating this vagueness and disinterest toward Asia and Asians was possible given that Cold War Orientalism provided the ideological sea change that allowed American citizens to imagine Asians as potential family members. Furthermore, while the social death of the displaced Korean child facilitated his or her legal adoption, the marketing of the social orphan at death's door provided the sense

Figure 23. A young girl falls asleep on a GI's shoulder after a long day of partying. Images such as this worked to naturalize the parental bond between Korean children and white American bodies. Still image. Paramount News. National Archives at College Park.

of emergency that compelled average American citizens to act. Stories of militarized humanitarianism became pedagogical tools as they taught civilians how to gaze at the postwar Korean orphans and how to get involved in the rescue mission. The sponsoring of children for a small monthly fee and the donations of food, money, and clothing eventually evolved into a "permanent rescue mission" via transnational adoption. Yellow desire fueled this permanent rescue mission: it created a discourse around Asian bodies that made them more worthy, more suitable for rescuing. These are the conditions that facilitated the evolution of "GIs and the Orphans" into the "Holt Family Portrait."

The marketing of children to make them appealing to Americans only increased as the years went by. As the immediate crisis of the war orphans' plight began to wane and as American troops began to withdraw, more direct strategies were developed to inspire American citizens to adopt these children. Transnational adoption became increasingly promoted as the only way to provide permanent help to the orphans of South Korea. This project was spearheaded by Harry Holt. In the next chapter, I explain how the adoption of Korean children flourished under Holt's leadership and how he came to institutionalize this practice. As a result of institutionalizing Korean adoption, increased attention was paid to make Korean orphans adoptable (that is, American and normal) in the eyes of Americans. Thus, processes of Americanization and normalization replaced militarization, which became the new modi operandi within the walls of the orphanages. How these two processes turned unadoptable orphans into adoptees is the primary focus of my next chapter.

4 NORMALIZING THE ADOPTED CHILD

So far, I have identified the material conditions that have made possible the emergence of the Korean orphan. I examined the construction of the Korean orphan in the militarized scene of the orphanage, in the fantasies of the U.S. military, and in the humanitarian desires of American civilians. In this chapter, I return to the orphanage to investigate further the material conditions that enabled the configuration of a new American family, as depicted in the "Holt Family Portrait." Specifically, this chapter concerns itself with how an orphan becomes an adoptee. How does a seemingly unwanted orphan become a desirable Korean adoptee? I ask this question to suggest that the term *adoptee*—as I demonstrated in the first three chapters with the term *orphan*—is not a natural, transparent, and inherently knowable category of identity. Rather, this chapter, along with the next one, illustrates that it takes ongoing work, time, energy, and resources to construct an adoptee—to turn an orphan into an adoptee. Thus, these two chapters focus on the subject formation of the Korean adoptee.

Drawing on Holt Adoption Program newsletters and documents from other adoption agencies, such as administrative files, letters, and memos, I investigate the functions and inner workings of the orphanage and its effects on the orphans during the 1950s and 1960s. Although the orphanage was a site of militarization that produced Korean orphans as militarized subjects during and immediately after the war, the withdrawal of American troops at the end of the war resulted in the waning imprint of militarization within the orphanages. Processes of normalization and Americanization replaced militarization as efforts to recruit Americans as adoptive parents became increasingly prioritized. Thus, I argue that the orphanage—now a site of normalization—worked to normalize orphans in order to make them adoptable. It is here, within the walls of the orphanage, where the subject formation of the adoptee takes shape.

The images and the discourses that circulated around the postwar Korean social orphan—as discussed in the previous chapter—may suggest that the orphans in South Korea were ready for adoption as they were. This chapter suggests otherwise, as I attend to the behind-the-scenes labor that was expended to not only turn orphans who were categorized as unadoptable into adoptable children but also to prepare adoptable children for American life. Although the extra effort to make these children desirable may not have been necessary for servicemen who had preexisting relationships with their adoptive children before their adoption, these added initiatives were necessary to spark and sustain the interests of civilians back home who did not have any prior contact with these children. Indeed, it was seeing and touching these children that prompted American GIs to adopt the orphans with whom they had contact.[1] Because the average civilian in the United States did not have access to these children in the same way that GIs did, more labor needed to be exerted to get civilians halfway around the world to bring them into their family. This extra care and effort to make orphans desirable and adoptable is the subject of this chapter.

I begin by explaining how the withdrawal of U.S. military forces opened up a new sphere of influence. If the U.S. armed forces assumed control of Korean orphans during and immediately after the Korean War, then American civilians like Harry Holt quickly took charge of the orphan situation during the postwar years. By establishing the Orphan's Foundation Fund and Holt Adoption Program in 1956, as well as working with legislators to change Asian immigration laws, Holt institutionalized Korean adoption in the United States. He also built his own orphanage in South Korea, which directly supplied his adoption agency with orphans for adoption.

Because Holt's orphans were specifically slated for adoption (rather than sponsorship) in the United States, he implemented policies and procedures to help prepare the orphan for travel to the States. Part of this had to do with visa requirements (such as passing medical examinations), but much of it had to do with making the orphan appealing to Americans. Therefore, in the second section, I examine Holt's Il San orphanage as a processing station that prepared Korean orphans for adoption. More specifically, I identify and examine the various techniques used to turn orphans into adoptees. These techniques—or technologies of power, as Michel Foucault calls them—were centered on processes of normalization.[2] The orphanage, as an institution of discipline, worked to normalize the Korean orphan into an adoptee. Not surprisingly, the physical health and body of the child were scrutinized upon his or her entrance into the orphanage. The orphan's body was subjected to different methods of biopower—techniques and procedures that governed life and subjugated bodies and that worked to protect the health and appearance of incoming orphans so that they may be made useful (that is, adoptable).[3]

Because the end goal is adoption by Americans, the final section examines the ways in which the orphans' regulation was tied to the process of Americanization. The processing station of the orphanage not only turned unadoptable orphans into adoptees, but it also prepared them for life in the United States by helping them transition into American culture and lifestyle. Thus, the orphanage can be seen as an institution where South Korea's social outcasts were manipulated and shaped into useful subjects for the state. As adoptees, they become economically profitable for South Korea and politically beneficial for the United States. In this way, the work that Holt engaged in can be regarded as a civilizing project of modernity. As hallmarks in the modernization, and therefore the civilization, of South Korea, Americanization and Christianity were deployed to help transform what Holt called the "discards of society" into productive American citizens, ensuring the success of Korean adoption as a racially integrative project.

Harry Holt and the Rise of Korean Adoption

From 1950 to 1953, a total of 5,720,00 men from the American armed forces were sent to the southern portion of Korea.[4] With the conclusion of major combat in 1953, American soldiers began leaving the war-torn country by the thousands. As GIs exited South Korea, so too did the money that they contributed to support and sponsor orphanages because, as William Asbury points out, "the too-generous support of the military is impossible to maintain." He explains the reasons behind the tenuous nature of GI support in his 1954 survey of Korean orphanages:

> The military support to orphanages in Korea . . . if it is sustained over any long period of time, depends upon the interest of one or a very few individuals in nearby military establishments. This highly personalized interest often ceases when the individual or individuals are transferred [or sent back home]. The highly mobile nature of military personnel render[s] support to children's homes as anything but dependable.[5]

This "out of sight, out of mind" nature of soldier support resulted in the plummeting of GI financial contributions to orphanages after the war.

John C. Caldwell even mentions that while stories of Americans supporting orphanages and adopting children were commonplace during the war years, "such stories now are much less frequent" since the soldiers left. Caldwell recalls an Eighth Army public relations officer telling him that "it is frequently necessary now [1955] to improvise or to actually invent a good-deed story."[6]

As military aid to South Korea decreased, government financial aid increased steadily after the war. U.S. government aid to South Korea rose rapidly each year by millions of dollars from 1950 to 1957. Beginning in 1958, however, economic aid began to steadily decline. In spite of this, U.S. aid made up 52 percent of the total South Korean budget in 1961. Ten years later (1971), the U.S. government ceased providing economic aid to South Korea, except for assistance in the form of loans.[7] Despite the increased funds allotted to South Korea after the war, very little of that money was set aside to support orphans and maintain orphanages. To be sure, the South Korean government allotted 5 won per month for each child residing in an orphanage.[8] At this time, 5 won equaled about half a cent. As one orphanage superintendent observed, "That is not even enough to buy the sugar to put in a cup of coffee!"[9] Even though the South Korean government did very little to support its orphanages, it did not stop them from taxing these institutions. In 1955, the Christian Children's Home in Anyang paid 450,000 won in taxes—an amount considered astronomical in the postwar economy.[10] These taxes, along with the majority of the financial aid received from the U.S. government, were used to support South Korea's armed forces.

Because the South Korean government, according to Asbury, "cannot support the large number of orphanages it will be left with if the American and Allied military establishments leave Korea," other solutions were created once direct combat ended.[11] For example, World Vision began a sponsorship program after collecting background information and pictures of 1,200 Korean orphans.[12] Christian Children's Fund (CCF) also helped to offset the loss of GI support by assisting orphanages in South Korea through their sponsorship program. In 1954, CCF took 104 orphanages under its wing, financially supporting 15,694 children.[13] By 1956, the number of orphanages that CCF supported rose to 140. In addition, nearly 18,000 children were sponsored by 11,000 Americans that same year.[14] Although sponsorship succeeded in replacing GI aid, transnational adoption emerged as an increasingly popular method to take care of orphans after the military support of orphanages dwindled in postwar South Korea.

Harry Holt, a fifty-year-old farmer from Oregon, decided to sponsor several orphans through World Vision after listening to Bob Pierce of World Vision describe the dire situation of Korean War orphans. He, like thousands of Americans, sent $10 a month to the organization to help feed and take care of Korean children. Sponsorship turned to adoption, however, during a visit to South Korea on May 30, 1955. There, Holt observed over "2,000 GI-fathered and abandoned infants . . . in particular need of assistance."[15] During this trip, Holt came to conclude that adoption by American families was the best way to help these orphans. Indeed, he selected and adopted eight mixed-race Korean children, despite already having six children of his own, before he left South Korea.[16] In becoming the ultimate figure of the Good Samaritan, he chose four girls and four boys who "[weren't] so attractive" and were the "least fortunate" of the group.[17] This act marked the so-called birth of Korean adoption.

Upon his return to the United States, Holt launched a full-fledged mission to find Korean orphans homes in the United States. Through the use of different media outlets, Holt promoted adoption as the best way to help Korean orphans, rather than donating materials or sponsoring them. His personal adoption of eight Korean orphans gained much publicity. His story was especially sensational because he adopted so many: adopting eight children at one time was unprecedented. It was, in fact, illegal because the Refugee Act allotted only two Korean orphans per American couple. New legislation was created specifically for Holt in order to permit his adoption of all eight children.[18] His story appeared in newspapers all over the country. He was also featured in *Life* magazine. *Paramount News* even documented his journey, beginning in South Korea, where the children were prepared for travel, and ending in the United States, where the children were shown adapting to their new life and home in Creswell, Oregon.[19] The media attention surrounding Holt's adoption led to increased interest in adoption by Americans. According to one newspaper article, aptly titled, "Mr. Holt 'Moves the World,'" "So heartening was the Holt story, that it brought appeals from 1000 additional American families willing to make homes for orphans."[20] Holt was indeed moving the world toward the transnational adoption of these children.

With the incorporation of the Orphan's Foundation Fund (OFF) and the establishment of the Holt Adoption Program (HAP) in 1956, Holt pioneered the institutionalization of Korean adoption in the United States. OFF was a nonprofit corporation that used funds from public and private donations to "pay expenses of hospitalization, housing, nursing, and care of Korean

War orphans while they are being processed for adoption by Americans, and paying expenses relating thereto."[21] HAP was the organization that oversaw the logistical and bureaucratic portion of matching Korean orphans with prospective adoptive parents (PAPs) in the United States. Under this program, over 1,000 Korean children were placed in American homes from 1955 to 1958. By 1960, almost 2,000 children had been placed through HAP.[22] Seven years later, that number doubled to 4,000.[23] In comparison, the International Social Service (ISS) averaged about twenty placements per year so that by 1960, the organization had matched about 100 Korean children with American families in the United States.[24] By 1965, this number rose to 100 placements per year.[25] As ISS general director Paul R. Cherney admits, Holt "place[d] many more children from Korea than all other agencies combined."[26] As the largest adoption agency, about half of all Korean adoptees were placed through HAP.[27]

The reason why Holt was able to achieve such high numbers (compared to ISS, for example) is because he dealt with proxy adoptions. Because the Refugee Relief Act was about to expire on December 31, 1956, Holt used this unorthodox procedure to bring as many Korean orphans into the United States before the termination date as possible. In proxy adoptions, a representative of the adoptive parents travels to South Korea and completes the adoption in the Korean court. Consequently, adoptions are completed sight unseen between the adopted child and adoptive parent in order to speed up the adoption process.[28] This practice was criticized by established social welfare agencies such as ISS and local state welfare departments because proxy adoptions did not provide a trial period wherein the child lived with the new family before the adoption was finalized. This trial period was protocol among licensed adoption agencies because, according to social workers, it protects the child.[29] For HAP, getting the children to the United States as quickly as possible was more important than finding the best match.[30] As an independent adoption organization, Holt eschewed these minimum standards that licensed social service agencies and state welfare departments considered to be necessary. Holt did not think that "man's rules" applied to him because he believed that he received a prophecy from the Lord concerning the rescue of Korean children.[31] Furthermore, reading and hearing stories of Korean orphans perceived to be at death's door legitimized his cutting of bureaucratic corners as he became "impatient of any social agency procedures necessary to protect the children."[32] Indeed, John E. Adams, who took over as executive director of HAP after Holt's death, admits that the organization is "dedicated to placing as large a number of children for adoption from Korea, as they can possibly manage, with at least minimal protection."[33]

Despite the numerous criticisms Holt received concerning his adoption practices from social welfare agencies, including the threat of taking legal action against him, he was respected and admired by people all across the nation, especially by those in positions of power. For example, the U.S. embassy, in its show of support, allotted Holt with special privileges. Although most adoption agencies could only process adoptions on a certain day of the week, Holt was given a special desk at the embassy and was allowed to process children on a daily basis.[34] The State Public Welfare Commission of Oregon also acknowledged Holt's favorable reputation: "We . . . believe that because of the favorable publicity and community support that Mr. Holt has received through this state as well as nationally, any attempt to take legal action would only increase his efforts and the public support accorded him."[35]

Not only did the American people embrace Holt's activities, but so too did South Korean president Syngman Rhee. As early as 1956, Holt "undoubtedly gained great status in Korea and ha[d] the cooperation of officials in that country." According to Holt, ISS and other American social welfare agencies "lost face in Korea" because of "their slowness and lack of cooperation in adoptions."[36] Holt, on the other hand, proved to be efficient, sending several charter planes full of orphans back to the United States. In the spring of 1957, Holt had established a receiving station that impressed Rhee with its speed and efficiency in processing children for adoption overseas.[37] According to ISS director William T. Kirk, the reason why President Rhee supported Holt and not ISS was because the South Korean government was "interested only in getting rid of the children by the quickest means and without concern for the long-run consequences." Kirk recalls that President Rhee had been quoted as saying, "Get these children out of Korea," and "[I] don't care if they throw them in the sea."[38] These sentiments certainly were not held by Holt; however, for both parties, "speed was the most important factor in this situation."[39] HAP expedited the removal of orphans out of South Korea faster than any other social welfare agency. And Holt was generously rewarded. In 1958, the South Korean government bestowed him with the highest award given to civilians for his work with Korean orphans: the Medal for Public Welfare Service.[40] However, perhaps the greatest reward came from knowing that the South Korean government, according to one of his daughters, "would do almost anything he asked." As proof, she recounts how the South Korean government changed its zoning laws in order to accommodate the building of Holt's orphanage, despite its dangerously close proximity to a powder factory.[41] Furthermore, in 1961, the South Korean government codified an adoption law that normalized proxy adoptions—the type of adoption for which Holt was infamous.[42] (Ironically, the U.S. Congress banned proxy adoptions that same year, making the new adoption law in South Korea inoperable.)

The building of another orphanage by Holt may seem like overkill in a country that quadrupled the number of orphanages after the war; however, the number of orphans was increasing rather than decreasing after the war. In 1955, 53,000 children were housed in 496 orphanages.[43] In 1965, approximately 67,000 children resided in over 600 orphanages.[44] The majority of these children in 1955 were indeed direct products of the war; however, this was not the case by 1961. The rapid industrialization of South Korea during the 1960s led to increased numbers of abandoned children by poor and working-class single mothers who were fighting poverty and the cultural stigma of being unwed.[45] Ironically, the practice of transnational adoption did not work to reduce these numbers. On the contrary, the rate at which Korean children were abandoned increased rather than decreased after the institutionalization of Korean adoption, from 715 abandoned children in 1955 to over 9,000 children in 1964.[46]

According to ISS–American Branch director Paul Cherney, the exponential increase in child abandonment can be attributed to two factors: the devastated economy after the war and the postwar financial support of Korean orphanages and orphans from Americans.[47] This second factor created a viscous cycle in which financial support fueled abandonment. At least 75 percent of the children in Korean orphanages were supported by Americans through sponsorship. The money supported the child being sponsored and was also used to take care of those who were not sponsored. As Cherney points out, "It is reported that many parents abandon their children to the orphanages knowing the children will receive better physical care and education than the family can provide. Whenever a sponsored child leaves the orphanage the income for his care stops so the incentive is to hold the children rather than try to reestablish them with family or relatives."[48] Cherney seems to equate the orphanage as a place where abandoned children are housed, when clearly many parents leave their children with the confidence that they will receive better care at the orphanage than at home. Abandonment implies that parents do not care about their children. On the basis of Cherny's words, most parents dropping off their children at the orphanage did so because they cared deeply for the welfare of their children. Thus, I want to reframe the discourse of abandonment as a discourse of separation. *Separation* is a more accurate term because many of the children were separated from their parents rather than abandoned (in the literal sense of the word).

Another reason fueled the separation between parent and child: the South Korean government's lack of prioritizing social welfare and family services. By 1976, over 40 percent of South Korea's national budget was still allotted to defense. Social welfare and social service spending, on the other hand, continued to be given the lowest priority in the national budget.[49] Because of the South Korean government's lack of financial investment in providing social services for its citizens, both the number of foreign orphanages and the number of children separated from their parents rose. Consequently, Korean orphanages became social welfare and social service centers rather than solely institutions of abandoned children, a place where struggling families went to get financial relief.

This reliance on American money—which supported Korean orphanages through sponsorship and adoption programs—fueled the separation of children from their families as it became the primary method of social welfare service and family planning offered to single mothers and poor families. Ironically, what began as a mission to solve the orphan problem actually stimulated child separation and provided the South Korean government with strong incentives to abrogate its social welfare responsibilities to Westerners. Korean adoption, according to Patricia Nye's report on her visit to Korea in 1976, "brings substantial money to Korea" and "sets a precedent of how Korea can transfer it welfare responsibilities to other countries."[50]

The South Korean government's lack of interest and lack of financial support in providing social welfare services to orphaned children, abandoned children, separated children, single mothers, and poor families—along with the exuberant financial support offered by Americans—created a perfect storm in which the number of orphanages and children residing in them would increase long after the Korean War. When Holt broke ground to build his orphanage, it is difficult to say whether he was meeting a growing need or fueling the separation of Korean children from their parents. Perhaps he was doing both. What is clear is that in constructing the Il San orphanage, he not only secured his very own supply of orphans (now composed of orphaned, abandoned, and separated children) for his adoption agency, but he also laid the foundation for a highly efficient system of processing orphans for overseas adoption.

By 1965, the Il San orphanage had developed into its own miniature city within the larger city of Il San. As a self-sustaining city, it had its own "power, water, laundry, heat, fuel supply, warehouses, medical dispensary, kitchen and dining hall, offices, school and chapel." It housed the orphans in eleven large buildings.[51] It even had its own rice mill, soybean processing plant, and macaroni manufacturing plant.[52] In contrast to the economically devastated and war-torn South Korea in which this miniature city existed, the Il San orphanage distinguished itself as a productive, organized, and well-maintained facility that was prepared to receive and discipline orphaned, abandoned, and separated children for adoption. Indeed, it was described by a journalist as a "processing station for children being adopted by foreign families."[53] In the next section, I examine the various techniques used to process orphans for adoption.

Making the Unadoptable Adoptable: The Docile Body of the Adoptee

Foucault's corpus investigates the relationship between technologies of power and the management of populations and the self. In scrutinizing the medical clinic, mental institutions, and prisons, Foucault gazes on the margins of society in order to gain knowledge about the relationship between technologies of power and the operations of the self. By investigating this relationship, he ultimately explains how the normal is differentiated from the abnormal. As such, his theories are useful in examining how adoptable orphans are differentiated from the unadoptable. To be sure, not all orphans are considered adoptable; many are considered unfit and unsuitable for adoption by Americans. So what makes an orphan suitable for adoption? What is the difference between a child who is unadoptable and a child who is adoptable?

In *Discipline and Punish,* Foucault narrows in on one specific technology of power: discipline. Discipline is a method used to control whole populations by meticulously controlling the movement and operations of the body, which "assure[s] the constant subjection of its force and impose[s] upon them a relation of docility–utility."[54] This relation—docility–utility—signifies the belief that the more obedient an individual is, the more useful, skillful, and therefore productive he or she will become. Discipline turns a useless, disobedient body into a docile body.

The following equation sums up Foucault's definition of a docile body: analyzable body + manipulable body = docile body. A docile body is not only one that can be examined and scrutinized but also one that can be "subjected, used, transformed and improved"; it can be shaped and trained for the purposes and uses of the state.[55] The body, as it is disciplined, becomes docile, making it manipulable and useful for the purposes of the state. This same logic of docility–utility permeated in the orphanage in order to improve the "useless" orphan (according to the South Korean nation) and turn the orphan into a productive, useful subject who can contribute to the state's economic expansion and well-being. Thus, the orphan's body was subjected to different methods of biopower, which worked to protect the health and appearance of incoming orphans so that they may be made useful—that is, adoptable.

The physical examination of the orphan's body became a fundamental way of disciplining the orphan. The creation of a medical history for each child began the moment he or she stepped inside the orphanage. For practical reasons, children who were in dire need of medical care needed to be identified so that they could be treated immediately. However, collecting medical information has as much to do with standardizing health as it has to do with treating the sick. In *The Birth of the Clinic*, Foucault explains how medical knowledge was utilized in a way that normalized the healthy body. Because the well-being of bodies became directly linked to the health of the government and nation, medicine was used to establish "the positive role of health, virtue, and happiness" in one's life.[56] As a result, medicine was no longer confined to curing ills but was also concerned with compiling knowledge of what it meant to be healthy, to be normal.[57] Because medical knowledge began to concern itself with normality (that is, the standard functions of the body, the organs, and so on), it normalized physical health.

Physical health was not only a concern for doctors and medical professionals; it was also a concern for the state. The relationship between the state and physical fitness is acutely seen in U.S. government standards for immigration.[58] According to Nayan Shah, "The immigration medical exam . . . sought to measure fitness and detect defects in a broad spectrum of the population." Consequently, the medical examination established certain health norms, which became the criteria that determined who could and could not enter.[59] Thus, the visa standards of health immediately became the orphanage's standard of health because a child could not be assigned to an adoptive family without having passed this physical examination. The visa physical examination included "stool examination, blood examination, chest X-ray, TB skin test and a complete physical examination by the doctor."[60] Appropriately, these were the same tests that orphans at Il San orphanage underwent.[61] Those who passed the examination were allowed entrance into U.S. borders and categorized as adoptable. Those who failed the test were denied access and were thereby categorized as unadoptable. Because the examination results were valid for only six months, repeat examinations were necessary. Consequently, the physical health of orphans was constantly scrutinized and tested. Accumulating knowledge about an orphan's body facilitated the regulation of that body because it helped orphanage workers prescribe the appropriate methods for improvement in order to make them adoptable. Knowledge is indeed power.

Without the medical examination, it would be easy to misdiagnose a child. Lee Van, who rolled up in a dilapidated city hall truck with several other babies, stood out from the rest because he looked especially thin. Appearing in HAP's 1960 newsletter, he looks to be extremely sick, at least on the basis of his picture and the accompanying description. He is described as looking like a "little old man with an animal-like face." In addition, "the corners of his mouth were cracked from vitamin C deficiency. His stomach was puffed out and his legs were skinny and knobby at the knees and so weak that he couldn't stand." However, during his physical examination, they found nothing wrong: "Tuberculin skin test was negative, and he had no intestinal worms. His chest X-ray was normal." He was just malnourished. All he needed, according to the newsletter, was "lots of food and some love and attention." In two weeks' time, his stomach grew larger, and "we could see that he was putting on a little meat over some of his bones." Indeed, he was described by his caretaker as *donk-donk,* or fat.[62]

Although the child's physical health was a priority, the child's physical appearance also became the object of scrutiny within the walls of the orphanage. Physical appearance becomes especially important for Holt because these children must attract rather than repel potential adoptive parents. From experience, Holt had seen PAPs chose more physically appealing children over the less attractive ones.[63] Consequently, in the same 1960 newsletter that featured the "animal-like face" of Lee Van, Holt makes a special effort to thank those who adopted ugly children: "We are thankful for the many wonderful Christian people who have accepted a baby whose pictures shows a thin, dark, unhappy orphan."[64] Here we see how racist logic informs the standards that adoption workers used to categorize the ugly from the beautiful: dark-skinned children are considered ugly and harder to adopt, while light-skinned children are considered beautiful and easier to adopt. However, being at the orphanage transforms these "thin, dark, unhappy orphan[s]" into healthy, attractive babies. Regarding Lee Van, one orphanage caretaker states, "I have been avoiding him all this time because I couldn't stand to bear the sight of him before." After he received some attention and food, Lee Van is described as "a wonderful baby boy and whoever adopts him will indeed be fortunate."[65] Lee Jeffie also blossomed under the care given to him at the orphanage. Once a child whom Holt felt sorry for because "frankly, [he was] a little ugly," Holt explains that "Jeffie had suddenly, along with losing his dark skin and becoming fat, became beautiful."[66] Whereas previous PAPs had chosen other children over him, Jeffie— having undergone this transformation—finally had been adopted by an American couple by the time the newsletter was published.

The HAP newsletters played a fundamental role in recruiting adoptive parents for the orphans residing at Il San orphanage. The newsletters functioned as an effective tool to advertise their product, as descriptions of the child's personality would accompany their picture. Caseworker Letitia DiVirgilio points out that it was usually upon seeing the child's photograph and reading their social history that PAPs decided on an individual child.[67] According to ISS senior case consultant Margaret Valk, the photograph and the "picturesque quality of the descriptions" were extremely effective in soliciting interest from PAPs because they helped the child "come alive to the adoptive parents."[68] In this way, the photograph and the personality description served as a proxy of the child. Unable to see and touch the child for themselves (which GIs turned adoptive parents were able to do), the photograph and descriptive text worked to create conditions in which PAPs could feel like the child was standing before their very eyes.

Another effective marketing tool was to show before-and-after pictures of the children. Unlike World Vision and CCF, which primarily displayed the "before" picture of the child, HAP included the "after" picture, highlighting the child's transformation. Juxtaposing the "before" image with the "after" photo and accompanying this imagistic pair with a narrative of improvement created a visual progress report for Holt's readers. This progress report not only revealed the docile body of the adoptee but also acted as evidence that these children were malleable and therefore assimilable. For example, in the same newsletter in which the stories of Lee Van and Lee Jeffies appear, there are three pairs of before-and-after pictures that show sullen, malnourished babies change into smiling, plump babies. The caption, or narrative of improvement, for these pictures reads: "The transformation of bewildered, undernourished abandoned children to healthy, happily adjusted boys and girls, is a joy to watch and a privilege which to have a part."[69] The visual progress report relies on the orphans' weakened condition before entering the orphanage because highlighting the worst qualities of the children as they enter the orphanage makes the changes they undergo during their stay all the more dramatic. In this way, the visual progress report—a combination of the before-and-after pictures plus the narrative of improvement—doubled the impact of Holt's message.

The public face of HAP and the image of the orphanage as an institution of cleanliness, health, and progress become disrupted when we go behind the scenes, however. Bertha Holt's diary, published decades after Il San orphanage was established, is filled with accounts of children dying in the orphanage. Her husband reasoned that the high death rate at his orphanage was because "City Hall gave us only their dying children."[70] However, there are other underlying causes that the HAP newsletters and annual reports fail to mention. For example, in an effort to lower operating costs, Holt cut his nursing staff. According to Bertha Holt, "To save money, Harry discharged 19 hospital nurses so there were only two left. He brought in several teenagers to help, but they were not qualified or experienced to care for critically-sick babies."[71] This took place on August 4, 1961. For almost a year, only two nurses looked after the hundreds of sick children. By May 28, 1962, Bertha Holt was the only nurse (and she was technically not a nurse) at the orphanage.[72] Even in the wake of increased infant deaths, Holt continued to discharge more and more employees.[73] Because they were understaffed, the Holts relied on the older orphans to help take care of the infants. This led to more deaths. Bertha Holt explains: "I drew a diagram of a throat, lungs, and stomach to warn them [the teenagers] to never leave babies sucking a bottle as they can strangle or inhale vomitus. Two had died recently from suffocation."[74] In addition, because they repeatedly forgot to disinfect dirty diapers, germs became widespread and resulted in more infant deaths. On one occasion, Bertha Holt recalls her husband yelling, "Murderer!" to the wash lady because she had "put a load of diapers into the machine without washing out the stools or soaking them in disinfectant."[75]

Holt compromised the care of infants not only by dismissing qualified and experienced health workers but also by scrimping on baby food. Bertha Holt writes: "Harry decided to make formula from skim milk, corn oil and syrup to save money." His effort to economize proved to be disastrous, as Dr. Lim, the resident doctor, informed the Holts: "many babies were dying with bloody diarrhea" from Holt's improvised concoction.[76] The babies were eventually given whole milk fortified with vitamins, which reduced the number of illnesses and deaths. Stories such as these expose the contradictions between the public face of the orphanage and its private activities. They interrupt the narrative of progress that HAP promulgated in their newsletters. These setbacks, however, motivated Holt to perfect the disciplining and care of orphans.

Examining the intricacies of orphanage procedures concerning the bodies of Korean orphans dismantles the preconceived notion that all orphans are the same. The very process of discipline presumes heterogeneity because discipline is used to regulate diverse (not homogeneous) populations. Within the pages of HAP newsletters and files, we witness children being funneled back and forth among various categories: adoptable, unadoptable, handicapped, and handicapped/adoptable. This becomes the new taxonomy of Korean orphans, developed from the knowledge–power dyad established by orphanage workers, adoption agents, and U.S. immigration officials. Because the adoptable category is the most profitable one for adoption agencies, much time and energy is devoted to classify as many orphans into this category.

The primary goal of the orphanage was to transform the unadoptable orphans into adoptable children. Making them adoptable was to make them normal by Western standards. After all, as Foucault points out, the regime of disciplinary power works to normalize.[77] Physical health became one marker to distinguish between the normal and abnormal. The process of normalization turned a sickly body into a healthy one, as seen in the transformations undergone by Lee Van and Lee Jeffie. In addition, signs of progress and development at an average or higher rate were also qualities that made a child normal. HAP's 1965 newsletter notes, "Several, who formerly lay like vegetables have started to crawl or walk and talk."[78] This was cause for celebration among the workers because the marked progress in physical development allowed them to be considered normal and therefore adoptable. Disability scholar Douglas Baynton explains that "normality was implicitly defined as that which advanced progress (or at least did not impede it). Abnormality, conversely, was that which pulled humanity back toward its past, toward its animal origins."[79] Walking and crawling were signs of normal physical development. Under the disciplinary power of the orphanage, Korean orphans could become normal children.

Because the normal child is a healthy child, defects and irregularities often prevented a child from being adopted. Children with such irregularities were classified as handicapped. According to HAP, children labeled handicapped have qualities that include "paralysis or twisted limbs from polio or other causes, birthmarks, short limbs (meaning crutches), malfunctioning eyes or slight harelips."[80] It may be puzzling to label a child with a birthmark or harelip as handicapped, but disability scholars have noted that one's appearance has historically been equated to one's function. Visible abnormalities were regarded as a sign of a hidden functional abnormality.[81] Furthermore, whereas a disability, as defined by the United Nations, is the restriction or inability to perform an activity due to an impairment (physiological or psychological), a handicap is the disadvantage that results from the disability.[82] Consequently, any defect in a child's appearance that made him or her look abnormal—and therefore disadvantaged the child from being adopted—marked the child as handicapped even though the superficial flaw did not affect the child from functioning normally.

Having a handicap, however, did not necessarily mean that these children were unadoptable. HAP had a category of children labeled handicapped /adoptable.[83] Handicapped (unadoptable) orphans could move into the handicapped/adoptable category by undergoing corrective surgery. In *Replaceable You: Engineering the Body in Postwar America,* David Serlin discusses how technology became a normalizing tool by transforming, through surgery and other medical procedures, individuals who deviated from the norm. These procedures, because they worked to normalize the abnormal body, served as "tools of consensus building" around ideas of the normal body and ideals of beauty.[84] In his chapter concerning the Hiroshima Maidens project, he discusses how, because "the Maidens' physical scarring from the bombing impaired their ability to appear normal," cosmetic surgery restored their ability to lead normal lives.[85] Not unlike the Hiroshima Maidens, who underwent plastic surgery to restore their beauty, plastic surgery was performed on these orphans to erase the aesthetic flaw that marked them abnormal and therefore handicapped. In the case of Park Song Ja, her handicap was a burn scar on her face. Her narrative of improvement reads like a classified ad:

> Park Song Ja #3135 (December 1, 1960) is one of our Lord's special jewels. Abandoned because she had a burn scar on her face, she was brought to our orphanage in March 1962. Though she was very shy at first, her pomo [orphanage caretaker] gave her special attention which caused her own gentle, loveable, kind nature to blossom. A year ago, surgery accomplished much to restore her natural beauty, but much more can be done for her if she were in this country. She is a friendly, active child, top student of her class, knows many songs and games and is happy with her roommates. She would bring immeasurable joy to the right family.[86]

This narrative suggests the power of surgery. The burn scar led to the child's abandonment, but surgery helped her to overcome her handicap and has enabled her to thrive. Surgery restored her *natural* beauty, while the loving care she received during her stay at the orphanage restored her "gentle, loveable, kind *nature*." This narrative also naturalizes the Asian female body as an Oriental doll by stating that surgery restored her seemingly innate Oriental doll-like qualities. The implication is that she will assimilate smoothly into her new American family. She is therefore ready to be adopted, as suggested by the advertisement-like quality of her story.

Serlin posits that "physical rehabilitation became an allegory of national rehabilitation" in postwar 1950s America.[87] Using the Hiroshima Maidens project as an example, he explains how the United States took responsibility over the rehabilitation of twenty-five Japanese women who were disfigured when American air forces dropped the A-bomb in 1945. Ironically, ten years later, American air forces transported these women to the United States, where a team of plastic surgeons awaited them at the Mount Sinai Hospital in New York City.[88] The project itself was perceived by many as a "shining expression of medical humanitarianism that attempted to repair some of the physical and political scars left by World War II."[89] In more blunt words, literary critic Edmund Wilson remarks, "We have tried to make up for our atomic bombs by treating and petting the Japanese women whom we disfigured or incapacitated."[90] In a similar way, Americans tried to rehabilitate the national image of the United States by rehabilitating the bodies that were injured as a direct result of American action during the Korean War. Both civilians and military men donated hundreds of thousands of dollars to amputee children. Prosthetics were even donated to orphans to help them function normally. In addition, the corrective and plastic surgeries that the children underwent at orphanages were completed by American surgeons or American-trained Korean doctors. Technology and Western medicine became the tools used to normalize the war-ravaged Korean body and hence repair the political scars left by the Korean War.

Fixing the Korean child worked to rehabilitate the national image of the United States, as well as repair the Korean nation-state. The purpose of correcting abnormal, imperfect Korean bodies in the orphanage was so that they could be placed for adoption. The amount of resources it took to feed, clothe, care for, and prepare the children for adoption was significant. Adoption agencies cannot make money on unadoptable children. By turning unadoptable orphans into adoptees, adoption agencies were able to recoup the money they invested into the child. In a correspondence between HAP and ISS, we learn how this particular financial investment can lead to possessiveness. In a 1967 letter, HAP tells ISS that they are reluctant to turn over a case involving twin girls to ISS for adoption: "We have already invested a lot in preparing these children for adoption. Our Korean office informs us that they were not in good condition when we received them. Therefore, we are somewhat reluctant to simply turn them over to another agency at this point."[91] Because the twins "were not in good condition when we received them," they needed more medical care and attention than the average orphan. This meant that HAP spent more money than usual to get them ready for adoption. Consequently, HAP is hesitant to hand this case over to ISS because that would mean that they would lose money rather than make money—or at least recoup the money they already spent on making these twins healthy and adoptable. Although agencies such as HAP and ISS claim that they were never in the adoption business to make money, the foreign adoption of these children eventually became big business, bringing in millions of dollars. Improving the body of the Korean orphan became one way of rehabilitating the South Korean economy. Indeed, the profits that came from the adoption of South Korean children by Western- ers helped reinvigorate a fledgling economy, so that by the 1980s, Korean adoption was bringing in $15 to $20 million a year, leading some to link South Korea's "economic miracle" to the exportation of Korean children.[92] That figure is now up to $35 million per year.[93]

Despite the availability of Western medicine and technology to improve orphans with disabilities, not all handicapped children could be fixed. These children fell into the category of being severely disabled or mentally handi- capped. Being placed in the unadoptable category, however, did not stop them from undergoing the project of docility–utility. For example, in 1965 HAP installed new beds and organized their living quarters so that better care could be provided.[94] The home for handicapped children was even equipped with low toilets (for easier access) and large tubs for water exer- cises.[95] These adjustments, along with a special diet, helped them to de- velop into more normal children. Emotionally disturbed children were also prescribed tranquilizers, making them "much calmer and far easier to care for."[96] By 1967, HAP had a resident psychiatrist at the orphanage who worked with the mentally challenged, and they had even more handi- capped children undergo surgery.[97] Implementing modern medicine and techniques of care had some miraculous results: "We have been blessed to see a number of these children that were considered hopelessly unadoptable and mentally retarded, develop into seemingly normal children and we hope in the future will be adoptable." For those whose results were not as transformative, medicine and medical technology still proved to be useful.

Many of the orphans who were severely handicapped made improvements—such as no longer eating clothes or climbing walls—but not enough to be adoptable.[98]

There were some children with no apparent physical or mental handicap who were considered unadoptable. These children were of African American descent and were older. In regards to age, HAP reasoned that older children were handicapped simply because "most people want babies."[99] I would also add that it was because older children were less manipulable. In a 1962 newsletter, Holt explains to his readers the decision to curtail their program with teenage orphan girls: "We have so many that they have kind of formed a gang on us and we can hardly control them anymore. . . . We feel that they have been in institutions too long and are not developing into normal women and have no opportunity to join in the normal social life of the Korean people."[100] The problem, according to Holt, was that these teenage girls refused to be normal. Their abnormality came from their unwillingness to be controlled. Even when HAP arranged marriages for some of the older girls, they refused. This refusal to comply, in the eyes of HAP, proved their deviance. Their aloofness toward marriage—which was supposedly the hallmark of a normal woman—rendered them abnormal and queer in the sense that they resisted proper gender and domestic roles. Furthermore, these girls were apparently too old to be trained and disciplined. Holt explains: "They are weak and undisciplined and untrained. We have done the best we could in the last two or three years that we have had them, but training should take place early in life and it is pretty difficult to do it after they are older."[101] Because these teenagers were unaffected by the disciplinary power of the Il San orphanage, they became unruly and queer, rather than docile and normative, subjects. Consequently, they were ejected from the orphanage.[102] Their age (arriving at the orphanage too old, too late) became both a liability and disability—not only because PAPs wanted infants, but also because they were unaffected by the disciplinary powers of the orphanage. Entering the orphanage past toddler age thwarted the older orphan's ability to become docile subjects, rendering them unadoptable.

As it relates to Korean Negro children, HAP states that they were considered handicapped because there was a lack of Negro families wanting to adopt.[103] HAP's policy concerning Korean Negro babies was that only African American families could adopt.[104] Although this limited the pool of PAPs, application records showed that many African Americans wanted to adopt; however, because adoption agencies included selection criteria that insisted that adoptive mothers not work outside the home, many black couples were rejected on this criterion alone.[105] Furthermore, black couples were scrutinized much more closely than white couples, especially when it came to their financial status. Consequently, they were rejected at a higher rate than white couples.[106]

HAP's explanation also obscured the implicit racist belief that mixed-race children, especially those of African ancestry, were considered racially inferior. Selection patterns reflected the racial hierarchy of the United States that situated whites at the top, Asians in the middle, and blacks at the bottom: Korean Caucasian children were the most desired (because they were racialized as white), and Korean Negro children were the least desired (because they were racialized as black).[107] Korean children who were not of mixed ancestry fell in between these two categories.[108] The way in which mixed-race orphans were categorized reveals the extent to which Korean orphans were understood through an American racial ideology. U.S. racial politics was exported to South Korea along with Christianity, social welfare procedures, and Western medicine. The black–white binary for which the United States is well known was so influential that it had the power to elide the Asian race even in South Korea.[109]

To reiterate, orphans classified as unadoptable were those with "severe physical handicaps" and "mental retardation," those who were Korean Negro, and those who were older. Because these children often became the permanent responsibility of the orphanage (until they turned eighteen years of age), "they [were] therefore in need of constant campaigning for support."[110] This is why most of the children who were advertised in HAP newsletters were handicapped, mixed race, older children, or some combination of these. Highlighting certain children in the newsletter proved to be an effective way to find homes for these hard-to-place children. For example, Yoo Sei Chun and Lee Johnny were adopted after their pictures appeared in the newsletter. Holt explains, "We had such a good response from those wanting to adopt these boys that we thought it well to let you know about others who also need good homes."[111] It seems like a contradiction that children labeled unadoptable would appear in the newsletter as available for adoption. This inconsistency, along with the fact that children could move from unadoptable to adoptable status, suggests that being unadoptable did not necessarily mean a life sentence at the orphanage. This category is not as fixed as it sounds; it is quite fluid and dynamic. Children who fell in the unadoptable category simply required more work and more resources to get them adopted. They needed "constant campaigning," unlike the normal children who were readily adopted by Americans without direct advertising.

As the man who placed more Korean children in American homes than all adoption agencies combined in the decade after the war, Holt perfected the docility–utility relationship. He was also able to persuade civilians halfway across the world to adopt Korean orphans, even after the postwar orphan crisis subsided. He accomplished this through the presentation of visual progress reports that made use of the children's bodies. In narrating the changes that a particular child underwent while at his orphanage, he was able to demonstrate just how manipulable and improvable these children could be.

The Americanization of the Adoptee

As a processing station that prepared orphans for transnational adoption, Holt's orphanage worked to normalize the body to make the orphan adoptable, which was and continues to be the primary goal of orphanages in general. Along with improving the child's health to gain legal entrance into the United States, as well as improving the child's appearance to solicit desire from PAPs, the orphanage also prepared the adoptee for American life. In this way, the processing station of the orphanage was also a center of Americanization, where adoptable orphans were trained for life in the United States. Thus, preparation to be an American began in South Korea before the adoptee's entrance into U.S. borders.

Despite the fact that the orphanage was located in South Korea, the diet of the Il San orphans resembled an American diet rather than a Korean one. Besides rice and kimchi (standard Korean fare), they ate peanut butter and peanut brittle (made from the peanuts planted and harvested by the children), Jell-O, Boston baked beans, bread, pudding, sweet potatoes, cinnamon rolls, pies (especially pumpkin), cobblers, pork, and rabbit.[112] South Korean babies and toddlers even sampled Gerber baby food—the iconic American baby brand—through generous donations made by the corporation.[113] The traditional Korean diet does not include baked goods because most Korean homes lack ovens; therefore, we can assume that the Boston baked beans, pies, cinnamon rolls, and peanut brittle tasted "almost the same, but not quite" because the ingredients and preparation of the food cannot be exactly replicated.[114] Indeed, Bertha Holt boasts, "I have learned to make 24 pies at a time, without lard, eggs, or sugar. They even tasted like pumpkin pie and were a delicacy for children who had never tasted it before."[115] Here, Bertha Holt unwittingly reveals the limitations and ambivalence surrounding this project of normalizing the Korean child through Americanization. As she tries to reform these children by disciplining their taste buds to be the same as Americans' taste buds, the process of mimicry simultaneously produces difference.[116] The very fact that these Korean children cannot tell the difference between a real pumpkin pie versus an imitation reveals that this project can never be complete and that difference will always remain. In this way, this event acts as a foreshadowing of what is to come for these children as they enter white American homes in which they are expected to assimilate. For example, Korean adoptee artist Mi Ok Song Bruining writes, "I was convinced I was going insane because I felt so inauthentic. I did not feel white, as I had been raised. I did not feel Asian, as I clearly looked & was."[117] Korean adoptee memoirist Jane Jeong Trenka echoes Bruining when she explains, "What I longed for was wholeness, for my body to be as white and Northern Minnesotan as my mind. I longed to be normal."[118] These adopted Korean artists reveal the ways in which Korean adoption as a project of normalization creates ambivalence, fragmentation, and incoherence. It creates the dilemma of being "almost the same, but not quite"—almost the same, but not white.[119] I discuss further the limitations of such a project for Korean adoptees in the next chapter.

More than diet was targeted in the goal of preparing adoptable children for American homes; bathroom habits were also addressed. In a letter to adoptive parents regarding their adopted child's initial period of adjustment, HAP explains that while Korean toilet habits are "casual" (that is, they relieve themselves in public, and they do not use flush toilets), their child has been taught "western toilet manners" in the orphanage; however, "if he forgets and urinates in public or outdoors, merely remind him quietly that in his new home the custom is to use the bathroom."[120] Worrying about the diet and bathroom habits of the orphans may seem trivial, but discipline requires meticulous attention to detail. As Foucault reminds us, "Discipline is a political anatomy of detail." Details are the foundation on which discipline flourishes. To neglect the little things would be dangerous because "little things lead to greater [things]."[121] Furthermore, the regulation of customs and habits related to health are integral components of biopower. As a result, the mundane is attributed great significance.

Although I have focused primarily on the policies and procedures of HAP and its Il San orphanage, other adoption programs and orphanages participated in the Americanization of Korean orphans as a way to prepare them for adoption. For example, even though CCF is not an adoption agency, according to its founder J. Calvitt Clarke, CCF "has a section in one of its Korean orphanages devoted to the preparation of Korean children for legal adoption. They are prepared for life in America by some of the wives of the American Armed Forces who donate their time."[122] The specifics of this preparation are unmentioned by Clarke; however, a report written by ISS may shed some light on this matter. Because ISS did not have orphanages of their own, they relied on other existing orphanages in South Korea for the preplacement care of orphans who were placed through them.[123] The two institutions that provided the most preplacement care for children adopted through ISS were World Vision Reception Center and Choon Hyun Orphanage, a CCF orphanage.[124] Sometimes children spent their preplacement care with missionary families living in South Korea who "[taught] the children some English and prepare[d] them for living in an American home."[125] The preparation that these American missionaries provided for ISS was probably similar to the preparation that the wives of American military soldiers provided for CCF. The preplacement care most likely included learning some English words and phrases; learning how to eat with a knife and fork (versus chopsticks); and becoming acquainted with sleeping in a bed (versus on the floor), using a flush toilet, and eating at the dinner table while seated in a chair (versus sitting on the floor).[126] The Americanization of those children adopted through ISS and CCF does not sound as institutionalized as HAP; however, even their cursory attempts at preparing the child for American life demonstrate that they too were conscious about molding potential adoptees who could assimilate smoothly into their new American homes.

This is another way in which Korean orphans and camptown women intersect: Korean orphans who were slated for adoption and camptown women who were slated for marriage to American soldiers both underwent processes of Americanization. In her discussion of how the *yanggangju* becomes a GI bride, Grace Cho notes that *yanggangju* women who were scheduled to marry American GIs attended USO Bride School to prepare them for American life. At this school, future GI brides were schooled on American cuisine and cooking—for example, how to make a lettuce salad, Jell-O, and pumpkin pie. Ultimately, the Bride School, according to Cho, worked to "ease Korean women's assimilation into American culture, reinforcing the notion that escape from the camptown and assimilation into the United States are two sides of the same coin."[127] The same could be said for the Korean child in the orphanage: escaping the orphanage and assimilating into the United States are two sides of the same coin—the coin in this case being adoption. It is precisely the child's potential for smooth assimilation that strengthens his or her adoptability status.

In preparation for American life, Korean orphans were also raised to be Christians. Because Korean orphanages were predominately run by missionaries and religious organizations, the majority of the orphanages were concerned not only with the physical well-being of the children but also with their spiritual well-being. Bertha Holt says of her husband, "He was impelled by a vision from God to save Korea's lost children and God used him to give life to many."[128] Because South Korea's children were lost physically (because they were considered unwanted) and spiritually (because they were pagan), saving Korean orphans took place on both these levels.[129] The goal of disciplining the soul was to convert the orphans into Christians and prepare them for life with their new Christian American families in the United States.[130] Thus, like the body, the orphan's soul was under constant supervision and regulation at Il San orphanage. The activities of their soul were controlled and organized by a religious program that was developed by Holt and his personnel. It included "Sunday school and church services on Sunday, Bible classes throughout the week in school, and Child Evangelism classes conducted each Monday."[131] After Holt's death, the religious program continued because, according to the new executive director, Louis O'Conner Jr., "It is our feeling that more important than the physical needs of the children are their spiritual needs."[132] As a result, church services increased from once a week to three times a week. As the orphans underwent the religious program, they were "encouraged to make personal decisions for Christ, to give their testimonies, read their Bible, memorize scriptures and to pray daily." Apparently the religious program was successful because "many of the children have already made a decision for Christ."[133]

The indoctrination of Christianity at Holt's Il San orphanage may not be surprising; Holt was infamous for his religious fervor. His was not the only orphanage, however, where Christianity was instilled. The *Pacific Stars and Stripes* reported that the Air Force observed "children receiv[ing] Christian teaching" at the Korean orphanage they were visiting.[134] At the Myung Chin Sa orphanage, Eighth Army captain H. R. Jones listened to the children sing "Jesus Loves Me" in English.[135] Eighth Army soldiers also recorded a children's choir at the Buk Han San orphanage, singing the "Hallelujah Chorus."[136] The Department of Defense film crew captured a prayer meeting/Bible study that took place at a boy's orphanage.[137] Christian training even made its way into a refugee camp for orphans, as reported by *Pacific Stars and Stripes*:

> More than 100 hungry orphan children . . . marched quietly into the mess hall and seated themselves in an orderly fashion before a breakfast of milk, cereal, eggs,

and fruit. But not a single child started to eat. Instead, each bowed his head and clasped his hands together in an attitude of prayer. Masking his surprise, Chaplain (1st Lt.) William G. Davanney, 24th Div. assistant chaplain, grasped the situation, bowed his head and repeated the words to the grace. With the "amen," the well mannered children began their repast.[138]

In this short article, we learn that the Christianizing force that swirled around Korean orphans extended to places with seemingly no ties to missionaries or churches. This is because a new kind of secular religion was becoming popular at the time: what Arissa Oh calls Christian Americanism. Christian principles became fused with American values such as individual responsibility and dedication to family, culminating into a belief that "equated being a good Christian with being a good American," and vice versa.[139] As a result, Christian training became an integral part of Americanization.

The ultimate purpose of disciplining the body and soul of the orphan was to create an adoptee who will become a proper American citizen who integrates and assimilates seamlessly into American society and homes. In this way, the practice of white couples saving Asian children from an Asian nation is akin to a civilizing mission. Oh puts it another way: Korean adoption became "yet another iteration of the white man's burden . . . by bringing them into their homes and inculcating them with the values of Christianity and the American way of life."[140] Civilizing the "discards of society" through the regulation of the orphan's body and soul begins not when the child arrives on American soil but in the processing stations of orphanages in South Korea. Once adopted into a white American Christian family (which is usually the case), the adoptee further undergoes the normalizing process as this new family works to erase the signs of racial and cultural difference and replaces them with middle-class white American Christian values, beliefs, and ideology. As I will demonstrate in the next chapter, the adoptee, while accessorized to look like a heteronormative subject is in fact a nonnormative subject. Even though the adoptee is made to perform like a white American subject, she will never be completely consolidated into the white heteronormative family because this structure is dependent on whiteness. That is to say, as a nonnormative subject, the adoptee—as she is being normalized and Americanized—transgresses the very heteronormative boundaries of race, nation, and family. As a result, the adoptee's presence in a Western adoptive family will always disrupt the heteronormative ideal of the nuclear family. Even though the orphanage disciplines orphans into normative adoptees, it cannot do so completely.

5 "I WANTED MY HEAD TO BE REMOVED"

The Limits of Normativity

IN HER AWARD-WINNING and celebrated memoir *The Language of Blood* (2003), Korean adoptee writer Jane Jeong Trenka theorizes Korean adoptee identity by way of a recipe. She writes:

> Home chef, the modern alchemist, starts not with base metals but old chicken hearts and livers, broken backs and flightless wings. . . . Extract the undesirable parts; accent the desirable flavors. Serve up consommé, chicken liver pâté with toast and apple rings, aspic in half-globes with carrot flowers suspended in amber.
>
> Consider another recipe: Start with a girl whose blood has been steeped in Korea for generations, imprinted with Confucianism and shamanism and war. Extract her from the mountains. Plant her in wheat fields between the Red River and the Mississippi. Baptize her. Indoctrinate her. Tell her who she is. Tell her what is real.
>
> See what happens.
>
> Witness a love affair with freaks, a fascination with hermaphrodites and conjoined twins, a fixation on Pisces and pairs of opposites. Trace a dream that won't die: a vision of an old woman slumped on a bench, her spirit sitting straight out of the body, joined to the corpse at the waist.[1]

Framing the formation of Korean adoptee identity within the confines of the kitchen laboratory, Trenka exposes the experimental qualities of Korean adoption. She implies that Korean adoption is an experimentation with identity, whose base ingredient is Korean children. Like most scientific experiments, highly controlled variables are set in place ("Indoctrinate her. Tell her who she is. Tell her what is real.") in order to achieve the desired results: to make the adoptee normal. However, it turns out that the recipe did not quite produce the intended effect: the Korean adoptee, who is now fascinated with freaks, is not normal. You can almost hear the whispers of orphanage personnel, social workers, adoptive agents, and adoptive parents in the observation suite: How did this happen? What went wrong?

Rather than assuming that things went wrong with the experiment, I am more interested in teasing out why the architects and endorsers of Korean adoption are so invested in constructing it as a project of normativity. Why are the practitioners of Korean adoption constantly laboring to normalize the adopted child? The answer, I suggest, resides in a core anxiety concerning the racial, cultural, national, and biological difference between the adopted child and her adoptive parents. In this chapter, I am devoted to investigating the nonnormative components that have been actively disavowed and/or shunned in Korean adoption and how this denial has shaped Korean adoptee subjectivity and identity.

In the previous chapter, I examined the processes of normalization and Americanization that orphans underwent in order to become categorized as adoptable. I used the case study of the Holt Adoption Program's Il San orphanage to examine this transformation, wherein the orphanage became a site of Foucauldian discipline that normalized abnormal and handicapped bodies in order to make them adoptable by Westerners. In this chapter, I follow the adoptee to the United States, where we observe that the strategies used to normalize the child become more varied and prolific (rather than ceasing altogether) inside her new American home. Even though the adoptee is disciplined in the orphanage to seamlessly assimilate into her new adoptive family, the very presence of the adoptee's body within the adoptive family disrupts the semblance of the all-American (read white) heterobiological nuclear family. It is this disruption that is the focal point of this chapter, and it is this disruption—the failure of being indoctrinated and told who she is (that is, white American), along with the excesses that "won't die"—that signals the queer dimensions of Korean adoption.

David Eng indexes Asian transnational adoption as a part of the queer diaspora because it challenges conventional organizations of kinship where families are chosen rather than units into which they are born.[2] For Eng, this form of adoption becomes a site to envision what he calls a "new global family," with space for two mothers—and perhaps even more.[3] Although I agree that Asian transnational adoption has the potential to create radical new forms of kinship that eschews the biological imperative of family making, it is important to point out that historically this has not been the case. Indeed, as this chapter will show, the goal for adoptive families during much of the fifty-year history of Korean adoption has been to be the same as other normal (read white, middle-class, and heterobiological) families rather than subvert or challenge this standard. The practitioners of Korean adoption were not trying to challenge normative constructions of kinship; rather, they were trying to make Korean adoptive families normal and normative.[4] They were trying to fit Korean adoption into the model of heteronormative kinship rather than radicalize family, at least in its original conception.[5]

Given this context, Korean adoption, while certainly having the possibility to radicalize family, was first conceived as a regime of the normal rather than a queer kinship formation. It is important that we recognize this original conception and examine the inner workings of the normative dimensions of Korean adoption so that we do not reproduce this same logic when envisioning the radical potential of Korean adoption as a queer formation of family—one where, as Eng describes, at least two mothers of different races can coexist and one where an "ethical multiculturalism that rejects the model of white heterobiological nuclear family" becomes the organizing principle.[6] Thus, I use queer critique primarily to investigate the normative investments in Korean adoption rather than to frame Korean adoption as part of the queer diaspora.[7]

Although of course there are Korean adoptees who identify as lesbian, gay, transgendered, or queer, they are not my subject here. For the purposes of this chapter, I use *queer* to signal a process and a critique rather than an identity. My definition of queer is informed by the recipe that opened this chapter. As I illustrate in this chapter, Korean adoptees have been subjected to different kinds of violence in their new adoptive families—both ideological and epistemic—precisely because they have been scripted into white normativity.[8] However, despite the pervasive qualities of this field of power, white normativity, as with all forms of power, is not totalizing. If it were, the recipe would have produced the desired results. Instead, it failed to turn the Korean child into a normal white American girl; she is now obsessed with objects that are excessively abnormal: hermaphrodites, conjoined twins, a corpse with her spirit joined at her waist. Thus, the adoptee can be read as being produced by white normativity while also being a sign of its failure. It is from this core contradiction that I draw my definition of queer and my approach to queer critique. I define queer as not only that which is nonnormative but also that which is in excess to or a failure of the white heteronormative.[9] I use queer critique to illuminate the ideological and epistemic violence that comes from compulsory white heteronormativity, as well as the contradictions that emerge from such a project. Given my approach to queer critique, I am less interested in how Korean adoption queers conventional

structures of family and more concerned about fleshing out the heteronormative investments within queer formations. What queer critique can
do for Korean adoption studies, then, is illuminate the ways in which the
heteronormative not only works to absorb but also fails to assimilate completely nonnormative bodies—for example, the Korean birth mother and
the Korean adoptee.

By utilizing this particular reading practice, I hope to bring to the fore
how heteronormativity coalesces with whiteness and middle-class respect-
ability as a way to cover up anxieties concerning differences in race, culture,
and biology. Heteronormativity is not only a sexual discourse but also a
racial, gendered, and classed discourse. In "Punks, Bulldaggers, and Welfare
Queens: The Radical Potential of Queer Politics?" Cathy Cohen complicates
the definition of heteronormativity as simply heterosexual privilege by illustrating the ways in which heteronormativity is defined in and through
structures of race, gender, and class. The particular ways in which heterosexuality intersects with these other structures is what produces the heteronormative. According to Cohen, heteronormativity is not only rooted
in heterosexuality but also in white supremacy and dominant middle-class
values and norms.[10] Linking heteronormativity to whiteness and middle-
class sensibilities is particularly significant for me because Korean adoption has tried to gain legitimacy as a normative kinship structure not
just through heterosexual formation but also, and primarily, through the
reproduction of white middle-class norms. Indeed, as I illustrate in this
chapter, upholding white middle-class norms becomes the path to heteronormativity, not only for Korean adoption (as a familial structure) but also
for the Korean adoptee. The anxieties concerning racial, cultural, and biological difference are assuaged through a cleaving to white heteronormativity. As the recipe indicates, the presence of the nonwhite Korean body in
the white American family is always already a reminder of how shaky the
facade of Korean adoption as a normative kinship structure is. As a result,
the adoptee herself enables the queering of Korean adoption. In other words,
her very presence exposes the contradictions of white heteronormativity. Because the presence of the adoptee is what queers Korean adoption
and the white American (adoptive) family, the regulation of the adoptee's
racial, gender, and sexual normativity is incomplete and therefore ongoing.
(As we shall see later on, the degree to which Jane's adoptive parents are
diligent in upholding racial and sexual normativity reveals the unstable
nature of the normative facade of transnational adoption. They must continually invest in this because the facade could collapse at any moment.)

Thus, what Korean adoption does for queer critique is reveal a partnership between heteronormativity and queerness that is cyclical, mutualist, and enabling. In addition, Korean adoption becomes a useful site to examine the multiple ways in which heteronormativity and whiteness are mutually constitutive.

Thus far in this volume, I have tried to provide alternative genealogies of Korean adoption that attend to its geopolitical history and function. By situating it within the context of American neocolonialism during the era of Cold War politics, I elucidated how Korean adoption, proposed as a humanitarian mission, was conceived from American military domination and quickly became an arm of American empire. In this chapter, I situate Korean adoption within the field of queer studies to provide yet another genealogy of Korean: one that is rooted in projects of white heteronormativity. Doing so helps us to reassess Korean adoption and Korean adoptee subjectivity, as well as reexamine the relationship among adoptees, their adoptive parents, and their birth parent or parents.

What does a queer reading of Korean adoption and Korean adoptee subjectivity reveal? One of the first things it exposes is the anxiety produced by the presence of difference. Because the architects of Korean adoption (state- and national-level officials, social workers, adoptive agents, and adoptive parents) are so invested in projecting Korean adoption as a heteronormative kinship structure, this very investment suggests that Korean adoption is not so normal. For example, their repeated efforts in trying to make racial difference a nonissue reveal that race is an issue; the denial of race calls up race. The first part of this chapter focuses on the anxieties surrounding Korean adoption and how these anxieties are assuaged by the assimilation imperative as seen in the pages of Holt Adoption Program (HAP) newsletters from the 1960s and 1970s.

The second part of the chapter continues to examine the ways in which the nonnormative dimensions of Korean adoption are elided by focusing on the ways in which difference is absorbed. As a way to disavow the contradictions and disruptions that are produced by the presence of the Korean birth mother and adoptee, their bodies are constantly regulated and disciplined in such a way as to make the adoptive family seem like a normal white nuclear family. In addition, this section investigates the psychic and emotional effects of forced assimilation—or compulsory white normativity—as experienced by the adoptee protagonist Jane in *The Language of Blood*.[11] These psychic and emotional effects become queer reminders; they not only remind the Korean adoptee that she is not white but also remind the adoptive parents that Korean adoption is not a normative formation of kinship.

Although the queer figures of the Korean birth mother and adoptee are disciplined in such a way as to simulate a white normative kinship formation, these same figures—like Cohen's punks, bulldaggers, and welfare queens—also hold the key to reviving the radical queer politics of Korean adoption. Therefore, I end this chapter by talking about how Jane revives the queer possibilities of Korean adoption through her short story, "A Fairy Tale." Jane resuscitates the nonnormative figures of the birth mother and the adoptee to labor on the side of Korean adoption as a queer formation of kinship rather than a pseudo form of the white heterobiological nuclear family. By presenting a vision of Korean adoption that is organized by an "ethical multiculturalism"—a multiculturalism that negotiates difference in a way that does not privilege or prioritize whiteness, middle-class values, and heteronormativity—Jane uses the fairy tale to serve as a blueprint for how Korean adoption can reach its full potential of becoming a radical form of queer kinship.

A Note on Primary Sources

As I explained earlier in my introduction to this book, a large body of knowledge has been produced about the Korean adoptee by nonadoptees (for example, social workers, adoptive agents, case consultants, social scientists, and adoptive parents). This body of literature has depicted the adopted Korean as a model minority par excellence, who has easily and seamlessly assimilated into his or her white American family and into mainstream American society. A key figure who promoted this image of the Korean adoptee was none other than Harry Holt. As we saw in the previous chapter, the HAP newsletters served as recruiting tools by advertising, through the visual progress report, the docile bodies of Korean orphans. The visual progress report demonstrated to potential adoptive parents just how manipulable and malleable they were.

The newsletters (composed primarily by Bertha Holt) also informed readers of the "many miracles" that God accomplished through HAP as a way to encourage people to participate in the activities of the program—for example, by becoming adoptive parents, providing donations, or recruiting other families to adopt.[12] Inside these pages, one could read about the expansion of the program, the hiring of new staff members, or the latest information on adoption procedures and policies. One could also learn about Korean customs and language, educating both present and future adoptive families about the culture of the orphaned children displayed within their pages. In short, these newsletters focused on the growth and successes of the program in order to assure its readers that HAP was making a positive difference in the lives of Korean children.

As the adopted children of HAP grew to become graduating high school seniors or married couples, the updates on Holt's adoptees served as visible evidence of the successful, assimilated model minority Korean adoptee. These updates became another manifestation of the visual progress report, this time in regard to the improvement and normalization of the adoptee. If Holt's Il San orphanage was an institution of normalization that worked to normalize Korean orphans before their immigration, then the newsletters updates served as proof that Korean adoptees were normal and "like other American teenagers in many respects," as Dong Soo Kim concluded in his study.[13] Put another way, in the same way that Holt's Il San orphanage was a prime site in which to investigate the normalization of the Korean orphan, the HAP newsletter updates are a key site in which to investigate the normalization of the Korean adoptee.

The cultural production of Korean adoptees, on the other hand, often offers a more nuanced, complicated, and contradictory narrative of identity than the one touted by HAP. Therefore, I juxtapose my examination of HAP's newsletter updates with the Korean adoptee memoir *The Language of Blood* not only to illuminate the different investments in each but also to expose the queer dimensions of Korean adoption. What the newsletter updates elide, Trenka highlights; what the newsletter updates attempt to deny and hide, Trenka exposes and brings to light. As a result, we must attend to these contemporary writings by adult Korean adoptees in order to peel back the layers of heteronormativity that conceal the radical queer politics of Korean adoption.

In using Trenka's memoir to tease out the complexities and contradictions of Korean adoptee identity, I am suggesting neither that her story is the experience of all Korean adoptees nor that she speaks for Korean adoptees everywhere; however, despite the particularities of her experience, there are aspects of her story—certain themes, issues, events—that are typical of the Korean adoptee experience, particularly the expectation felt by the adoptee to assimilate into a white American family and society. It is precisely because her story resonates with so many Korean adoptees worldwide that her book has received so much attention in the global Korean adoptee community. The emblematic quality of her memoir is one of the major reasons why I chose this text over other Korean adoptee memoirs.

Finally, the distance in publication dates between the HAP newsletters (from the 1960s through the 1970s) and *The Language of Blood* (2003) may suggest that there is a large historical gap between my primary sources. On the contrary, because Jane, the protagonist in the memoir, was adopted in the early 1970s, her story is historically situated in a similar moment as the Holt adoptee updates on which I focus. The ideology of color-blindness and compulsory white normativity has structured Korean adoption for nearly fifty years. Only since the 1990s has a slow ideological shift taken place, in which the discourse of multiculturalism has been promoted in conjunction to color-blindness. The rising number of Korean culture camps, motherland trips, and "roots" tours attest to this shift, as the adoption industry tries to reeducate adoptive parents about the importance of nurturing a cultural and racial identity that takes into account Koreanness. The adoptees I examine (in the HAP newsletters and *The Language of Blood*) were adopted and raised before this shift, which locates them in a similar moment in Korean adoption practice and policy.

Assimilation Stories: Holt Adoption Program Newsletters

Because Korean adoption is a queer construction of family, there has been a constant effort to naturalize and normalize Asian transnational adoption, which reveals an anxiety around this particular kind of kinship. This anxiety is assuaged not only through the construction of Korean adoption as heterosexual reproduction (only married heterosexual couples have been allowed to adopt) but primarily through the obliteration of racial and national difference.[14] More specifically, it replaces nonwhiteness with whiteness; it replaces a Korean identity with a white American one. This is most poignantly demonstrated in the section where adoptive families provide updates of their adoptive children in the newsletters published by HAP. In effect, these updates serve to illustrate the seemingly smooth and successful assimilation of the adoptees.

Along with a new family comes a new American name and identity. In the May–June 1965 newsletter, we see names such as Nancy Ferridino and Betty Birosel attached to the pictures of two Korean American women.[15] They both have stylish hairstyles that represent the era, and they appear happy. They look completely assimilated into American culture, as captured by their high school graduation pictures. "Graduations and weddings in the

Holt families' children will be of great interest to all of us in the years ahead" is the line that concludes their update. Choosing to highlight graduations and weddings is significant because these two events symbolize not only successful assimilation but also the attainment and perpetuation of heteronormativity. Graduations signal a future wherein which adoptees will become respectable middle-class citizens. For women, it is the first step to becoming a good wife; for men, it is the step to landing a good job, making them good husbands. Weddings signal the active reproduction of heteronormative unions and family making. Accomplishing these markers works to ease the anxiety that queer kinship—that is, Korean adoption—will produce unassimilated, nonconforming members of society.

Adopted Korean Jeanne Wickes is also the picture of successful assimilation, graduating with honors from Wheaton Academy. Her article "The Day My Faith Meant Most to Me" earned her a $500 scholarship award. According to the newsletter, her "helpful parents and faith in God" led her to achieve these scholastic accomplishments.[16] While her handicap of being blind may have prevented her from achieving similar accomplishments in South Korea, it did not stop her from becoming successful in the United States. Bertha Holt, in recalling her trip to visit "happy parents of contented adopted children in Iowa," describes the transformative power of adoption. She writes, "It was a joy to see the pride of the parents and the transformation that has taken place in the children. They have changed from frustrated, love-hungry babies to secure, satisfied, and adorable children."[17] Bertha Holt's account, along with Ferridino's, Birosel's, and Wickes's update, attempt to prove that transnational adoption is effective: it has led to the successful normalization of once lost Korean orphans. Indeed, their stories and pictures appear alongside the story and picture of Park Song Ja, the little Korean orphan with a burn scar. The strategic placement of her among those who have already been adopted sends a powerful message to readers that she could be like any of these successful ladies, if only she were given the opportunity (via adoption).[18] Furthermore, it assuages whatever fears and doubts prospective adoptive couples might have by assuring them that Park Song Ja will turn out just like Nancy, Betty, or Jeanne.

These newsletter updates serve as a recruiting tool to potential adoptive parents, but they also function to cover up Korean adoption's nonnormative structures. This is accomplished by highlighting and celebrating normative gender roles and sexual relations in an effort to forgo racial difference altogether. By the 1970s, the updates in the HAP newsletters become more elaborate and are formally organized under the heading "Grandma's

Brag Book" (the grandma being Bertha Holt).[19] The Korean adoptees who are featured in this section are successful in school (honors students, high school graduates, college bound), in religion (practicing Christians), and to paraphrase a line from *Flower Drum Song*'s starlet Linda Low (played by Nancy Kwan), successful in their gender.[20] For example, in the January–February 1973 newsletter, siblings Marsha and Dennis Ruder are featured. The "Report on the Ruders" begins this way: "A happy, busy, productive life is the story of Marsha and Dennis Ruder."[21] This brother-and-sister pair, however, are busy and productive in quite different ways. Along with receiving all A's, playing first chair clarinet in her high school band, and winning a state competition in piano, Marsha is also described as "an excellent home-maker, and a knitting champion." Dennis, like his sister, is also accomplished, but his future is quite different. A member of the National Honor Society for two years running, he sings and plays piano, is a member of the drama club, writes for the school newspaper, and plays football. But unlike his sister, law school is what lies in his future.[22] Even the photos that accompany this report reify white middle-class gender norms: Marsha looks feminine, with her soft smile and long, flowing hair. She wears a simple turtleneck and vest, adorned with an understated necklace. Her photograph exudes a friendly, warm, maternal energy. Dennis, on the other hand, looks like the picture of heteropatriarchy, with his thick-framed glasses, well-groomed hair, suit, and tie. His edges are much sharper than his sister's, as his unsmiling face and demeanor evinces an attitude of masculine authority and seriousness. They both look the part, she the housewife and mother, he the lawyer.

Like Marsha and Dennis, the Korean adoptees who make it into "Grandma's Brag Book" are so successful in their gender and in their new American lives that one could possibly forget that they are not white. (Or, if one can't forget, it doesn't matter because they are so normal in other ways.) Their hypernormativity acts as a substitute for their racial lack (that is, whiteness). The narratives that the updates provide are so thoroughly codified in white American middle-class norms that it becomes difficult to not see them as white. But this is precisely the point, after all. By focusing entirely on the seemingly smooth and easy assimilation of Korean adoptees in white American homes, HAP overcompensates in the area of gender, class, and sexual normativity to hide the nonnormative racial foundations of Korean adoption.

It is important that Korean adoptees be successful in their gender because gender normativity is a central component of heteronormativity.

The women whose accomplishments are highlighted in the newsletters could be classified as good girls primed for marriage: they are attractive, obedient, and talented. They are interested in feminine work such as nursing or candy striping at a nursing home. Likewise, the men who are featured could be categorized as good husband material. They are handsome, ambitious, and interested in masculine occupations such as serving in the military or becoming doctors and lawyers. It is certain that these soon-to-be professionals will easily provide their future families with a financially stable home. Indeed, these updates have the quality of personal ads, in which readers can envision and locate potential wives and husbands in their perusal of this section. However, thinking about these adoptees as marriage partners is quite different from seeing them as good students and obedient children. It is when one envisions Korean adoptees as sexual partners that race starts to become an issue and when racial difference must be taken into account.

In the context of marriage, the issue of race is revived. One only needs to look at who is and who is not getting married. The wedding announcements primarily show female Korean adoptees getting married. Furthermore, they are not getting married to other Korean adoptees or other men of Asian descent; they are marrying white men.[23] Within the context of compulsory assimilation, this is logical. After all, if complete assimilation is the goal, then marrying another Korean adoptee would defeat this purpose, no matter how assimilated the Korean adoptee might be. Whiteness is the goal not only in terms of identity but also in marriage. However, there are some unintended effects that arise with this particular pairing. In the wedding pictures, the presence of the white male body next to the Asian female body does not make her appear more white; it makes her less white. In the presence of whiteness, her nonwhiteness becomes more apparent. In addition, this particular coupling—although it could be read as evidence of successful assimilation—evokes multiple histories that belie such a reading. First, militarized sexuality is indexed, reframing this union as another by-product of U.S. militarism in South Korea.[24] If we took these wedding pictures outside the context of the HAP newsletter, the couple would more likely be perceived as an American soldier with his Korean military bride rather than an assimilated Korean adoptee with her white American husband. In this way, the wedding pictures have the unintended effect of evoking the militarized genealogy of Korean adoption. Second, it recalls the uneven ways Asian bodies have been racialized and gendered in the United States. The racialized and gendered fantasy of the Asian female as simultaneously hypersexual and docile, erotic and submissive, positions Korean adoptee women into the status of prime marriage partners. In the contemporary context of the white women's liberation movement, the fantasy of the sexually attractive, docile Asian woman becomes even more desirable.[25] In contradistinction, Asian men have historically been constructed as yellow perils who threaten national security or have been cast as feminine and asexual. Neither characterization makes for good marriage material. The overachieving Korean adoptee men who emit masculinity and heteropatriarchy in the pages of the newsletter, it seems, cannot compete with these preexisting stereotypes of Asian men; the stereotypes are simply too powerful. It is because of these uneven histories of war, sexuality, race, and gender that have made the partnering of Asian women with white men more common than Asian men with white women. Put simply, in marriage matters, race matters, which is one reason why racial difference cannot be as easily displaced by heterosexual union as it was by gender normativity. The other reason is because, as previously explicated, normative heterosexuality is codependent on whiteness; consequently, it is more difficult for Korean adoptees to achieve heteronormativity through marriage (because the whiteness of their partner accentuates their nonwhiteness) than through the attainment of normative gender roles.

These narratives and photographs that highlight white normativity, gender and middle-class norms, and heteronormativity work to alleviate the racial aberration that is Korean adoption. These stories seem to indicate that despite the queer construction of white Americans parenting nonwhite foreign children, white adoptive parents have nothing to worry about because adoption will transform these children into successful and responsible Americans with all the accoutrements of white middle-class values and norms. Furthermore, the assimilation project often includes the component of entering into normative gender roles and heterosexual relations with white Americans. White heteronormative reproduction becomes another way to mitigate, albeit to varying degrees, the anxieties concerning the queer dimensions of transnational adoption.

Queer Reminders in *The Language of Blood*

In stark contrast to the stories promoted by HAP, Korean adoptee narratives can often disrupt the picture of seamless assimilation as conveyed in the newsletters. By sharing their experiences of growing up and being raised in predominately white communities, Korean adoptee artists like Trenka expose the contradictions that emerge from white normative projects that try to suppress difference. Adopted Koreans reap the contradictions that erupt from projects that try to deny difference in the quest for sameness. Because adoptees live with and within these contradictions, their personal narratives often address rather than repress difference. As a result, their narratives tend to expose the queer dimensions of Korean adoption.

Because the goal is to make Korean adoption a normative structure of kinship, the regulation of the Korean birth mother and child become key strategies used to elide the nonnormative aspects of Korean adoption. The first step in regulating the birth mother is to make deviant her gender and sexuality. When the local pastor visits the Brauers—Jane's soon-to-be adoptive parents—he hands them a brochure with Korean children pictured. He explains:

> These children could have been aborted, but their mothers chose life for them. Often the mothers are prostitutes or teenagers, and they cannot take care of their own children. But these babies need homes and parents who love them. . . . Lutheran Adoption Service . . . believes [that] every child has a right to permanent parents who can provide an atmosphere of love, acceptance, and supportive care. . . . They also believe married couples . . . should have the opportunity to experience the satisfactions and responsibilities of parenthood.[26]

This reeducation concerning the basic ingredients to make a family (married couples willing to provide needy children a permanent home, regardless of skin color and nationality) may sound like an effort to radicalize normative kinship structures; however, its reproduction of and reliance on white heteronormativity forecloses the potential radical queer politics of Korean adoption. It does so by framing Korean adoption as a white heteronormative formation of family. On the basis of the requirements of the brochure, the prospective adoptive parents have to be married Christians. In addition, the financial responsibility it takes to not only adopt the child but also to raise and support her presumes at least a middle-class standing. Although whiteness is not a written requirement, the overwhelming majority of adoptive parents are white—not just in the United States but also in Canada, Europe, and Australia—because this style of family building, according to Kristi Brian, is "cost-prohibitive for low-income families. . . . Thus, the promotion of KAA [Korean American adoption] is primarily 'targeted' at white, middle-class, heterosexual couples."[27] Significantly, the criteria to adopt Korean children reflect the main pillars of heteronormativity: whiteness, middle-class values and norms, normative gender roles, and normative heterosexual practices.

In stark contrast to the presumably financially stable married couple with Christian values and middle-class sensibilities is the figure of the Korean birth mother, who is depicted as a prostitute or an unwed teenage mother. Her supposed sexual deviance from a prescribed norm—in this case, exchanging money for sex, being unwed at the time of pregnancy, or having sex at an inappropriate age—renders her unfit to take care of her own children.[28] The Korean birth mother, according to the pastor's narrative (which is also the narrative promulgated by adoptive agents), falls short of being a proper woman and mother. Juxtaposed against this nonnormative heterosexual figure is the married white American couple who exude gender and sexual normativity, even if they are unable to reproduce. Their heteronormative lifestyle gives them the right to "experience the satisfactions and responsibilities of parenthood" (partly because marriage supposedly signifies permanence and stability), whereas the nonnormative heterosexual lifestyle forfeits the Korean birth mother's right to parent. Consequently, the white American couple is presumed to be the best choice—and eventually the natural choice—to take care of these Korean children.

What becomes evident here is that white heteronormativity becomes the alibi used to situate white Americans as more fit for parenthood than the Korean birth parents. Even though Jane's birth mother was neither a prostitute nor an unwed teenager, framing Korean adoption as a normative kinship formation relies on the presence and labor provided by a nonnormative subject: in this case, the supposedly deviant Korean birth mother (rather than the infertile American couple).[29] Fabricated or not, the figure of the birth mother as prostitute or unwed teenage mother becomes the key to help legitimize the parenthood of childless white middle-class couples.[30] Thus, Korean adoption as a normative kinship formation (rather than queer) is constructed in and through the repudiation of the birth mother.

Another way that practitioners of Korean adoption try to cover up the nonnormative dimensions of Korean adoption is by framing it as a bastion of heteronormativity, where at-risk children who may be doomed to replicate the lives of their nonnormative birth mothers are saved. Social workers and adoptive agents constructed a popular narrative about the Korean birth mother that they passed onto adoptive parents, who eventually passed the story onto their adoptive children. In this narrative, the birth mother is not only sexually licentious but also immoral, which makes her a dangerous influence on the child.[31] According to HAP, the children of these women "end up as child-servants or as teen-age concubines."[32] The construction of the Korean birth mother as gender and sexually deviant, along with the perceived danger that these traits will be passed onto the child, launches the adoptive parents to Christlike status—not only in their absolution of the mother's original sin but also in saving the child—further fueling the discourse of adoption as an act of rescue. As Jane explains, the rhetoric of adoption says that she had been "rescued by adoption; had I stayed in Korea, I would have been institutionalized, after which I would have turned into what Asian girls tend to turn into if left to their own devices: a prostitute."[33] In her film *Searching for Go-Hyang* (1998), Tammy Tolle echoes the same sentiment when she explains that she and her twin sister, Amy, "were told we should be grateful to them for adopting us. . . . It if wasn't for them, we would either be dead or be prostitutes on the streets of Korea."[34] For Jane, Tammy, and Amy, adoption would not only provide them with proper parents but also save them from prostitution.[35] Korean adoption is propped up as a training ground where at-risk (at risk of becoming prostitutes) Korean children turn into good girls. Within the domain of Asian transnational adoption, Korean children who are born from supposedly sexually perverse behavior and fated to repeat this cycle are given the chance to become normative sexual subjects; their deviant sexual past can be erased through the normative powers of transnational adoption. Thus, Korean adoption gains legitimacy as a normative formation of kinship through its reproduction and reinforcement of middle-class norms and values concerning sexuality and gender.

So far we have seen that the construction of Korean adoption as a normative kinship formation depends on both the queering (that is, figuring her gender and sexually deviant) and disciplining (that is, taking away her parental rights) of the Korean birth mother. However, there is another queer figure that requires discipline: the Korean adoptee. As I mentioned before, disciplining the Korean child does not end after she leaves the orphanage; on the contrary, the adoptee's entrance into her new white American family destabilizes the semblance of the conventional white nuclear family so that her body becomes a site of even more scrutiny and regulation. New circumstances require new tactics of discipline. Because the goal is to make Korean adoption a heteronormative structure of kinship, the regulation of the adopted child's sexuality and race becomes yet another tool to elide the nonnormative dimensions of this new family.

As they enter the sphere of their new adoptive family, Jane and her sister, Carol, undergo rigorous regulation of both their sexuality and race, although in different ways. For example, after catching the girls masturbating during the dead of night in their bedrooms at the ages of four and eight, respectively, their adoptive mother is thrown into a frenzy about their supposed rampant sexual energy.[36] The older sibling, Carol, is particularly targeted because she was "pretty, popular, and smart—right from puberty."[37] Assuming her "wickedness" from the start, Mrs. Brauer calls her eldest adoptive child a "slut" and a "whoring sinner." She even solicits a house call, asking the Lutheran pastor for divine intervention to keep Carol on the straight and narrow.[38] However, Carol had not deviated from the straight and narrow path, and so the good reverend leaves their house unalarmed. Despite the lack of evidence that Carol is a slut or whore, the adoptive mother continues to obsess and worry about her seemingly sexual improprieties with around-the-clock vigilance.[39] It seems that the stereotypical construction of Asian women as whore, along with the fabricated narrative that made her birth mother a prostitute (even though she wasn't), is too powerful an image to forget. Consequently, the regulation of the adoptee's sexuality becomes an important aspect of normalizing the adopted child.

If the regulation of Jane and Carol's sexuality resulted in the adoptive mother's hyperawareness of their sexual activity, the regulation of their race entails quite the opposite. Schooled by the practitioners of Korean adoption at this time, the Brauers try hard to make race a nonissue: the Holt Adoption Program "sees him as a child and human being first, and as being of a particular nationality or race as secondary."[40] Despite convincing themselves that race did not matter—that they could see beyond race—race is the first thing they see when they pick up their newly adopted children at the airport. Their response to seeing race is to not see race; their response, like the entire industry's response to racial difference, is to be color-blind—that is, blind to every shade but white.

In *The Language of Blood,* we see the systematic regulation of the adopted child's racial identity in order to create the facade of the white American nuclear family. Unlike the Korean birth mother—whose difference was highlighted—the regulation of the Korean adoptee hinges on the ability to erase the racial, cultural, and national characteristics that mark her different in an effort to make her white.[41] This erasing process takes place in the form of assimilation and requires recruitment. In "Highway 10," a play embedded in *The Language of Blood,* sounds of airplanes taking off and landing open the play.[42] After ten minutes, the scene transitions into a rural highway. Sitting in the car are Fred and Margaret (the adoptive parents) and their newly arrived adopted children, Mi-Ja and Kyong-Ah, who are instantly renamed Carol and Jane. Four-and-a-half-year-old Carol sits alone in the backseat, while Margaret holds baby Jane in the passenger seat. The entire play consists of just three lines: two questions and an assertion.

FRED: [*Looks into the rearview mirror to see* Carol.] How you doin' back there?
[Carol *continues to scan audience*]
MARGARET: [*Pats baby gently but constantly, like a nervous tic. Turns head to look at Carol but is unable to see her. Speaks over her shoulder.*] Are you okay?
[*Long pause*]
FRED: [*Louder*] Your mother asked you a question.
[Carol *does not look at* Margaret *but searches the faces in the audience, looking for a Korean face, any Korean face. Finding none, she closes her eyes and decides to forget.*][43]

In this scene, the "color-blind" father and mother interpellate Carol as their adopted child.[44] More precisely, heteropatriarchy—as a stand in for the nation-state—hails Carol, while the white mother plays a supporting role. Even though Carol does not understand English and therefore does not comprehend the actual words that are spoken, she does recognize that the words are meant for her. Specifically, she knows intuitively that they are recruiting her to be someone else: not Mi-Ja, a Korean girl, but Carol, an American girl whose identity and life are just beginning. We know that she knows that she is being recruited not by the words she says (she remains silent for the entire duration of the play) but by the internal decision she makes. Her response: "she closes her eyes and decides to forget." She understands that the words spoken by her adoptive father and mother are not only directed at her but are also soliciting a response that requires conversion.

Louis Althusser admits that the interpellation process seems inexplicable because even with a whistle, "the one hailed always recognizes that it is really him who is being hailed."[45] However, the reason why we respond to the hail, according to Althusser, is because "individuals are always-already subjects."[46] Even before birth, a child has always already been configured as a subject via the expectations created by the familial ideology: "Before its birth, the child is therefore always-already a subject, appointed as a subject in and by the specific familial ideological configuration in which it is 'expected' once it has been conceived."[47] In the case of Carol, the ideology of adoption—the core of which is color-blindness and white normativity—has always already interpellated her as a white racial subject. Despite the fact that she is four and a half years old, the ideology of adoption states that she is reborn as an American child. "The existence of ideology and the hailing or interpellation of individuals as subjects are one and the same thing," according to Althusser.[48] That is why there is no time lag between the construction of Mi-Ja and Carol. Fred and Margaret expect Carol, not Mi-Ja, to arrive at the airport; they hail Carol, not Mi-Ja.

This transformation from Korean to American girl is not without violence or trauma. As the newly formed family makes the trek from the airport to their rural Midwestern home, the audience not only feels what Carol feels but also witnesses Carol's transformation on a historical, cultural, and emotional level. The play is organized in real time: it is four hours long, the time it takes to drive from the airport to Carol's new house. Like Carol, who is trapped in the car for the entire time, the audience is also trapped. Once the play begins, all the theater exits are locked, preventing anyone from leaving until all four hours of the play are completed. By recreating similar physical and temporal conditions, Trenka replicates in the viewer how Carol must have felt: anxious, scared, confused, overwhelmed, and reticent. In so doing, Trenka dismantles the picture of adoption (as promoted by adoption agencies and social workers) as a smooth, seamless process of assimilation; rather, the audience begins to understand the kind of psychic and emotional violence that takes place when a child is expected to forget the past in order to begin anew.[49]

Indeed, later in the memoir, Jane recalls a memory from her childhood that captures the graphic violence of assimilation. The scene is the annual slaughter and processing of chickens on her grandparent's farm. As she witnesses the beheading of chickens, Jane's contempt for her own face turns masochistic when she fantasizes about chopping it off with her grandpa's ax:

> I wanted my head to be removed, a metaphor so strong that only later did I realize that it was not a death wish at all. I dreamed about it, fantasized about it, imagined the mercy of a guillotine. My body was separated from my mind in a dualism so ridiculous that I almost flew apart at the shoulders.
>
> What I longed for was wholeness, for my body to be as white and Northern Minnesotan as my mind. I longed to be normal, to not have to emotionally excavate myself to find my place. I wanted to be like my normal cousins who took after their normal parents or grandparents, who inherited the family colons and noses.[50]

The assimilation story is most commonly understood as a teleological narrative that moves the alien or foreign subject from darkness into light, from savagery into modernity. It is depicted by those in power as a benign, peaceful project. Jane's re-memory of her assimilationist fantasy, however, revises this progressive, benign journey of assimilation by capturing the violence that accompanies such a project. The graphic violence of this scene becomes the critique. If taken literally, assimilation leads to death, not life. Seen another way, Jane, through this shocking tale of memory, provides the backstory to the seemingly smooth and painless narratives of assimilation recounted in HAP's newsletter updates. The psychic violence that compulsory white normativity entails is made explicitly clear in this remembering.

In "Highway 10," we witness the psychic effects of the assimilation imperative on Carol. After Carol "decides to forget"—which is her response to the hail—a reel-to-reel home movie is projected above and behind the car. It consists of scenes from Mi-Ja's (Carol's) life in South Korea, ranging from playing with her sisters and friends to sleeping with her mother to saying good-bye—less than twenty-four hours ago—to her family at Kimpo Airport. Eventually, the memories of her past life in South Korea become "blank frames and white noise."[51] The process of assimilation is put on fast-forward as we observe the name, language, family, and history of one Korean child diminish into complete erasure. The ideology of adoption necessitates this erasing process in order for her conversion from Korean child to American girl to take place: "Carol has willed herself to become a girl with no history and is now ready to start her new life."[52]

However, Carol is not completely without history. Trenka seems to have miswritten, because the movie turns into a series of "illuminated scratches and other imperfections" rather than a blank screen. Scratches and imperfections are not nothing. In this case, they are the etchings that remain from her past. In the same way that a pencil's imprint on paper cannot be completely rubbed away with an eraser, four and a half years of life experience cannot be wiped out so thoroughly. Even if on the surface the pencil marks have been wiped away, the grain of the paper's pulp has been forever changed. On the surface, it may look like Carol has completely erased her past, but deep in her psyche, her life in South Korea has made an impression that cannot be undone. For example, although Carol "assimilated well, just as Mom and Dad were promised she would," she "spoke one Korean word repeatedly and for no visible reason."[53] That word was *apun,* "pain." Significantly, Carol uses Korean to identify not a physical pain but a psychic pain. For many Korean adoptees who undergo processes of historical erasure, traces of their Korean past reside in the psychic world rather than the material or physical world.[54] According to Judith Butler, this is because the psyche houses the price that is paid for normative subjectivity: "Every ritual of conformity to the injunctions of civilization comes at a cost, and that a certain unharnessed and unsocialized remainder is thereby produced. . . . This psychic remainder signifies the limits of normalization."[55] In Carol's case, *apun* is a psychic remainder that signifies the limits of transnational adoption as a normalizing process. This slip of the tongue signals the impossibility of complete assimilation. Jacqueline Rose contends that "the unconscious constantly reveals the 'failure' of identity—'failure' is something endlessly repeated and relived. . . . It appears not only in the symptom, but also in dreams, in slips of the tongue . . . which are pushed to the sidelines of the norm."[56] For Carol, it is the slip of her Korean tongue that signifies the failure of complete assimilation. For Jane, it is within her dreams where this failure manifests itself.

Jane's psychic remainders are housed in her dream world. After reuniting with her birth mother in South Korea and living with her for a week, she begins to dream in Korean:

> Although I couldn't understand it, there it was—a full-fledged Korean language dream complete with Korean women talking and me having no idea what they were saying. And then something quite extraordinary happened: the dream seemed to dissolve, although I didn't wake. And what was left was a kind of heightened reality, from which there emerged a very loud voice that asked, "What is your name?" And I said to it, "My name is Kyong-Ah. It never used to be, but it is now. My name is Kyong-Ah."[57]

Her ability to dream in Korean proves the limits of the normalizing powers of transnational adoption. However, even more significant is the new level of awareness she achieves about herself. In this "heightened reality," Jane experiences a "coming to" in which she comes to consciousness about her Korean identity—an identity that has been squelched and rescinded since her adoption. Indeed, taking back her Korean name, Kyong-Ah, is remarkable considering that she used to check "white" on all her college forms.[58]

If the psyche, as Butler suggests, is where the excesses of normativity are housed, then it is also in psychic space where queerness takes its first breath. Butler argues that transforming into a normative subject comes at a cost, and this cost is accounted for in the unconscious, in the psyche. There is another way we can interpret this: in conforming to the injunctions of normativity, queerness gets displaced in the psyche. Psychic remainders become queer reminders, and these queer reminders are consciousness raising. For both Carol and Jane, psychic remainders remind them that they are not white, and this particular queer reminder aids Jane in "coming to" identify as Korean rather than white.

Korean adoption makes whiteness compulsory.[59] Because the Brauers are committed to portraying Korean adoption as a conventional structure of family, Jane tells us that she was raised in a house where "The a-word, adoption, was not mentioned in our house. Neither was the K-word, Korea."[60] The "a-word" and the "K-word" are unmentionable because they would expose the secret that Jane's adoptive parents are so committed to locking away: the secret that Jane is different from them racially, culturally, and biologically. These unmentionables would shatter the dream of raising them "the way they were supposed to—like we were their own."[61] Jane becomes complicit in trying to keep this secret and tucks away her Korean self behind a bulletin board: "I took down the bulletin board in my bedroom and with a thumbtack scratched my Korean name (which I had cunningly memorized years before) into the paint on the wall and then replaced the bulletin board so I would not be found out."[62] She also engages in a variety of activities to whiten her appearance: she bleaches her hair blonde, alters her face with makeup, and dates only white men.[63] However, after she returns from her South Korea trip where she "came to," she begins to see herself no longer as "Jane the Twinkie, the Pan-Asian fraud."[64]

Jane describes the process in which she affirms her nonwhite Korean identity as "coming out of the closet."[65] Even though Jane herself uses the discourse of the closet to frame her renewed sense of self, I provide an alternative discourse to understand this event. Rather than reproducing the problematic logic of the closet that has organized much of canonical queer theory,[66] I suggest that Jane engages in a process of coming to rather than coming out.[67] Because the coming-out narrative creates strict binaries such as closeted/visibility, secrecy/disclosure, and oppressed/liberated, it produces a teleological narrative of identity where the subject moves from inauthentic self to true self. The process of coming to, however, evokes an altogether different trajectory of identity. Unlike "coming out," the phrase "coming to" is less teleological, more fluid; it eschews binary production. Not only does it connote a coming to awareness or consciousness—which is emblematic in Korean adoptee memoirs—but it also evokes a movement toward something or some person. Because the "to" is left open-ended, "coming to" connotes multiple directions, which signifies that identity formation is multiply inflected, multidirectional, multifaceted, and continuous. In short, coming to is not so much about declaring or achieving some end result (like coming out implies) but about confronting one's circumstances and conditions in order to achieve a more nuanced and complex understanding of oneself. By reframing Jane's narrative of identity as coming to, I not only offer an alternative to the coming out narrative that is less teleological, normative, and essentialist but also provide a more nuanced rendering of Korean adoptee identity formation.

By coming to, Jane recovers what was taken away during the interpellation process via her Korean mother. In a letter that she writes to her now-dead Umma ("mom" in Korean), she recounts the ways in which she has reclaimed a Korean identity: being able to read Korean, dream in Korean, cook Korean food, and engage in Korean rituals to properly mourn her passing. By filling herself with these aspects of Korean culture, she proclaims, "I take you back, and I take back all the things that were stolen, back inside my body." She even signs the letter—for the first time—with her given Korean name: "Your daughter, Kyong-Ah."[68] Here, she reverses the losses associated with heteropatriarchy's hailing of Kyong-Ah as Jane through the figure of her Umma.

By pointing out the ways in which Jane has recovered her nonwhite identity via her coming to, I am neither suggesting that Jane's formation of identity is complete nor suggesting that she is a whole person because she has reclaimed her origins. To be sure, her sister Carol also returned to South Korea on a separate trip, and she had no such coming-to experience.[69] I am suggesting, however, that Jane's coming to is significant because it not only proves the limits of Korean adoption as a heteronormative project but also revives the radical potential of Korean adoption as a queer formation of family, where there is room for at least two mothers and where white heteronormativity is not privileged.

Despite achieving this new level of self-understanding, Jane realizes that coming to may destroy her relationship with her parents because that very relationship has been founded on the belief that she is not (racially or biologically) different from them. Her validation of her Korean identity names that difference and in so doing disturbs the white normative world in which she lives. She ponders whether to reveal her newfound awareness of self:

> I know that announcing "Mom, Dad, I'm K-K-Korean. No you don't get it, I mean, I'm *Korean*," is a lot more difficult than deciding to become a pianist. And after I acknowledge that I'm Korean—or at least an adopted one. . . . I am not going to magically "move on" or become "normal."[70]

Here we see that part of Jane's coming-to process requires an act of enunciation, where she proclaims her Korean identity in the hopes of having it recognized and acknowledged by her adoptive parents. This recognition by her adoptive parents is particularly important if the radical queer politics of Korean adoption is able to reach its full potential; however, just as the white heteronormative standard of Korean adoption has disciplined the adopted child, so too has it disciplined the adoptive parents. Predictably, when Jane proclaims her affiliation with Koreanness over the phone, she is met with hostility and then silence.[71]

When Jane introduces herself to her adoptive parents as Korean, she doesn't say directly "I'm K-K-K-Korean," as she rehearsed in her mind; rather, she relies on the reclamation of her Umma to signify her new identity as Korean to her adoptive parents. After receiving news from South Korea that her Umma died from brain cancer, Jane decides to organize a memorial service in her honor because she cannot attend the funeral in South Korea. She contemplates whether to invite her adoptive parents for fear of getting hurt if they reject the invitation. In the end, her optimism wins over, and she asks her parents. She telephones her adoptive mother and says, "It would mean a lot if you would come."[72] Her adoptive mother says she's planning a shopping trip to Wal-Mart that day. Jane pleads with her, "Mom, please come. I want you to come. It would mean so much to me." This time, her adoptive mother is more direct: "not interested" is her answer.[73] At this moment, Jane takes stock of the situation:

> She [Mom] is unaffected by my mother's death; it didn't happen, *she* didn't happen. In my mom's mind, I don't come from somewhere else, I don't have a birth mother, I don't, I don't.
>
> I take another deep breath and weigh my choices. I can continue the charade or I can be true to myself. I opt for the latter. I'll say it. I'll name this illusion, this intractable lie.
>
> . . . "Can't you fucking come for the woman who gave you your children?" . . .
>
> "*Say.*"[74] She snaps it like a whip across my face . . .
>
> She has done it again. She can cow me into submission with a single word. I politely tell her, voice shaking, that I will not talk to her for a while. Good-bye.[75]

Jane, in uttering the words "the woman who gave you your children," is evoking the unmentionables—the "a-word" and the "K-word"—at the same time. She is, in fact, exposing the illusion of Korean adoption as a normative formation of family in order to shatter it. Because the dominant ideology of Korean adoption depends on making the Korean birth mother disappear, it is not surprising that her reappearance (even as a corpse) threatens the facade of Korean adoption as a white heterobiological structure of kinship. What is unexpected, however, is that Jane uses her Umma to signify her coming to Koreanness: "Can't you fucking come for the woman who gave you your children?"[76] By aligning herself as the child of the newly deceased Korean woman, Jane resuscitates the disappeared Korean birth mother and reemploys her—this time—to disclose Korean adoption as a queer kinship formation.

At first glance, the adoptive mother seems to be more incensed by Jane's use of profanity ("fucking") than the actual meat of her words ("the woman who gave you your children"). Indeed, when Jane tries to solicit sympathy from her adoptive father—"Please come to the memorial service, even if Mom doesn't. Do you remember how sad you were when your mom died? I feel like that now. That's why I would like you to come"—his only response is, "You swore at my wife. We're not coming."[77] I wonder, however, which is more obscene for the Brauers: the word *fucking* or Jane identifying herself as Korean. Perhaps both are equally obscene. After all, fucking—as a reference to sex, as well as the vulgarity of the word itself—could act as a condensation of all that the Brauers associate with Koreanness and the Korean birth mother: improper sexuality, gender deviance, and immorality.[78] Or perhaps even more profane than this is being outed by Jane: Mrs. Brauer is not the natural mother. This may be obvious; however, the dominant ideology of Korean adoption tries to construct the adoptive mother as the natural mother, as the real mother, because she is the one raising the child.[79] Korean adoptee filmmaker Deann Borshay Liem has noted that there simply is no room for two mothers in the adoptee's mind.[80] The rhetoric of Korean adoption does not allow for more than one mother to exist at a time because having two mothers would make visible the queer dimensions of Korean adoption. Consequently, each mother's role is regulated in such a way that only one emerges. In this case, the adoptive mother gains the status of the real mother. The Korean mother is displaced so that the white American woman can assume her rightful role as the maternal figure. By evoking her Korean mother, Jane shatters the fantasy that allows her adoptive mother to imagine herself as the natural mother, which authorizes Korean adoption to be seen as a white heterobiological structure of kinship.

Put another way, the reclamation of her Umma destabilizes the white heteronormative foundation upon which the adoptive family has been built. Jane's coming to has brought with it a host of queer reminders, shaking that very foundation. But what precisely are those reminders? Jane ends up reminding her adoptive mother that she, Jane, has another mother. If it weren't for this mother, Mrs. Brauer may have never become a mother. In this way, Jane reminds her adoptive parents of their infertility: "We [Jane and her adopted sister] are reminders that something is wrong with someone's womanhood or someone's manhood. We are reminders of inadequacy, or incompleteness."[81] Furthermore, because the birth mother is Korean,

Jane also reminds her adoptive mother that she is not white: "Mom, I am not from you; I will never be fully yours. I will never have peachy skin or blonde hair; I will never see the world through blue eyes."[82] All these reminders work to dismantle an ideology of adoption that is founded on white normativity, color-blindness, and assimilation; an ideology that privileges white motherhood over third world and nonwhite mothers; and an ideology that disappears the nonwhite mother in an effort to make Korean adoption a pseudobiological kinship formation so as to make it appear normal and natural. By coming to via her Korean mother, Jane stops the cycle of racial, cultural, reproductive, and maternal violence that is done for the sake of upholding white heteronormative kinship structures. Preserving white middle-class norms will no longer be at the expense of Jane's sense of identity and well-being. The suppression and repression of her racial and cultural identity is no longer a valid form of payment for keeping up appearances and keeping alive the "adoption is wonderful" rhetoric.[83]

"A Fairy Tale": Reviving the Radical Queer Politics of Korean Adoption

It is apt that the very subjects who have been queered and disciplined by Korean adoption are the very subjects to radicalize Korean adoption. Rather than being used to normalize Korean adoption, their presence and labor are now being redeployed in Trenka's memoir to revive the queer politics of Korean adoption. Even though Jane's parents refuse to recognize and acknowledge Korean adoption as a queer formation of kinship, the radical possibilities of Korean adoption that were resuscitated with Jane's coming to are not entirely foreclosed. Instead, they are rerouted and reinvested in herself rather than in her adoptive parents.

Because so many nonadoptees consider the reclamation of a Korean identity as an act of rejection (of whiteness, Americanness, or adoption), Jane is often asked by strangers and friends, "Would you rather have been raised in Korea?"[84] As a way to answer this question for herself, Jane composes a fairy tale that is at once "completely plausible and also completely false."[85] Entitled "A Fairy Tale," Jane begins her story with a mother who loved her two Korean girls very much but could not take care of them. So she sends them to people who have the resources to support them. The people who adopt these girls help them to become healthy and strong. But more importantly, they raise them to be conscious of their Korean past:

They honored the girls' Korean heritage as they grew, helping them to remember the things they had forgotten. Together they rediscovered Korean language and food, clothing and customs. They proudly displayed in their home the gifts sent by the Korean mother. Most importantly, they talked about the Korean family and made them a part of their own family. In their prayers at the dinner table, they asked God to bless their food, their family, and their extended family in Korea.[86]

Rather than ignoring the material realities of racism, this tale tells of local schoolchildren calling these girls hurtful names. In Jane's fairy tale, however, an effective solution is created: the adoptive parents collaborate with the schoolteacher to implement a curriculum where a different child's heritage would be learned and celebrated each month. The fairy tale continues: when the two girls are old enough to travel back to South Korea, their adoptive parents join them. When their birth mother becomes sick and dies, the adoptive mother holds a memorial service for her, honoring the ways in which these two families—which have now become one—are bound together through her. In effect, in this story, "The two girls never felt ashamed of their heritage. They felt proud to be both American and Korean."[87]

It matters very little whether this story is true or false, or based on fact or fiction. As Jane points out, there are many kinds of truth: partial truths, covered truths, emotional truths, and multiple versions of truth.[88] Obtaining the truth about her personal history or identity is neither her intention nor the goal because the quest for truth is always already marked by impossibility and incompleteness. What matters instead are the creative possibilities that blossom by garnering fragments and pieces of truth, both factual and fictional. In this case, Jane weaves both fact and fiction to rewrite the dominant script of Korean adoption. Through her fairy tale, Jane provides an alternative blueprint for kinship where there is room for two mothers and space enough for two families of different races, nationalities, and cultures to coexist and even become one. In effect, she embraces the queer dimensions of her family by disidentifying with a notion of kinship (that is, Korean adoption) that makes assimilation compulsory, that privileges whiteness over nonwhiteness, that privileges the adoptive mother over the Korean mother, that privileges sameness and homogeneity over heterogeneity, and that privileges the normative over the queer.[89]

Interestingly, the queer possibilities provided by her fairy-tale vision present her with the opportunity to recycle and reuse her names in a way that befits her new vision of family.[90] After she gets married, Jane is given the opportunity to select whatever name she wants and thus to "choose who I wanted to be."[91] She considers reclaiming her given Korean name, Kyong-Ah Jeong; keeping her given American name, Jane Marie Brauer; or combining her American name with her married name, Jane Brauer Trenka. She finally decides on "Jane Jeong Trenka: one name from each family."[92] She explains:

> I wear it like a scar and a badge, the same way others wear their names, adapting language to reflect reality. I deliberately choose my name, my clan, my place in the world as it has borne me and created me. I choose to wear my joy and my pain in these words that signify me, and from this name you will know who I am.[93]

Perhaps the fairy tale she envisioned is not so much a world of make-believe than it is reality. To be sure, Jane's fairy tale has come true, despite her fraught relationship with her adoptive parents, via her new name. She has come to embody the ideology constructed by her fairy tale through her new identity. Put another way, her invented tale has carved a path toward an identity that is composed of her Korean heritage, her adoption experience, and her marriage to a white American man. These raw materials are recycled to embody an identity that encompasses her past, present, and future, all at the same time. Rather than discarding the trauma and pain that has informed much of her adopted life—extracting the undesirable parts—she incorporates them and invests them with new meaning; she wears her pain and struggle like a badge to signal her strength, growth, and perseverance rather than failure, shame, and guilt. Like her fairy tale, her chosen name makes room for her white adoptive family, her Korean family, and this new family that she is creating with her husband.

Within this context, the results of the recipe that introduced this chapter are far from being a failed experiment with undesirable results; rather, fresh discoveries and insights have been made through these unintended effects. These insights have become the very ingredients for a new recipe: it is called "A Fairy Tale." With the revised list of ingredients and directions offered by her fairy tale, Jane has created an ideology of Korean adoption that is organized by the vision of an "ethical multiculturalism." Perhaps, one hopes, this modified recipe that is formulated by Jane will become the new set of instructions that Korean adoptee practitioners and policy makers—those in the observation suite—will follow instead and thus bring to fruition the radical queer politics of Korean adoption.

EPILOGUE

Tracing Other Genealogies of Korean Adoption

AS A GENEALOGICAL INVESTIGATION of Korean adoption, this project has offered multiple beginnings, entry points, and divergences concerning the discourses that have shaped Korean adoption.[1] In an attempt to unsettle the dominant narrative of Korean adoption as a natural consequence of the Korean War and as an institution of normalization and successful assimilation, I situated Korean adoption within militarized humanitarianism, the geopolitics of Cold War Orientalism, and the radical politics of queer kinship formations. By attending to the shifting political, economic, and social conditions that have shaped Korean adoption, I not only destabilized its relationship to the Korean War but also disrupted the perception of the Korean orphan and adoptee as ahistorical figures. Attending to the shifting discursive and ideological forces that have enfigured Korean orphans and adoptees illuminated the multiple ways in which they have been constituted by empire- and nation-building projects, revealing the important roles they have played in fortifying militarized humanitarianism and white heteronormative constructions of family and nation.

Tracing the numerous discursive strands that have shaped Korean adoption via the figures of the Korean orphan and adoptee is also important because it is precisely here—on their bodies—where the conditions, effects, affects, and contradictions of war, empire, militarized humanitarianism, and compulsory assimilation are inscribed. Foucault explicates the importance of the physical body to the project of genealogy: "Genealogy, as an analysis of descent, is thus situated within the articulation of the body and history." This is because the "body manifests the stigmata of past experience and also gives rise to desires, failings, and errors."[2] As descendents of American imperialism and militarized humanitarianism whose bodies have been inscribed by particular crises, tensions, and conflicts, Korean orphans and adoptees do indeed serve as markers of certain critical moments and shifts in history. Although their bodies have been used to build and strengthen American neocolonialism in South Korea, their bodies have also articulated the excesses, shortcomings, and paradoxes of empire. The Korean orphan who called out "Number 1" instead of "Thank you" to the GI; the orphans who ran away from orphanages and instead became mascots and spies for the U.S. military; the boys who fired back at the militaristic gaze of the camera; the little boy who returned the gaze; the teenage girls who refused to be disciplined and domestically tamed during their residence at the Il San orphanage; the infants who accidently died because of Holt's cost-saving measures; and Jane, the adult adoptee, who fantasized about beheading herself—all these bodies have signaled the slippages, discrepancies, and failures of the seemingly totalizing power of empire and projects of discipline and normalization.

Furthermore, investigating the genealogies of the orphan and the adoptee also helped us to illuminate the ways in which the past continues to persist and shape the present. Although I for the most part agree with Foucault's theorization of genealogy, I do not fully agree with what he says about genealogy's relationship to the past and present. Foucault states that it is not the project of genealogy to "demonstrate that the past actively exists in the present, that it continues secretly to animate the present."[3] Given that the dominant narrative and image of Korean adoptees, which has framed them as well-assimilated model minorities, has become a strategy to efface the national memory of U.S. militarism, occupation, and racialized sexual violence in South Korea (projects that continue to this day), it becomes an important task to blast through the past in order to understand why Korean adoption continues and why it may now be expanding. A congressional bill was introduced on April 8, 2011, to facilitate the adoption of "stateless" North Korean children into American homes. This act, H.R. 1464, the North Korean Refugee Adoption Act of 2012, would legalize transnational adoption between the United States and North Korea. Interestingly, the discourse of humanitarian rescue, along with the availability of interested Americans, becomes the justification for why this act should be approved. As the September 2012 version of the bill states, "(1) Thousands of North Korean children do not have families and are threatened with starvation and disease if they remain in North Korea or as stateless refugees in surrounding countries [and] (2) thousands of United States citizens would welcome the opportunity to adopt North Korean orphans."[4] Here we see the atavistic return of Cold War, humanitarian, and consumer capitalist logics that are now being used to legitimize Americans as the rightful parents to North Korean children. The House of Representatives passed this bill in September, with the Senate following in January 2013.

Even though Congress passed this bill, a critical mass of Korean adoptee activists and allies have protested it during its various iterations. For example, Christine Hong and Jennifer Kwon Dobbs spearheaded the destruction of this bill in their coauthored policy brief, *The Case against the North Korean Refugee Adoption Act of 2011.* In this document, Hong and Kwon Dobbs dismantle the first part of this bill by pointing out that these North Korean children do in fact have families.[5] The children are typically mixed race, with a Chinese father and a North Korean migrant mother. Furthermore, referring to these children as "North Korean refugees" and "stateless refugees" is a misnomer because they are Chinese citizens: not only were they born in China, but at least one parent is Chinese, making them Chinese citizens according to Chinese law. This bill also violates the Hague Adoption Convention, which stipulates that a child is only considered adoptable after the state has exhausted all efforts to place the child in his or her birth country.[6] And finally, Hong and Kwon Dobbs cogently point out that rather than being "in the best interests of this child," this bill actually turns children with intact families into orphans: "In effect, instead of 'saving' orphans, the North Korean Refugee Adoption Act of 2011 will create 'orphans' by legitimizing the movement of children across borders with little to no documentation—in essence, child-trafficking."[7] In the same way that U.S. militarism caused Korean children to become social orphans during the 1950s, the North Korean Refugee Adoption Act will produce orphans by creating familial, cultural, and national upheaval for these Chinese–North Korean children. This bill will increase, not mitigate, the violent separation of these children from their families. In so doing, it will turn Chinese–North Korean children who already have parents into social orphans. Unfortunately, these kinds of discrepancies and ironies become overshadowed by the powerful tone of humanitarian rescue and the seductive image of needy Asian children. It is precisely the silences and contradictions that continue to gather around the bodies of orphans and adoptees that signal our need to examine the relationship between "moment[s] of danger" in the past and the "state of emergency" in the present.[8]

In using history as a theoretical armature of the present, I have sought to provide reasons for why Korean adoption continues to exist today.[9] If in blasting through the past we are better able to make sense of the present, I have also suggested—through my incorporation of Korean adoptee cultural production—that the contemporary works of Korean adoptee artists can endeavor to change the past as a way to alter the future. The imaginative re-creation of Korean adoption via Jane Jeong Trenka's "A Fairy Tale" espoused a new discourse and ideology of adoption that embraced the radical queer politics of transnational adoption and thereby revealed the limits of constructing Korean adoption as a white heteronormative and pseudoheterobiological formation of kinship. Indeed, her coming-to process exposed the material and psychic effects and consequences of such a project. By paying attention to the experiences, insights, and imaginative re-creations of Korean adoptee artists, we may enter a future in which the coming-to process is absent from the formation of the adoptee's identity. After all, the point is to create conditions in which the coming-to process is altogether unnecessary.

New Directions in Critical Adoption Studies

In the November 2011 issue of *Foreign Policy,* U.S. secretary of state Hillary Clinton notes that it is time for the United States to be a "Pacific power."[10] The piece, entitled "America's Pacific Century," begins with a tone that Amy Kaplan would describe as symptomatic of imperial melancholy.[11] Rather than feeling relief as the wars in Iraq and Afghanistan come to a close, Clinton expresses a mix of pensive regret and an eagerness for more political engagement in her opening paragraph:

> As the war in Iraq winds down and America begins to withdraw its forces from Afghanistan, the United States stands at a pivot point. Over the last 10 years, we have allocated immense resources to those two theaters. In the next 10 years, we need to be smart and systematic about where we invest time and energy, so that we put ourselves in the best position to sustain our leadership, secure our interests, and advance our values. One of the most important tasks of American statecraft over the next decade will therefore be to lock in a substantially increased investment—diplomatic, economic, strategic, and otherwise—in the Asia–Pacific region.[12]

It could be argued that since the turn of the twentieth century (rather than a new agenda item), the United States has attempted to become a Pacific power through its military occupation, and in some cases through its colonization of countries such as the Philippines, Guam, Hawaii, Japan, South Korea, and Vietnam. Clinton does acknowledge that the United States has had an active presence in Asia throughout the twentieth century; however, rather than seeing this history as problematic, Clinton sees this as a "strong tradition" upon which our current engagement with the Asia–Pacific can be built. However, since losing the Vietnam War, many have questioned the United States' "staying power around the world." Now that our engagement in the Middle East has declined, Clinton argues that it is time for the United States to reengage with the Asia–Pacific region to prove that "America has the capacity to secure and sustain our global leadership in this century as we did in the last."[13] Clearly, U.S. diplomatic, economic, and military involvement in the Asia–Pacific region will increase rather than decrease in the twenty-first century. In a direct response to the imperial melancholy suffered by the U.S. nation-state, Clinton's words work to reassure our nation and its citizens that we will "extend the history of imperial time."[14] We will do so by flexing our economic and military might in the Asia–Pacific region.

Grace Cho points out that various Asian immigrants—such as Filipinos, Koreans, Vietnamese, Cambodians, Laotians, and Hmong—arrive "primarily through the means of American military domination." As such, these Asian immigrants have "bodies bearing the marks of militarization."[15] Because the United States is invested in becoming a Pacific power in the next sixty years,[16] more and more Asians and Pacific Islanders will bear the marks of militarization as the United States increases it security and military power in that region. It is for this reason that Asian American studies in general, and critical adoption studies more specifically, must renew its investment in analyzing the ways in which U.S. militarism affects the bodies, identities, and cultural production of Asian Americans and Asian adoptees.

In addition, critical adoption studies must continue to privilege the narratives, voices, and perspectives of adoptees over nonadoptees. Their cultural production—including literary, visual, and cinematic work—often provides more nuanced and complex understandings of adoption because many of their works reveal the contradictions of adoption. The insights garnered by Korean adoptee activists and artists provide opportunities to delve into other genealogies of Korean adoption that go beyond the scope of this book. For example, an increasing number of newly produced adoptee narratives center around search, reunion, and repatriation. Jane Jeong Trenka's second memoir, *Fugitive Visions: An Adoptee's Return to Korea* (2009), is not only about her reunion with her birth family but also about her repatriation back to Korea as she struggles for acceptance in the land of her birth. Katie Hae Leo's play *Four Destinies* (2011) ruminates on race, identity, and genetic code, as she explores the experiences of four adoptees, one Korean, one African American, one Latin American, and one white American, all of whom are named Destiny. Leo continues her exploration of the adoptee experience in her one-woman show "N/A," which debuted with Sun Mee Chomet's one-woman show "How to Be a Korean Woman" at Dreamland Arts in June 2012.[17] Headlined under *The Origin(s) Project*, Leo's one-woman show recounts the experience of having to write "N/A" ("not applicable"; "no answer") on documents that ask for her medical history after numerous failed attempts to locate her birth family. She weaves this particular experience with a mysterious physical condition that remained undiagnosed for years. In an attempt to fill in the missing information of her genetic past, she relies on Korean folklore and mythology to provide an alternative genealogy of her family history. In the second act of *The Origin(s) Project*, Chomet investigates the complexities of search and reunion as she recounts her reunification with her Korean mother, grandmother, and aunts in "How to Be a Korean Woman." Although being reunited with her Korean family brings immeasurable joy, it also produces confusion, disappointment, and depression as Chomet grapples with more questions than answers after the reunion. In her physically and emotionally demanding one-woman show (she plays not only herself but also social workers, a child welfare worker, a Korean translator, her grandmother, her birth mother, and her aunts), Chomet reveals the desires, failings, and impossibilities in the search for origins, illustrating how messy genealogical excavation can be. Furthermore, she suggests another genealogy of Korean adoption: one that is rooted in the practice of human trafficking.[18] Attending to these new shifts that are taking place in the contemporary literature of Korean adoptees will help us to theorize other related genealogies that come from adoptees themselves.

Finally, I suggest that critical adoption studies move towards an examination of the necropolitics of adoption. Because the overwhelming majority of adoption scholarship in general, and Korean adoption scholarship in particular, focuses on the adoptee, the biopolitics of adoption have been a significant point of inquiry in these fields. This is not to say that we should stop investigating the biopolitics of adoption. Reading the biopolitics of Korean adoption via new primary sources (as I hope that chapter 4 illustrated) can be productive. However, if we want to examine other emergences and other genealogies of Korean adoption, we must attend to other figures in Korean adoption. These other figures are birth mothers and birth fathers. Given that Korean adoptees are indeed reuniting and building relationships with their birth families, the birth parent or parents are increasingly becoming significant figures in their cultural production. A striking feature in Chomet's "How to Be a Korean Woman" is the inclusion of the birth mother's subjectivity and narrative, as she literally embodies her birth mother on stage. Furthermore, increasing attention is being paid to birth mothers (and, more recently, birth fathers) as Korean adoptee activists such as Jennifer Kwon Dobbs and Jane Jeong Trenka push for new policies, procedures, and programming on their behalf in South Korea. Tellingly, a Korean documentary film entitled *Miss Mama*, released in 2012, focuses on the experiences of Korean unwed mothers. The film works to confront the prejudice that Korean society has toward unwed single mothers, shattering the stereotypes associated with them. Focusing on birth mothers (and birth fathers) lends itself to examining the necropolitics of adoption, whereas the focus on adoptees lends itself to the biopolitics of adoption. I have attempted to gesture toward the necropolitics of adoption not only by pointing out the process of social death that the adoptee undergoes but also by discussing how the heterobiological investments in Korean adoption have relied on killing off the birth mother in *The Language of Blood* (chapter 5). In pointing out these three trajectories, I am not suggesting that these are the only sites that will help grow the field. Rather, given my theoretical and methodological investments, I believe that attending to alternative conditions (militarism) and new figures (birth parents), as well as continuing to privilege the perspective of adoptees (through their cultural production), will help us sharpen the critical edge in critical adoption studies.

The genealogies of Korean adoption are multiple and varied. By introducing new primary sources and reading against the grain of traditional history and hegemonic notions of Korean adoption, I have attempted to provide other sites of emergence and other points of entry to analyze the significance and persistence of Korean adoption. More work needs to be done in teasing out not only other genealogies concerning Korean adoption and its orphans and adoptees but also the ways in which militarized humanitarianism continues to animate U.S. imperial power, continues to be wielded in different contexts, and continues to be dispersed to other sites, such as Iraq, Afghanistan, Haiti, and the Chinese–North Korean border. I hope that my work has served as one model for how this can be done.

ACKNOWLEDGMENTS

WHEN I WAS STRUGGLING to find a research topic during graduate school, I remember a professor telling me, "Write the book that you always wished you could have read in college." I started to reflect back to my undergraduate years, thinking about the holes and gaps in my own secondary education. "If only I had been able to read a book on Korean adoption, maybe I would have a better understanding of who I am," I thought. It was at this moment that I began to conceive my dissertation project, which was the first iteration of this book. As I underwent the process of turning my dissertation into a book, the words of my graduate professor reverberated in my mind. Now, having read the final version of this book, I feel like I have indeed written the book that I have always wanted to read. So many people have supported me along the way. I want to thank them for helping me finally write the book that I had longed to see on my bookshelf those many years ago.

First, I want to thank the members of my two dissertation writing groups, who helped me formulate and polish my ideas: Sonjia Hyon and Harrod Suarez, who dedicated their time and energy to make our writing group productive and active despite our long distance from each other; and Kandace Creel Falcón and Alex Mendoza from the Kitchen Table Collective, a writing group for women of color. They read draft after draft of my chapters and were there every time I needed to think through an idea or test out an argument. The extremely insightful and critical feedback I received from these four colleagues undoubtedly made this book stronger. I also want to express appreciation for my graduate school friends at the University of Minnesota, who fostered a rich and stimulating environment for intellectual inquiry. In addition to Alex, Harrod, Kandace, and Sonjia, I want to thank Pamela Butler, Michael David Franklin, Nalo Johnson, Jason Ruiz,

Heidi Kiiwetinepinesiik Stark, and Tlahtoki Xochimeh for their friendship and support.

During my tenure at the University of Minnesota, I couldn't have asked for more dedicated and nurturing faculty members. I especially want to thank Jigna Desai and Rod Ferguson for advising me. They both pushed me and challenged me at just the right times and in just the right ways. Thanks to Jigna, Erika Lee, and Jo Lee for being excellent role models in showing me how to negotiate the demands of family life with the rigors of academic pursuit. These three scholar–teacher–mothers have demonstrated to me that motherhood can actually make one a better teacher and scholar. I am so grateful to have had such wonderful examples in my midst.

Several fellowships from the University of Minnesota funded the research and writing of my dissertation. The Leonard Memorial Film Study Fellowship and the Thesis Research Grant that I received from the graduate school, as well as the Scholarly Research Grant from the department of American studies enabled research travel. The Leonard Memorial Film Study Fellowship was particularly valuable: it provided me with not only the resources to conduct research at various archives but also the time to examine and analyze the materials I collected. Toward the later stages of my dissertation, a Summer Dissertation Writing Grant from the department of American studies and the Doctoral Dissertation Fellowship from the graduate school facilitated the completion my dissertation, providing me with invaluable time to write and revise. I am grateful to the various selection committees who chose to fund my project.

Thanks to Linnea Anderson and David Klassen for their assistance and guidance in helping me navigate the Social Welfare History Archives at Anderson Library at the University of Minnesota. In addition, I want to thank International Social Service, United States of America Branch Inc. (ISS-USA), for allowing me to use their records for my research. Thanks also to the staff at the National Archives in College Park, Maryland, particularly those working in the Motion Picture, Sound, and Video Records division and the Textual Archives Services Division, for their assistance in helping me locate materials. I am grateful to the various organizations, individuals, and artists who generously granted me permission to reproduce their work. I especially want to thank Bill Brewington at *Paramount News,* Brian Campbell at Holt International Children's Services, Max Crow at USS Whitehurst Association, George F. Drake at Korean War Children's Memorial, Mihee-Nathalie Lemoine, Martha Roby Stephens, Jenifer Stepp at *Stars and Stripes,* and Penny Zarneski.

Turning a dissertation into a book requires a new set of priorities, skills, and relationships. My heartfelt thanks goes to Mark Jerng for sharing his revision process with me. In so doing, he passed along tips and tools of the trade that helped me shape my research proposal and book manuscript for a broader audience. At the University of Minnesota Press, my deep appreciation and gratitude go to executive editor Richard Morrison and editorial assistant Erin Warholm-Wohlenhaus for believing in this project from the beginning, as well as finding it a good home in the Difference Incorporated series. Thank you to Grace Kyungwon Hong, the series editor, for her incisive comments, which brought clarity to the book. Finally, to the two anonymous readers, thank you so much for your generous, thoughtful, and insightful reader's reports. Your feedback helped me to strengthen my arguments and major interventions.

A heartfelt thanks goes to my friends, colleagues, and fellow mothers Taiyon Coleman, Kathleen DeVore, and Shannon Gibney for helping me during the revision process. I am so inspired by this fierce group of women who show courage, tenacity, and love in their lives and work. For me, our writing group was about more than just meeting deadlines; it was about the restoration of our souls and our humanity, as we work in institutions that were never made for us. Thank you, ladies, so much for the sustenance you provided me during this process. I also want to thank my dear friend Caren Umbarger, who offered up her home in Florida so that I could complete the book. Thank you for feeding both my stomach and spirit, and for giving me uninterrupted time and a quiet and beautiful place to write. A deep sense of gratitude goes to Krystal Banfield, who has shown me love and support over the years. Thank you for being my advocate and for being such a good friend.

I would like to acknowledge the new colleagues and friends who have entered my life during this process. A special thank-you to Jim Lee for his friendship, loyalty, and kindness. His insights on life, relationships, and academia have not only made me a better teacher and scholar but also a better human being. I am humbled by his generosity, compassion, and goodness. I strive to be the kind of mentor and advisor he is to his students. I want to thank Jennifer Kwon Dobbs for not only introducing me to Jim but also for being such a supportive and generous colleague and friend. I appreciate her fierce dedication to the field of critical adoption studies, as well as her activism regarding Korean adoptee and birth mother rights. Thanks also to Kale Fajardo for his friendship and collegiality. His support of my work—both inside and outside the classroom—has been humbling. Finally, I want to thank Karin Aguilar-San Juan, Duchess Harris, Jane Rhodes, and Kathie Scott for providing me with an intellectual home in the department of American studies at Macalester College as I finalized my revisions.

I want to close by acknowledging some of my friends and family who have not only sustained me throughout these years but have also brought great meaning to my life and work. First, I want to thank my sisters, Abby and Tam. To Tam, I thank you for always having an open heart and a listening, sympathetic ear. To Abby, I am inspired by your courage, determination, and persistence in trying to make our world a better place by focusing on the health of children and families who are underserved. Thank you for being my sister and for doing the work that you do. I also want to thank my dear friend and soul sister, Sun Mee, for her fierce dedication to our friendship, for being unwavering in moments of crisis, and for always grounding me during moments when I feel the earth shifting under my feet. You reflect and remind me of all things good. Your honesty, desire for truth, and love of life centers my soul.

Finally, I want to thank Alexs and my daughter, Sxela. To Alexs: your unceasing and unconditional support has been my sustenance throughout this journey. I could not have asked for a more patient and kind intellectual partner. Your creative brilliance and artistic courage continue to awe and inspire me. To Sxela: your very presence in my life has inspired me in ways unimaginable. I have learned so much from you, realizing early on that you are the real teacher in this relationship. You were with me from the very beginning of this project, keeping me company as I dug through the archives in Minnesota, Maryland, and Washington, D.C. As you tumbled about in my belly, you reminded me of how important it is to produce work that can benefit our community and society. You motivated me to finish what I started. You make me a better person. I hope Mama's journey and this book inspire you to fill in the gaps of your own knowledge by writing the book you've always wanted to read.

NOTES

Introduction

1. The official dates of the Korean War are 1950 to 1953. In 1953, the thirty-eighth parallel became the demilitarized zone (DMZ) upon signing a cease-fire agreement by both the United States and Soviet forces. Currently, as the most heavily militarized space in the world (with about a million North Korean soldiers on the northern side of the DMZ and about a million South Korean and U.S. soldiers combined), the term "demilitarized zone" is a truly a misnomer. Although the signing of the armistice signaled the end of the Korean War, it is important to point out that many Koreans—from both the southern and the northern portions of the peninsula, as well as Korean diasporic peoples all over the world—do not see this war as being over, even if direct combat has ceased. National division continues to plague the Korean people to this day.

2. While there is currently a push for North Korean adoption, the entire history of Korean adoption has involved South Korea. Therefore, when I use the phrase "Korean adoption," I am referring to the adoption of children from South Korea.

3. The Korean peninsula is divided into two nations: South Korea (Republic of Korea) and North Korea (Democratic People's Republic of Korea) were both officially formed in 1948. I use the terms "South Korea" and "North Korea" to refer to the two nations.

4. The fact that the practice of sending Korean children overseas for adoption has not ceased—despite many pronouncements made by the South Korean government to do so—also confirms that factors other than the Korean War are at work. To date, nearly 2,000 children are sent abroad every year. South Korea continues to be a leader in transnational adoption, moving from first place to being the fourth-largest sending country (after China, Ethiopia, and Russia) to the United States. See Tobias Hübinette, *Comforting an Orphaned Nation: Representations of International Adoption and Adopted Koreans in Korean Popular Culture* (Seoul: Jimoondang, 2006), and Jane Jeong Trenka, "A Million Living Ghosts: Truth and Reconciliation for the Adoption Community of Korea (TRACK)" (lecture, University of Minnesota, Minneapolis, February 11, 2010).

5. Christina Klein, *Cold War Orientalism: Asia in the Middlebrow Imagination, 1945–1961* (Berkeley: University of California Press, 2003), 16.

6. Ibid., 144–46.

7. "'The Lord is their sponsor': Korean Octet Gets a U.S. Home," *Life*, December 26, 1955, 58.

8. Letitia DiVirgilio, "Adjustment of Foreign Children in Their Adoptive Homes," *Child Welfare* 35 (November 1956): 15–21.

9. Ibid., 15. International Social Service, United States of America Branch Inc. (ISS-USA) is an organization whose mission is to "improve the lives of children, families and adults impacted by migration and international crisis through advances in service, knowledge and public policy" (www.iss-usa.org). They seek to provide social services to children and families separated by international borders. During the first half of the twentieth century, ISS-USA focused on migrants, refugees, and displaced persons from Europe. After the Korean War, however, they began participating in placing Korean orphans into American homes. See Cathy Choy, "Institutionalizing International Adoption: The Historical Origins of Korean Adoption in the United States," in *International Korean Adoption: A Fifty-Year History of Policy and Practice*, ed. Kathleen Ja Sook Bergquist et al. (New York: Haworth Press, 2007), 26–27.

10. Choy, *International Korean Adoption*, 20, 21.

11. Margaret A. Valk, "Adjustment of Korean-American Children in American Adoptive Homes" (paper presented at National Conference on Social Welfare, 1957), 4, in ISS-USA Papers, Box 10, File "Adjustment of Korean-American Children," Social Welfare History Archives (SWHA), University of Minnesota, Minneapolis. Of the ninety-three children, seventy-five were "Korean-Caucasian," fourteen were "Korean-Negro," and "four are probably of Korean-Mexican or Korean-American Indian." These descriptors are hers and not mine. Identifying four of the children as "probably Korean-Mexican and Korean-American Indian" reveals the slippage of racial categories. It also suggests that the fathers were unknown in these cases, so Valk is probably guessing what their parentage is on the basis of appearance, again indicating the inadequacy of racial categorization and perhaps the inaccuracy of these numbers.

12. Ibid., 18.

13. Dong Soo Kim, "Intercountry Adoptions: A Study of Self-Concept of Adolescent Korean Children Who Were Adopted by American Families" (Ph.D. diss., University of Chicago, 1976), 62.

14. Ibid., 165.

15. Ibid., 166. Dong Soo Kim does admit that as the adoptees grow older and have more interaction with people outside their family and communities, their racial difference may play a more significant part in their sense of identity.

16. Ibid., 170, 171.

17. Rita J. Simon and Howard Alstein, *Adoption across Borders: Serving the Children in Transracial and Intercountry Adoptions* (Lanham, Md.: Rowman and Littlefield, 2000), 106.

18. Jun Kim, "A Reel Reflection," *KoreAm Journal* 11, no. 5 (May 2000): 17.

19. Jane Jeong Trenka, Julia Chinyere Oparah, and Sun Yung Shin, eds., *Outsiders Within: Writing on Transracial Adoption* (Cambridge, Mass.: South End Press, 2006), 1.

20. Tonya Bishoff and Jo Rankin, eds., *Seeds from a Silent Tree: An Anthology by Korean Adoptees* (San Diego: Pandal Press, 1997), 2.

21. This isn't to say that before 1997 there were no artistic productions by Korean adoptees. On the contrary, notable works include Kim Su Theiler, dir., *Great Girl* (New York: Women Make Movies, 1994); Me-K Ahn, dir., *Living in Halftones* (New York: Third World Newsreel, 1994); and Me-K Ahn, dir., *Undertow* (New York: Third World Newsreel, 1995).

22. Other memoirs include *Ten Thousand Sorrows: The Extraordinary Journey of a Korean War Orphan* (2000), by Elizabeth Kim, and *A Single Square Picture: A Korean Adoptee's Search for Her Roots* (2002), by Katy Robinson. In addition, several anthologies have also been published since 1997, including *Voices from Another Place* (1999), edited by Susan Soon-Keum Cox; *After the Morning Calm: Reflections of Korean Adoptees* (2002), a collection devoted to the voices of adolescents and young adults edited by Sook Wilkinson and Nancy Fox; and *Parenting as Adoptees* (2012), an anthology on parenting by transracial and transnational adoptees edited by Adam Chau and Kevin Ost-Vollmers.

23. Eleana Kim, "Wedding Citizenship and Culture: Korean Adoptees and the Global Family of Korea," in *Cultures of Transnational Adoption,* ed. Toby Alice Volkman (Durham, N.C.: Duke University Press, 2005), 53.

24. Michel Foucault, "Nietzsche, Genealogy, and History," in *Language, Counter-memory, Practice: Selected Essays and Interviews,* ed. D. F. Bouchard (Ithaca, N.Y.: Cornell University Press, 1977), 145.

25. Ibid., 144–45.

26. Ibid., 148–49.

27. Walter Benjamin delineates the difference between historicism and historical materialism. Historicism is characterized by universalism and is unconcerned with the theoretical. It approaches history as "homogenous, empty time" that is waiting to be filled by data collected by historians. Historical materialism, on the other hand, is characterized by particularity and heterogeneity and situates history as a "theoretical armature" of the present (262). Indeed, history becomes deployed to make sense of the present. In this way, the job of the historical materialist is not to narrate a progressive, linear history that follows the "sequence of events like the beads of a rosary" (263), but to seize the "moments of danger" in the past in order to "bring about a real state of emergency" in the present (257). Benjamin, "Theses on the Philosophy of History," in *Illuminations: Essays and Reflections,* ed. Hannah Arendt, trans. Harry Zohn (New York: Schocken Books, 1969), 253–64.

28. Lisa Lowe, *Immigrant Acts: On Asian American Cultural Politics* (Durham, N.C.: Duke University Press, 1996), 41.

29. Benjamin, "Theses on the Philosophy of History," 255.

30. Jodi Kim, *Ends of Empire: Asian American Critique and the Cold War* (Minneapolis: University of Minnesota Press, 2010), 5.

31. Simon and Alstein, *Adoption across Borders,* 106.

32. I want to thank Grace Hong for helping me articulate this point.

33. See, for example, Toby Alice Volkman, ed., *Cultures of Transnational Adoption* (Durham, N.C.: Duke University Press, 2005); Sara Dorow, *Transnational Adoption: A Cultural Economy of Race, Gender, and Kinship* (New York: New York University Press, 2006); and Mark Jerng, *Claiming Others: Transracial Adoption and National Belonging*

(Minneapolis: University of Minnesota Press, 2010). These works all attend to the larger social, cultural, political, and economic contexts in which adopted children migrate and are incorporated into the national landscape. In addition, Trenka, Oparah, and Shin, *Outsiders Within* (2006), and Diane Marre and Laura Briggs, eds., *International Adoption: Global Inequalities and the Circulation of Children* (New York: New York University Press, 2009), have collected essays that address the unequal relations of power (regarding race, gender, class, and nation) within the transnational adoption industry.

34. Hübinette, *Comforting an Orphaned Nation,* was especially groundbreaking because it was one of the first monographs on Korean adoption that did not focus on adjustment issues and that did not use social scientific methods. Rather, it provided a postcolonial, cultural analysis of how the topic of Korean adoption and the figure of the Korean adoptee are depicted in Korean popular culture (e.g., music videos, films, and novels). Eleana Kim's *Adopted Territory: Transnational Korean Adoptees and the Politics of Belonging* (Durham, N.C.: Duke University Press, 2010), is the first comprehensive study on Korean adoptee community building. Combining both social scientific and cultural methods, Kim engages in an ethnographic study of adoptee networks (social, cultural, and geographical) that have been forged by Korean adoptees not only in their adoptive countries but also by adoptees who have repatriated back to South Korea.

35. See Seungsook Moon, *Militarized Modernity and Gendered Citizenship in South Korea* (Durham, N.C.: Duke University Press, 2003); Katharine Moon, *Sex among Allies: Military Prostitution in U.S.–Korea Relations* (New York: Columbia University Press, 1997); Elaine Kim and Chungmoo Choi, ed., *Dangerous Women: Gender and Korean Nationalism* (New York: Routledge, 1998); Ji-Yeon Yuh, *Beyond the Shadow of Camptown: Korean Military Brides in America* (New York: New York University Press, 2002); Grace M. Cho, *Haunting the Korean Diaspora: Shame, Secrecy, and the Forgotten War* (Minneapolis: University of Minnesota, 2008); and Chunghee Sarah Soh, *The Comfort Women: Sexual Violence and Postcolonial Memory in Korea and Japan* (Chicago: University of Chicago Press, 2008).

36. See Moon, *Sex among Allies,* and "Prostitute Bodies and Gendered States in U.S.–Korea Relations," in *Dangerous Women,* 141–74; Yuh, *Beyond the Shadow;* Cho, *Haunting the Korean Diaspora;* and Soh, *Comfort Women.*

37. See, for example, Jodi Kim, "An 'Orphan' with Two Mothers: Transnational and Transracial Adoption, the Cold War, and Contemporary Asian American Cultural Politics," *American Quarterly* 61, no. 4 (December 2009): 855–80; Eleana Kim, "The Origins of Korean Adoption: Cold War Geopolitics and Intimate Diplomacy" (Working Paper Series; Washington, D.C.: U.S.–Korea Institute at SAIS, 2009), 1–25; Patti Duncan, "Genealogies of Unbelonging: Amerasians and Transnational Adoptees as Legacies of U.S. Militarism in South Korea," in *Militarized Currents: Toward a Decolonized Future in Asia and the Pacific,* ed. Setsu Shigematsu and Keith L. Camacho (Minneapolis: University of Minnesota Press, 2010), 277–307; and Bongsoo Park, "Intimate Encounters, Racial Frontiers: Stateless GI Babies in South Korea and the United States, 1953–1965" (Ph.D. diss., University of Minnesota, 2010).

38. Holt founded and institutionalized Korean adoption through this agency. Holt Adoption Program newsletters, memos, and administrative papers that I examined were

part of the historical records of ISS-USA. These records are held at SWHA, University of Minnesota, Minneapolis.

39. "Harry Holt, Who Found Parents for 3,000 Korean Orphans, Dies," newspaper clipping, April 29, 1964, ISS-USA Papers, Box 10, File "Children—Independent Adoption Schemes, Harry Holt, 1960–1963, Vol. 3," SWHA, Minneapolis, Minn.

1. Militarized Humanitarianism

1. The USAMG ruled from September 1945 to August 1948, although it did not formally organize until January 4, 1946. The United States, however, began to set up military occupation of the southern half of Korea as early as September 1945. I am counting from this September date. It ended in August 1948, when southern Korea gained independence from the United States after Syngman Rhee became the new president of the Republic of Korea. The United States changed the title of administration from government-general to military government because the former denoted a colonial status. Although the appellation may be different, many Koreans came to realize that the name change meant little. See Jinwung Kim, "A Policy of Amateurism: The Rice Policy of the U.S. Army Military Government in Korea, 1945–1948," *Korea Journal* 47, no. 2 (Summer 2007): 210.

2. Dong Choon Kim, "Forgotten War, Forgotten Massacres—The Korean War (1950–1953) as Licensed Mass Killings," *Journal of Genocide Research* 6, no. 4 (December 2004): 525.

3. In February 1947, the Truman administration assembled this committee, which "included representatives from the State and War Departments and the Bureau of the Budget, to make recommendations on Korea." William Stueck, *Rethinking the Korean War: A New Diplomatic and Strategic History* (Princeton, N.J.: Princeton University Press, 2002), 45.

4. "Report of Special Interdepartmental Committee on Korea," February 1947, 17, Formerly Security-Classified Correspondence of Howard Peterson, December 1945–August 1947, Box 9, Folder 91—Korea, Modern Military Records, Record Group 107, Textual Archives Services Division, National Archives at College Park. This report served to provide policy recommendations concerning a general course of action in regard to the southern portion of Korea.

5. Ibid., 17–18.

6. Dong Choon Kim, "Forgotten War, Forgotten Massacres," 526.

7. "Report of Special Interdepartmental Committee on Korea," 17.

8. Ibid.

9. Donald E. Pease, *The New American Exceptionalism* (Minneapolis: University of Minnesota Press, 2009), 20.

10. General John R. Hodge to Joint Chiefs of Staff, memorandum, July 18, 1947, Formerly Security-Classified Correspondence of Howard Peterson, December 1945–August 1947, Box 9, Folder 91—Korea, Modern Military Records, Record Group 107, Textual Archives Services Division, National Archives at College Park.

11. Louise Yim, "A Plea to the War Department and to the American People," July 11, 1947, 2, Formerly Security-Classified Correspondence of Howard Peterson, December 1945–August 1947, Box 9, Folder 91—Korea, Modern Military Records, Record Group 107, Textual Archives Services Division, National Archives at College Park.

12. "Justification for a Grant-in-Aid Program for the Rehabilitation of South Korea Covering Fiscal Years 1948 through 1950," March 27, 1947, 12–15, Formerly Security-Classified Correspondence of Howard Peterson, December 1945–August 1947, Box 9, Folder 91—Korea, Modern Military Records, Record Group 107, Textual Archives Services Division, National Archives at College Park.

13. Joungwon Kim, *Divided Korea: The Politics of Development, 1945–1972* (Cambridge, Mass.: East Asian Research Center at Harvard University, 1976), 68.

14. Kim, "Policy of Amateurism," 211–12.

15. Ibid., 215, 229.

16. Quoted in ibid., 229.

17. In 1948, after three years of continued disagreement, the United States finally let the United Nations deal with Korea. It was decided that U.N.-supervised elections would be held in May of that year. Syngman Rhee took office in August 1948. See Joungwon Kim, *Divided Korea*, 79.

18. Joungwon Kim, *Divided Korea*, 60.

19. Dong Choon Kim, "Forgotten War, Forgotten Massacres," 526.

20. General John R. Hodge to Joint Chiefs of Staff.

21. Harry Savage to President Truman, April 22, 1947, Formerly Security-Classified Correspondence of Howard Peterson, December 1945–August 1947, Box 9, Folder 91—Korea, Modern Military Records, Record Group 107, Textual Archives Services Division, National Archives at College Park.

22. General John R. Hodge to Joint Chiefs of Staff.

23. Young-Iob Chung, *South Korea in the Fast Lane: Economic Development and Capital Formation* (New York: Oxford University Press, 2007), 307.

24. Edward Sagendorph Mason et al., *The Economic and Social Modernization of the Republic of Korea* (Cambridge, Mass.: Harvard University Press, 1980), 177, their table 34, "Economic Assistance to Korea, 1945–1953."

25. "Justification for a Grant-In-Aid Program," 1.

26. Ibid., 2, 10. According to Dong Choon Kim, many of these riots and loss of life were attributed to the rooting-out process spawned by the anticommunist paranoia that abounded within the Korean army and the military police. In 1948, the mass killing of civilians reached its height. In total, between August 1945 and June 1950 (when the Korean War began), more than 100,000 Koreans were killed and 20,000 were jailed under suspicion of being communist. Dong Choon Kim, "Forgotten War, Forgotten Massacres," 526–28.

27. "Justification for a Grant-In-Aid Program," 2, 10.

28. Ibid., 2.

29. Stueck, *Rethinking the Korean War,* 49, 51. Stueck states, "During late March and early April, numerous newspapers and radio commentators endorsed new aid for Korea" (51).

30. Mason et al., *Economic and Social Modernization,* 177, table 34.

31. Ibid., 172–73.

32. Ibid., 177, table 34.

33. Ibid., 181, 165.

34. William F. Asbury, "Military Help to Korean Orphanages: A Survey Made for the Commander-in-Chief, United Nations Forces, Far East, and for the Chief of Chaplains of the United States Army," 1954, 4, reprinted in Korean War National Museum, www.koreanchildren.org. Ashbury explains that as part of the Japanese imperial forces, Korean men became separated from their families, died in battle, became POWs, or were simply reported missing. In addition, after Korea gained independence from Japan, half a million Koreans remained in Japan. As a result of these various factors, families became broken, separated, or both, which created this orphan population. In addition, one could also presume that some of these orphans were the offspring of Japanese soldiers and Korean comfort women. See, for example, Cho, *Haunting the Korean Diaspora,* and Chunghee Sarah Soh, *The Comfort Women: Sexual Violence and Postcolonial Memory in Korea and Japan* (Chicago: University of Chicago Press, 2008).

35. Joungwon Kim, *Divided Korea,* 48.

36. Asbury, "Military Help," 1, 4–5.

37. Hübinette, *Comforting an Orphaned Nation,* 40.

38. Jung-Woo Kim and Terry Henderson, "History of the Care of Displaced Children in Korea," *Asian Social Work and Policy Review* 2 (2008): 14–17.

39. Ibid., 16. By offering up this history, Jung-Woo Kim and Henderson dismantle the popular belief that Korea, as a Confucian society, could not imagine kinship formations outside of having direct blood ties.

40. Ibid., 17–19.

41. Hübinette, *Comforting an Orphaned Nation,* 40. Many of the orphanages in South Korea after the war continued to be affiliated with a Christian denomination or mission work, with names like St. Francis Mission, Lady Kathryn Presbyterian Church School and Orphanage, and Children's Garden of Holy Mind Orphanage. See AFAK Command Construction Progress Reports, August–December 1954, Eighth U.S. Army Armed Forces Assistance to Korea (AFAK) Project Files 1954–1963, Box 2196, Folders "AFAK Project Completion Reports Sept. and Nov., 1954," Modern Military Records, Record Group 338, Textual Archives Services Division, National Archives at College Park.

42. Asbury, "Military Help," 14.

43. Jung-Woo Kim and Henderson, "History of the Care of Displaced Children," 18.

44. Asbury, "Military Help," 14.

45. AFAK Bulletin No. 1, January 4, 1954. Eighth U.S. Army AFAK Project Files 1954–1963, Box 2201, Folder "AFAK Bulletins 1–9, 1954," Modern Military Records, Record Group 338, Textual Archives Services Division, National Archives at College Park.

46. Asbury, "Military Help," 7.

47. See AFAK Command Construction Progress Reports, January–July 1954, Eighth U.S. Army AFAK Project Files 1954–1963, Box 2195, and AFAK Command Construction Progress Reports, August–December 1954, Eighth U.S. Army AFAK Project Files 1954–1963, Box 2196, Modern Military Records, Record Group 338, Textual Archives Services

Division, National Archives at College Park. Each monthly report also includes how much money each project cost, breaking down the costs of labor, materials, and so on.

48. "Helping Koreans Help Themselves," *Life*, October 12, 1953, 48.

49. Korean War National Museum, www.koreanchildren.org.

50. Asbury, "Military Help," 7.

51. Korean War National Museum, "Saving Lives," www.koreanchildren.org.

52. "Good Soldier Cited 'Best Missionary,'" *Pacific Stars and Stripes*, December 10, 1951, reprinted in Korean War National Museum, www.koreanchildren.org.

53. Asbury, "Military Help," 16.

54. Ibid., 12, 16.

55. Michael Barnett, *Empire of Humanity: A History of Humanitarianism* (Ithaca, N.Y.: Cornell University Press, 2011), 2, 104.

56. Ibid., 109.

57. Inderpal Grewel, *Transnational America: Feminisms, Diasporas, Neoliberalisms* (Durham, N.C.: Duke University Press, 2005), 132. Slavoj Žižek, "Turkey Is a Thorn in the Side of a Cosy Western Consensus," *Guardian*, October 23, 2007, www.guardian.co.uk.

58. Barnett, *Empire of Humanity*, 3–4.

59. AFAK Bulletin No. 1.

60. This quote appears at the end of each episode. *The Big Picture* aired from 1951 to 1971, with an episode on the first forty days of the Korean War inaugurating the series. For more information about this series, see *The Big Picture*, Army Pictoral Center: Signal Corps Photographic Center, www.armypictorialcenter.com.

61. See, for example, "Construction of AFAK Orphanage, Seoul, Korea," March 18, 1954, and "Buk Han San Orphanage, Seoul, Korea," April 5, 1954, Department of Defense, U.S. Army Audiovisual Center, Motion Picture, Sound, and Video Records, Record Group 111, National Archives at College Park; "War Orphans, Korea," September 18–20, 1953, Department of Defense, U.S. Army Audiovisual Center, Motion Picture, Sound, and Video Records, Record Group 111, National Archives at College Park; "Korean Orphan Story," reels 1, 2, 4, and 5, January–February 1952, Department of Defense, Department of the Air Force, Motion Picture, Sound, and Video Records, Record Group 342, National Archives at College Park; Epidemic Control Unit (USN), "Ullong-Do Korea," July 8, 1952, Department of Defense, U.S. Army Audiovisual Center, Motion Picture, Sound, and Video Records, Record Group 111, National Archives at College Park; and "Front Line Air Force Chaplain: Outtakes," n.d., Department of Defense, Department of the Air Force, Motion Picture, Sound, and Video Records, Record Group 342, National Archives at College Park.

62. Asbury, "Military Help," 7. See also "Christmas Party for Korean Orphans, IX Corps, Kinsal, Korea," December 24, 1953; "7th Division Christmas Celebration, Chorwon and Vijongbu, Korea," November 11, 1953; "Gen. Maxwell D. Taylor Visits Kyum Sam Orphanage, Seoul, Korea," December 20, 1953; and "Armed Forces Assistance to Korea Gifts of Clothing to Children, Yong Do (Pusan), Korea," December 22, 1954, Department of Defense, U.S. Army Audiovisual Center, Motion Picture, Sound, and Video Records, Record Group 111, National Archives at College Park.

63. Cho, *Haunting the Korean Diaspora*, 84.

NOTES TO CHAPTER 2

64. We might also see these charitable acts as attempts by soldiers to relieve their guilty conscience. After an eighteen-day-long trip visiting U.S. armed forces units in southern Korea and seeing pinup pictures riddling the bunker walls, Bishop Austin Purdue had this to say about the morals of American servicemen: "Charity covers a multitude of sins. And Americans in Korea are the most charitable services in the history of the world." See Ray Waterkotte, "Charity of U.S. Troops 'Fantastic,' Bishop Says," *Pacific Stars and Stripes,* February 7, 1953, reprinted in Korean War National Museum, www.koreanchildren.org.

65. "7th Division Christmas Celebration, Do Bong Orphanage," reel 3, November 11, 1953, Department of Defense, U.S. Army Audiovisual Center, Motion Picture, Sound, and Video Records, Record Group 111, National Archives at College Park.

66. Paul Dickson, *War Slang: American Fighting Words and Phrases since the Civil War* (Dulles, Va.: Brassey's, 2004), 250.

67. Novelist Chinua Achebe puts it another way: "Charity . . . is the opium of the privileged. . . . Let us not forget that the real solution lies in a world in which charity will have become unnecessary." Achebe, *Anthills of the Savannah* (New York: Anchor Books, 1997), 143.

68. Howard Rusk, "The GI's Give a Hand to the Koreans," *New York Times Magazine,* October 11, 1953, reprinted in Korean War National Museum, www.koreanchildren.org.

69. See, for example, Robert H. Mosier, "The GI and the Kids of Korea: America's Fighting Men Share Their Food, Clothing, and Shelter with Children of a War-torn Land," *National Geographic Magazine,* May 1953, 635–64, reprinted in Korean War National Museum, www.koreanchildren.org. Mosier, a technical sergeant in the U.S. Marine Corps, explains how witnessing and hearing about the charitable activities of the U.S. Marines, Navy, and Air Force during his stint as a photographer in the Korean War made him "feel pretty good to be an American."

70. Hübinette, *Comforting an Orphaned Nation,* 36–37, lists some exceptions, citing Antonio Corea, who is considered to be the first adopted Korean (adopted by an Italian salesman in the late sixteenth century), and Kim Kyu-sik. In the late nineteenth century, at six years of age, Kim Kyu-sik was adopted by Horace G. Underwood, the American missionary who is credited for introducing Protestantism to Korea.

71. Korean children displaced by the Korean War may have been adopted as early as 1950. Certainly, by 1952, formal adoptions of Korean children by U.S. servicemen were taking place. See Corporal Peter Steele Bixby, "No. 1 Sargy, Sambo Plan Life Together," *Pacific Stars and Stripes,* October 30, 1950, reprinted in Korean War National Museum, www.koreanchildren.org, and Bill Purdom, "Officer Wins Fight to Adopt Lad, Korean Boy Starts for U.S.," *Pacific Stars and Stripes,* September 23, 1952, reprinted in Korean War National Museum, www.koreanchildren.org.

2. Gender and the Militaristic Gaze

1. Korean War National Museum, www.koreanchildren.org.

2. Ibid.

3. I want to thank Eleana Kim, who generously shared with me her copy of this book.

4. George F. Drake and Al Zimmerman, foreword to *GIs and the Kids—A Love Story: American Armed Forces and the Children of Korea, 1950–1954* (Bellingham, Wash.: Korean War Children's Memorial, 2005).

5. Ibid., 1.

6. Ibid., back cover.

7. Mihee-Nathalie Lemoine, "Suck Me-Ho's First English Lesson," collage on paper, reprinted in *O.K.A.Y.: Overseas Korean Artists Yearbook* 1 (2001): 85.

8. Bruce Cumings, "Silent but Deadly: Sexual Subordination in the U.S.–Korean Relationship," in *Let the Good Times Roll: Prostitution and the U.S. Military in Asia*, ed. Saundra Pollock Sturdevant and Brenda Stoltzfus (New York: New Press, 1992), 170.

9. Ji-Yeon Yuh, *Beyond the Shadow of Camptown: Korean Military Brides in America* (New York: New York University Press, 2002), 14.

10. *Gijichon* is the Korean word for "camptown." Depending on which romanization system is being used, the spelling of this word varies. Some scholars write *kijich'on* (reflecting the older McCune-Reischauer system), and some write *gijichon* (reflecting the revised romanization system that was officially adopted by South Korea in 2000).

11. Lemoine, "Suck Me-Ho's First English Lesson," 85. The "Mr." that prefaces Me-Ho's last name may signify the sexist language of the workbook rather than the identity of the speaker. Lemoine may be alluding to how English grammar books (and texts in general) use masculine nouns and pronouns when the subject's gender is variable. Another possible interpretation could be this: as a queer adoptee who challenges gender normativity, the "Mr." could also signify Lemoine's playing around with gender categories, exposing it as a flexible, hybrid, and ambiguous construction rather than an innate biological essence.

12. Cho, *Haunting the Korean Diaspora*, 8.

13. Cumings, "Silent but Deadly," 170.

14. See Yuh, *Beyond the Shadow of Camptown*, and Cho, *Haunting the Korean Diaspora*. See also Moon, *Sex among Allies*.

15. Patti Duncan, "Genealogies of Unbelonging: Amerasians and Transnational Adoptees as Legacies of U.S. Militarism in South Korea," in *Militarized Currents: Toward a Decolonized Future in Asia and the Pacific*, ed. Setsu Shigematsu and Keith L. Camacho (Minneapolis: University of Minnesota Press, 2010), 285, 287. Jodi Kim, *Ends of Empire: Asian American Critique and the Cold War* (Minneapolis: University of Minnesota Press, 2010), 161.

16. Moon, *Sex among Allies*, 3, 28. Cho indicates that the practice of U.S. soldiers breaking into private homes and raping the girls living there also fueled the production of camptown prostitutes. Many girls who were raped by American servicemen turned to military prostitution as a means of survival.

17. Ibid., 85.

18. Cynthia Enloe, *Globalization and Militarism: Feminists Make the Link* (Lanham, Md.: Rowman and Littlefield, 2007), 145.

19. Ibid., 4.

20. See, for example, "Construction of AFAK Orphanage, Seoul, Korea."

21. See, for example, "Refugee Evacuation, Chunchon, Korea," October 22, 1952, Department of Defense, U.S. Army Audiovisual Center, Motion Picture, Sound, and Video Records, Record Group 111, National Archives at College Park, and "Korean Orphanage Supported by 502nd TAC Control Group," March–April 1952, Department of Defense, Department of the Air Force, Motion Picture, Sound, and Video Records, Record Group 342, National Archives at College Park.

22. "War Orphans, Korea," September 18–20, 1953, Department of Defense, U.S. Army Audiovisual Center, Motion Picture, Sound, and Video Records, Record Group 111, National Archives at College Park, and "Korean Orphan Story," reels 1 and 4, January–February 1952, Department of Defense, Department of the Air Force, Motion Picture, Sound, and Video Records, Record Group 342, National Archives at College Park.

23. "Epidemic Control Unit (USN), Ullong-Do Korea," July 8, 1952, Department of Defense, U.S. Army Audiovisual Center, Motion Picture, Sound, and Video Records, Record Group 111, National Archives at College Park, and "Korean Orphan Story," reel 2, January–February 1952, Department of Defense, Department of the Air Force, Motion Picture, Sound, and Video Records, Record Group 342, National Archives at College Park.

24. "Sec. of Army Robert T. Stevens at Orphanage Dedication, Seoul, Korea," January 19, 1954, Department of Defense, U.S. Army Audiovisual Center, Motion Picture, Sound, and Video Records, Record Group 111, National Archives at College Park.

25. "Korean Orphanage Supported by 502nd TAC Control Group," March–April 1952, Department of Defense, Department of the Air Force, Motion Picture, Sound, and Video Records, Record Group 342, National Archives at College Park, and "Armed Forces Assistance to Korea Gifts of Clothing to Children, Yong Do (Pusan), Korea," December 22, 1954, Department of Defense, U.S. Army Audiovisual Center, Motion Picture, Sound, and Video Records, Record Group 111, National Archives at College Park.

26. "Korean Orphan Story," reel 5, January 18, 1952, Department of Defense, Department of the Air Force, Motion Picture, Sound, and Video Records, Record Group 342, National Archives at College Park, and "Front Line Air Force Chaplain: Outtakes," n.d., Department of Defense, Department of the Air Force, Motion Picture, Sound, and Video Records, Record Group 342, National Archives at College Park.

27. "Christmas Party for Korean Orphans, IX Corps, Kinsal, Korea," December 24, 1953; "7th Division Christmas Celebration, Chorwon and Vijongbu, Korea"; and "Armed Forces Assistance to Korea Gifts of Clothing to Children, Yong Do (Pusan), Korea," December 22, 1954, Department of Defense, U.S. Army Audiovisual Center, Motion Picture, Sound, and Video Records, Record Group 111, National Archives at College Park.

28. "Korean Orphanage Supported by 502nd TAC Control Group" and "Christmas Party for Korean Orphans, IX Corps, Kinsal, Korea."

29. Cumings, "Silent but Deadly," 174.

30. "304th BN Orphanage in Seoul, Korea," March 27, 1953, Department of Defense, U.S. Army Audiovisual Center, Motion Picture, Sound, and Video Records, Record Group 111, National Archives at College Park.

31. "Sailors, Marine Unite to Garb Korean Tots," *Pacific Stars and Stripes*, November 30, 1952, reprinted in *Korean War Children's Memorial*, Korean War National Museum, www.koreanchildren.org.

32. "7th Division Christmas Celebration, Chorwon and Vijongbu, Korea."

33. Ibid.

34. "A New American Comes 'Home,'" *Life*, November 30, 1953, 25.

35. Michel Foucault, *Discipline and Punish: The Birth of the Prison* (New York: Vintage Books, 1995), 135–36.

36. Allan Punzalan Isaac, *American Tropics: Articulating Filipino America* (Minneapolis: University of Minnesota Press, 2006), 49, 75.

37. "A New American Comes 'Home,'" 28, 27.

38. Isaac, *American Tropics*, 75.

39. Ibid.

40. Unfortunately for Lee Kyung Soo, who was renamed Lee Paladino after his adoption, the fantasy did not become reality. In 1958, the *New York Times* published a follow-up story on Lee and reported that he had been handed over to the state welfare department after his bachelor father got married. Evidently friction developed between Lee and his stepmother. He lived with a foster family until he was legally adopted by his grandparents at the age of nine. Quoted in Eleana Kim, "Origins of Korean Adoption," 8.

41. The practice of incorporating local children into foreign military troops as mascots has, according to Arissa Oh, "existed at least since World War II," when Allied troops adopted European children as mascots. Oh, "Into the Arms of America: The Korean Roots of International Adoption" (Ph.D. diss., University of Chicago, 2008), 62.

42. An orphan's informal adoption as a troop's mascot would often eventually turn into a formal adoption by a serviceman. The inevitable would happen: a GI's tour would end, bringing him back to the States. The possibility of being separated forever from the child forced the GI to make a decision: to leave the child behind or to take the child with him. Possible separation became the catalyst that propelled many GIs to adopt their mascot. See "Korean Lad to Leave for U.S.," *Pacific Stars and Stripes*, August 23, 1952, reprinted in Korean War National Museum, www.koreanchildren.org; "24th Div. Sergeant Plans Adoption of 'Wild Bill,'" *Pacific Stars and Stripes*, July 7, 1954, reprinted in Korean War National Museum, www.koreanchildren.org; and Sergeant Robert L. Brown, "Orphan, 7, Leaves Korea for New Home in Texas," *Pacific Stars and Stripes*, June 15, 1954, reprinted in Korean War National Museum, www.koreanchildren.org.

43. Korean War National Museum, "Adopting the Children," www.koreanchildren.org.

44. Peter Linden, "Chocoletto: A Korean War Orphan Joins the Marines," April 14, 1953, reprinted in Korean War National Museum, www.koreanchildren.org.

45. Max Crow, "Pon Son See aka Jimmie Pusan," USS *Whitehurst*, usswhitehurst.org /Mascot.htm.

46. Andy Bisaccia, "Jimmie Pon Son See," USS *Whitehurst*, usswhitehurst.org/Jimmy.htm.

47. Ibid.

48. CETO, *Child Soldiers: Implications for U.S. Forces,* Seminar Report (Quantico, Va.: Center for Emerging Threats and Opportunities, Marine Corps Warfighting Laboratory, 2002), 7.

49. Ibid.

50. See, for example, P. W. Singer, *Children at War* (Berkeley: University of California Press, 2006); Michael Wessells, *Child Soldiers: From Violence to Protection* (Cambridge, Mass.: Harvard University Press, 2009); and Illene Cohn and Guy S. Goodwin-Gill, *Child Soldiers: The Role of Children in Armed Conflict* (New York: Oxford University Press, 1994).

51. The publication of Cohn and Goodwin-Gill's *Child Soldiers* was motivated by the killing of a U.S. serviceman (the first casualty of Operation Enduring Freedom) by a fourteen-year-old Afghan boy. This event spurred the U.S. Marines to discuss how U.S. forces should respond when confronted by armed children. CETO does acknowledge that child soldiers existed during World War II and the Vietnam War; however, they do so in a way that suggests that Germany and Vietnam used child soldiers and not the United States.

52. Although outside the scope of this study, it would be interesting to find out if the U.S. military's experience with Korean orphans as child soldiers informed or influenced its decision to employ Southeast Asian children during the Vietnam War. Korean children, like Hmong children during the CIA's so-called secret war in Laos, made excellent spies and informants because of their ability to blend into the enemy's territory. Hmong and Laotian children also fought in armed combat, receiving pennies a day for their work. Edgar Buell, U.S. Agency for International Development (AID) official working with Hmong mercenaries, gestures to one possible reason why these children were employed by the U.S. military: "Everyone [*sic*] of them (Hmong) that died, that was an American back home that didn't die." Quoted in Richard S. Erlich, "CIA's Secret War in Laos," *Global Politician,* July 25, 2006, www.globalpolitician.com.

53. Laura Mulvey, "Visual Pleasure and Narrative Cinema," in *Film Theory and Criticism: Introductory Readings,* 5th ed., ed. Leo Braudy and Marshall Cohen (New York: Oxford University Press, 1999), 843.

54. See, for example, "Construction of AFAK Orphanage, Seoul, Korea" and "Sec. of Army Robert T. Stevens at Orphanage Dedication, Seoul, Korea."

55. Moon, *Sex among Allies,* 2.

56. Ibid., 2, 85.

57. Yuh, *Beyond the Shadow of Camptown,* 25.

58. Quoted in Oh, "Into the Arms of America," 68.

59. Ibid., 67, 69.

60. Cho, *Haunting the Korean Diaspora,* 107, 108.

61. See, for example, "Want to Lead a Band?," *Pacific Stars and Stripes,* June 11, 1952, reprinted in Korean War National Museum, www.koreanchildren.org. Orphans play "Boogie-Woogie Bugle Boy of Company B" with improvised instruments, endearing them to the soldiers. See also "Korean Children Entertain," *Pacific Stars and Stripes,* n.d., reprinted in *Korean War Children's Memorial,* Korean War National Museum, www.koreanchildren.org. Two female Korean orphans are dressed up like sailors, dancing the

"Navy Dance" during "Operation Santa Claus." Finally, see *Pacific Stars and Stripes*, October 16, 1954, reprinted in Korean War National Museum, www.koreanchildren .org. A group of young Korean girls at Aerin Won Orphanage, dressed in *hanbok,* performed for Commanding General Richard S. Whitcomb as a gesture of appreciation for his "continued efforts and assistance in reconstruction and establishment of a number of the orphanage's buildings."

62. "Redlegs Adopt Korean Pin-up," *Pacific Stars and Stripes*, February 26, 1951, reprinted in Korean War National Museum, www.koreanchildren.org.

63. Devised by American soldiers stationed in post–World War II Japan, *Baby-san* was a term that "combined an American pick-up line ('Hey, baby') with an everyday Japanese title of respect ('san')." Baby-san became a popular cartoon character after being featured in naval reservist Bill Hume's illustrated, semipornographic cartoon series in the Far East edition of the *Navy Times*. In these cartoons, Baby-san was depicted as a sex kitten. His first collected volume of cartoons, *Babysan: A Private Look at the Japanese Occupation,* was published in 1953 and was a bestseller among GIs in South Korea. See Naoko Shibusawa, *America's Geisha Ally: Reimagining the Japanese Enemy* (Cambridge, Mass.: Harvard University Press, 2006), 35, 36.

64. "'Adopted' Korean Girl Loves Officer, Now Happy," *Pacific Stars and Stripes*, July 24, 1951, reprinted in Korean War National Museum, www.koreanchildren.org.

65. "Christmas Party for Korean Orphans, IX Corps, Kinsal, Korea."

66. See E. Ann Kaplan, *Looking for the Other: Feminism, Film, and the Imperial Gaze* (New York: Routledge, 1997). According to Kaplan, "the 'male' gaze and the 'imperial' gaze cannot be separated within western patriarchal cultures" (xi). This is because the imperial gaze, which assumes the centrality of the white Western subject, is almost always male—or at least is structured by patriarchal norms and ideology (78). The militaristic gaze shares this same structure by centering the white Western male, who in this particular case is a soldier.

67. Orientalism, as originally theorized by Edward Said, is a system of knowledge that constructs the Occident (the West) as superior to the Orient (the East) so that the Oriental Other is imagined as inferior, irrational, feminine, and exotic, which is in direct contrast to the rational, modern, masculine, and civilized Occident. Said, *Orientalism* (New York: Vintage Books, 1979).

68. In citing James Kincaid's *Erotic Innocence: The Culture of Child Molesting* (Durham, N.C.: Duke University Press, 1998), I do not mean to imply that all interaction between GIs and orphans were pedophilic. However, it is safe to assume that some Korean children were molested and sexually abused by U.S. soldiers, even though I could not find any formal records of this. This sort of data and these types of violations are usually not the kind that occupying forces collect; however, on two separate occasions, after I presented the information in this chapter, an audience member came up to me and shared that a family member was molested by a soldier during the Korean War. Citing this book is to gesture to this violation, as well as to suggest that their innocence is what made these children desirable, sexually or otherwise.

69. Ibid., 53.

70. Ibid., 15, 14.

71. Ibid., 17–20.

72. Because Orientalism is a contradictory process, its viewing practices are uneven. As pointed out earlier in the chapter, sometimes Orientalist tropes render Korean children adultlike (e.g., camptown women or soldiers). In other cases, like this one, it infantilizes them.

73. Harry D. Pratt and Kent S. Littig, *Lice of Public Health Importance and Their Control*, Training Guide: Insect Control Series (Atlanta, Ga.: U.S. Department of Health, Education, and Welfare, 1961), VIII-10, phthiraptera.info/Publications/46342.pdf.

74. "Epidemic Control Unit (USN), Ullong-Do Korea," July 7, 1952.

75. Ibid., July 8, 1952.

76. Ibid., July 13, 1952.

77. Ibid., July 8, 1952.

78. Ibid.

79. See, for example, "Christmas Party for Korean Orphans, IX Corps, Kinsal, Korea"; "7th Division Christmas Celebration, Chorwon and Vijongbu, Korea"; "304th BN Orphanage in Seoul, Korea"; and "Front Line Air Force Chaplain: Outtakes" (reel 4 of 9).

80. "Christmas Party for Korean Orphans, IX Corps, Kinsal, Korea."

81. "Armed Forces Assistance Korea (AFAK), South Korea," November 13, 1963, Department of Defense, U.S. Army Audiovisual Center, Motion Picture, Sound, and Video Records, Record Group 111, National Archives at College Park.

82. Malek Alloula, *The Colonial Harem* (Minneapolis: University of Minnesota Press, 1986), 13, 14.

83. Ella Shohat, "Imaging Terra Incognita: The Disciplinary Gaze of Empire," *Public Culture* 3, no. 2 (Spring 1991): 68.

84. "Epidemic Control Unit (USN), Ullong-Do Korea," July 8, 1952.

85. Moon, *Sex among Allies*, 8, 27.

86. For a fuller discussion on other factors that enabled GIs to adopt Korean children when an international adoption policy was absent in South Korea, see Eleana Kim, *Adopted Territory*, 51–53.

3. Marketing the Social Orphan

1. In addition, in 1946, on the eve of Philippine independence, Congress established immigration quotas from India and the Philippines, which commenced the dismantling of the Asiatic Barred Zone of 1917. Robert G. Lee, *Orientals: Asian American in Popular Culture* (Philadelphia: Temple University Press, 1999), 149.

2. Ibid.

3. Erika Lee, *At America's Gates: Chinese Immigration during the Exclusion Era, 1882–1943* (Chapel Hill: University of North Carolina Press), 245; Lee, *Orientals*, 149.

4. Caroline Chung Simpson, *An Absent Presence: Japanese Americans in Postwar American Culture, 1945–1960* (Durham, N.C.: Duke University Press, 2001), 43–75.

5. Ibid., 152–53, 155–56. Simpson argues that it was precisely these earlier projects of racially integrating Japanese Americans—through internment and resettlement programs—that enabled the depiction of Asian Americans as model minorities to form

during the 1950s and 1960s. For more information on the WRA Resettlement Project, see 152–64.

6. Klein, *Cold War Orientalism,* 9.

7. Said, *Orientalism,* 3–7. The evolution from Orientalism to Cold War Orientalism can be attributed to America's evolving ideas of race. Klein points out that Franz Boas's work shifted the concept of race away from biological difference to cultural difference, making the idea of a pluralistic model of society especially salient during America's fight against the Nazis in World War II. She goes on to explain that "Cold War ideologues mobilized this idea of a racially and ethnically diverse America in the service of U.S. global expansion" (11). As a result, racial tolerance and inclusion were key concepts in Cold War Orientalism. The primary distinction then between Orientalism and Cold War Orientalism is this: Orientalism denigrates and rejects difference, while Cold War Orientalism seeks to integrate difference.

8. Klein, *Cold War Orientalism,* 16.

9. Ibid., 144–46.

10. Jung-Woo Kim and Henderson, "History of the Care," 16.

11. Jodi Kim, "An 'Orphan' with Two Mothers," 857.

12. Giorgio Agamben, *Homo Sacer: Sovereign Power and Bare Life* (Stanford, Calif.: Stanford University Press, 1998), 8–9.

13. Signe Howell, *The Kinning of Foreigners: Transnational Adoption in a Global Perspective* (New York: Berghahn Books, 2006), 4, 5.

14. Arissa Oh, "A New Kind of Missionary Work: Christians, Christian Americanists, and the Adoption of Korean GI Babies, 1955–1961," *Women's Studies Quarterly* 33, no. 3/4 (Fall–Winter 2005): 164.

15. "Yank's Appeal Brings Flood of Donations," *Pacific Stars and Stripes* (Yokohama edition), February 11, 1955, reprinted in Korean War National Museum, www.korean children.org.

16. Bob McNeil, "Good Samaritans in Uniform," *Pacific Stars and Stripes,* December 15, 1953, reprinted in Korean War National Museum, www.koreanchildren.org; "Yank Funds to Aid Needy at Christmas," *Pacific Stars and Stripes,* November 24, 1953, reprinted in Korean War National Museum, www.koreanchildren.org.

17. "Mr. Holt 'Moves the World,'" *Oregonian,* April 9, 1956, and "Mrs. Holt Says Korea Tots Dying," *Oregon Daily Journal,* July 24, 1957, newspaper clippings, ISS-USA Papers, Box 10, File "Children—Independent Adoption Schemes, Harry Holt, 1955–1957, Vol. 1," SWHA, Minneapolis, Minn.

18. Eloise Dungan, "Orphan Homes: Mrs. Pettiss Tells of Adoption," *San Francisco News,* February 20, 1956, newspaper clipping, ISS-USA Papers, Box 10, File "Children—Independent Adoption Schemes, Harry Holt, 1955–1957, Vol. 1," SWHA, Minneapolis, Minn.

19. By pointing this out, I am not suggesting that these stories weren't true or that the situation involving these children weren't urgent; rather, I'm suggesting that GIs, missionaries, adoption workers, and journalists capitalized on this heightened sense of emergency to get Americans—who were halfway around the world—to act on behalf of these children.

20. Laura Briggs, "Mother, Child, Race, Nation: The Visual Iconography of Rescue and the Politics of Transnational and Transracial Adoption," *Gender and History* 15, no. 2 (2003): 180–81.

21. Ibid., 184.

22. This proclamation appears at the beginning of each *Paramount News* newsreel and serves as the opening shot.

23. Although the Korean War is primarily discussed in terms of a war between the Soviet Union and the United States, the United States relied on the United Nations to help keep their enemies on the northern side of the thirty-eighth parallel. As members of the United Nations, Canada assisted the United States both during and after the war. Airing this news story not only informed U.S. citizens about the neighborly actions of their Canadian allies, but it also may have worked to inspire Americans to act, so as not to be outdone by their Canadian neighbors.

24. "Hand of Mercy . . . Canadian GIs save Korean Orphanage," *Paramount News,* February 6, 1952, PARA: Paramount Pictures Inc., Motion Picture, Sound, and Video Records, National Archives at College Park.

25. Klein, *Cold War Orientalism,* 154. Dr. J. Calvitt Clarke, founder of Christian Children's Fund, goes so far as to say, "The hungry children of the world are more dangerous to us than the atom bomb" (quoted in ibid.).

26. Oh, "New Kind of Missionary Work," 171.

27. "Helping Koreans Help Themselves," *Life,* October 12, 1953, 48.

28. Klein, *Cold War Orientalism,* 152–59.

29. "Test Yourself!," *Look,* January 11, 1955, 56.

30. Valk, "Adjustment of Korean-American Children," 3.

31. Oh, "New Kind of Missionary Work," 164.

32. Dungan, "Orphan Homes."

33. Harry Holt, "Dear Friends," December 27, 1956, ISS-USA Papers, Box 10, File "Children—Independent Adoption Schemes, Harry Holt, 1955–1957, Vol. 1," SWHA, Minneapolis, Minn.

34. Briggs, "Mother, Child, Race, Nation," 181.

35. The 1924 Immigration Act is also called the Asian Exclusion Act. It established a quota system in which only 2 percent of the foreign-born people living in the United States in 1890 could immigrate. This, along with the provision in the National Origins Quota of 1924 (which stated that people ineligible for citizenship could not immigrate into the United States), restricted people of Asian descent from entering the country.

36. Tobias Hübinette, "Korean Adoption History," in *Community 2004: Guide to Korea for Overseas Adopted Koreans,* ed. Eleana Kim (Seoul: Overseas Koreans Foundation, 2004), 3, reprinted in www.tobiashubinette.se. In proxy adoptions, a representative of the adoptive parents travels to South Korea and completes the adoption in the Korean court. Consequently, adoptions are completed, sight unseen, between the adopted child and adoptive parent in order to speed up the adoption process. This practice was criticized by licensed social welfare agencies because it eschewed the minimum standards of adoption: investigation, supervision, and probation. The supervision and probationary periods were particularly important because it provided both parties a trial period in

which the child lived with his or new family before the adoption was finalized. Proxy adoptions eliminated these safeguards, which led to abuses and risky matches. I engage in a more detailed discussion of proxy adoptions in chapter 4. See Adoption History Project, "Proxy Adoptions," www.uoregon.edu.

37. Hübinette, "Korean Adoption History," 5.

38. U.S. Citizenship and Immigration Services, "Legislation from 1961–1980," www.uscis.gov. See also Adoption History Project, "Timeline of Adoption History," www.uoregon.edu.

39. Giorgio Agamben, *State of Exception,* trans. Kevin Attell (Chicago: University of Chicago Press, 2005), 3.

40. For more information on the 1950s production of the model minority, see chapter 5 in Lee's *Orientals* and chapter 5 in Simpson's *Absent Presence.*

41. Lee, *Orientals,* 8.

42. Ibid., 11.

43. As previously argued in chapter 1, because male orphans were made in the image of GIs, they took on the aesthetics of the military, including the shaved head.

44. "Hand of Mercy."

45. John C. Caldwell, *Children of Calamity* (New York: John Day, 1957), 29; Klein, *Cold War Orientalism,* 158; Caldwell, *Children of Calamity,* 29.

46. Interestingly, prospective adoptive parents (PAPs) would appropriate the language of department store orders by submitting their own orders. It was typical for PAPs to indicate the age and sex of the child they wanted. Some, like Mrs. Casey from Missouri, enclosed a clipping of a magazine article with the following request: "the child in circle is [the] one we are writing about" (quoted in 64). Eleana Kim, *Adopted Territory,* 63–65.

47. Naoko Shibusawa, *America's Geisha Ally: Reimagining the Japanese Enemy* (Cambridge, Mass.: Harvard University Press, 2006), 23.

48. Museum of International Folk Art, "Miss Yamaguchi," moifa.org/collections/aboutcollectionsyamaguchi.html.

49. Esther Singleton, *Dolls* (Washington, DC: Hobby House Press, 1962), 77.

50. Wechill, "Effanbee Patsy Dolls, Part I," www.angelfire.com/tx3/dollchat2/patsy1.html. After her debut in 1928, the original Patsy was called "Loveable Imp" and "Hit of the Year."

51. Caldwell, *Children of Calamity,* n.p.

52. Barb Lee, dir., *Adopted* (New York: Point Made Films, 2009). DVD. According to Korean adoptee Jennifer Fero, this was the first sentence in the letter to her adoptive parents from Holt Adoption Agency, regarding her adoption. It accompanied her photograph.

53. Karl Marx, *Capital: A Critical Analysis of Capitalist Production,* vol. 1, trans. Samuel Moore and Edward Aveling (Moscow: Progress Publishers, 1965), 72–73, 82.

54. "Party for 2,000 . . . GI's Host to Korean Orphans," *Paramount News,* October 22, 1954, PARA: Paramount Pictures, Inc., Motion Picture, Sound, and Video Records, National Archives at College Park.

55. Ibid.

56. The belief that the period of adjustment will be easy for the adoptee is an expectation that adoptive parents continue to have. In the film *Adopted* by Barb Lee, we witness Jacqueline and John Trainer—white Americans who just adopted a girl from China—discuss their perspective on their child's adjustment process. Jacqueline explains: "She did most of her grieving in China [3 days], which is remarkable and fast." John agrees: "She made it so easy . . . She's adjusted so well." Jacqueline adds: "Nobody believed that she cried . . . Yeah, we have a perfect child." It is this kind of discourse regarding the Asian orphan/adoptee that continues to fuel yellow desire and constructs Asian adoptees as model minorities. See Barb Lee, dir., *Adopted* (New York: Point Made Films, 2009). DVD.

57. "Party for 2,000 . . . GI's Host to Korean Orphans."

58. Quoted in Klein, *Cold War Orientalism*, 145.

4. Normalizing the Adopted Child

1. In one International Social Services (ISS) case, a soldier, who became "attracted" to a young orphan girl at a Christmas party, tried to get his parents to adopt her since he was single. (At this time, only married couples could adopt.) After finding out that the GI had romantic feelings for the girl, ISS rejected his request. See Marcia Speers to Margaret Valk, August 29, 1957, ISS-USA Papers, Box 42, Folder 8, SWHA, Minneapolis, Minn. ISS case files are filled with accounts like this: a GI becomes "attracted" (sometimes romantically) to an orphan boy or girl that he met at an orphanage or a GI-sponsored party and becomes interested in adopting the child. One U.S. ambassador reported that almost every day, he "received a letter from a returned Korean veteran who wanted legally to adopt a Korean child, or had a soldier still in Korea visit the Embassy who wanted to leave money for a child, or another who had returned [to the United States] who wanted to send money back to a child." See Asbury, "Military Help," 3.

2. See Foucault, *Discipline and Punish*.

3. Michel Foucault, *History of Sexuality: An Introduction*, vol. 1, trans. Robert Hurley (New York: Vintage Books, 1990), 140–45. Biopower, as defined by Foucault, is power that deals with living beings so that life itself can be mastered. The disciplining of the body and the regulation of populations make up the two axes of biopower.

4. Joungwon Kim, *Divided Korea: The Politics of Development, 1945–1972* (Cambridge: East Asian Research Center at Harvard University, 1976), 147.

5. Asbury, "Military Help," 17, 16.

6. Caldwell, *Children of Calamity*, 78.

7. Joungwon Kim, *Divided Korea,*147, 160, 226, 258, and 280. During the mid 1960s, South Korea began to take on private commercial loans and public loans from foreign nations, including the United States.

8. Caldwell, *Children of Calamity*, 78–79.

9. Quoted in ibid., 79.

10. Caldwell, *Children of Calamity*, 80.

11. Asbury, "Military Help," 17.

12. Choy, "Institutionalizing International Adoption," 30.

13. Korean War National Museum, "List of Orphanages in Korea Supported by Christian Children's Fund, Inc., 1954," www.koreanchildren.org.

14. Caldwell, *Children of Calamity*, 35, 37, 83.

15. "Creswell Man—Father of Six—To Adopt Korean War Orphans," newspaper clipping, ISS-USA Papers, Box 10, File "Children—Independent Adoption Schemes, Harry Holt, 1955–1957, Vol. 1," SWHA, Minneapolis, Minn.

16. Holt became so invested in the plight of mixed-race orphans in South Korea that some people believed that as long as there was a single mixed-blood child in South Korea, Holt would never leave the adoption industry. See Margaret A. Valk, "Visit to Korea—November 21–30, 1956," 14, ISS-USA Papers, Box 35, File "Reports and Visits to Korea, 1956–," SWHA, Minneapolis, Minn.

17. "Creswell Man—Father of Six—To Adopt Korean War Orphans."

18. Ibid.

19. See "The Lord is their sponsor," 58, and "Haven for Korean Orphans . . . 12 Waifs Make Journey to U.S.," *Paramount News*, October 19, 1955, PARA: Paramount Pictures, Inc., Motion Picture, Sound, and Video Records, National Archives at College Park.

20. "Mr. Holt 'Moves the World,'" *Oregonian,* April 9, 1956, newspaper clipping, ISS-USA Papers, Box 10, File "Children—Independent Adoption Schemes, Harry Holt, 1955–1957, Vol. 1," SWHA, Minneapolis, Minn.

21. "Articles of Incorporation of Orphan's Foundation Fund, Inc.," n.d., ISS-USA Papers, Box 10, File "Independent Adoption Schemes, Harry Holt, 1958–1959, Vol. 2," SWHA, Minneapolis, Minn.

22. Holt Adoption Program Inc., "1965 Annual Report," March 11, 1966, ISS-USA Papers, Box 10, File "Children—Independent Adoption Schemes, Harry Holt, 1960–1963, Vol. 3," SWHA, Minneapolis, Minn.

23. ELH to WCK, Memo, November 8, 1967, ISS-USA Papers, Box 10, File "Children—Independent Adoption Schemes, Harry Holt, 1960–1963, Vol. 3," SWHA, Minneapolis, Minn.

24. Director of ISS (American Branch), "Report of Visit to Korea, June 18–July 13, 1962," March 4, 1963, 16, ISS-USA Papers, Box 35, File "Reports and Visits to Korea, 1956–," SWHA, Minneapolis, Minn. In total, ISS averaged about sixty placements per year, but only twenty were placed in the United States. The other forty children were placed with Americans residing in Japan, Okinawa, and South Korea.

25. Paul R. Cherney, "Report to the Board of Directors of ISS, American Branch," June 8–July 10, 1965, 11, ISS-USA Papers, Box 35, File "Reports and Visits to Korea, 1956–," SWHA, Minneapolis, Minn.

26. Ibid., 15.

27. Holt Adoption Program Inc., "Annual Report 1969," 5, ISS-USA Papers, Box 10, File "Children—Independent Adoption Schemes, Harry Holt, 1968–1972, Vol. 4," SWHA, Minneapolis, Minn.

28. Harry Holt, "Dear Friends," n.d., ISS-USA Papers, Box 10, File "Children—Independent Adoption Schemes, Harry Holt, 1955–1957, Vol. 1," SWHA, Minneapolis, Minn.

29. William T. Kirk to Reverend Eugene Carson Blake, June 17, 1958, ISS-USA Papers, Box 10, File "Independent Adoption Schemes, Harry Holt, 1958–1959, Vol. 2," SWHA, Minneapolis, Minn.

30. Privileging speed and quantity over quality led to numerous unsuccessful adoptions, especially in the first ten years of HAP. At times, ISS stepped in to deal with these case breakdowns, as ISS called them. The reasons for these breakdowns ranged from petty reasons (such as a child being returned because he had an ear infection) to severe reasons (such as an adoptive parent abusing the adopted child). Dr. Pierce of World Vision said that out of 600 families adopting through HAP, "he doubts whether one out of five adoptive couples would be suitable—they were either too old or maybe unstable." See American Branch, ISS, Inc., "Proxy Adoptions," n.d., p. 6, ISS-USA Papers, Box 10, File "Proxy Adoptions, 1954–1956," SWHA, Minneapolis, Minn. The Holts themselves were rejected when they applied to adopt through a licensed adoption agency in Oregon because of their age. Some people speculate that this was one of the reasons why Holt started his own adoption agency—no other agency would allow him to adopt these children. Interestingly, HAP became known as the agency that approved everyone, including families who had been previously rejected by other adoption agencies.

31. Bertha Holt, *The Seed from the East* (Eugene, Ore.: Holt International Children's Services, 1956), 55.

32. Raymond W. Riese to Paul Martin, May 13, 1958, ISS-USA Papers, Box 10, File "Independent Adoption Schemes, Harry Holt, 1958–1959, Vol. 2," SWHA, Minneapolis, Minn.

33. ELH to WCK.

34. Patricia Nye, "Report on Visit to Korea, March 23–26, 1976," 2, ISS-USA Papers, Box 35, File "Reports and Visits to Korea, 1956–," SWHA, Minneapolis, Minn.

35. Raymond W. Riese to Paul Martin.

36. Andrew F. Juras to Susan T. Pettis, May 4, 1956, ISS-USA Papers, Box 10, File "Children—Independent Adoption Schemes, Harry Holt, 1955–1957, Vol. 1," SWHA, Minneapolis, Minn.

37. State Public Welfare Commission to Carl Adams, August 30, 1957, ISS-USA Papers, Box 10, File "Children—Independent Adoption Schemes, Harry Holt, 1955–1957, Vol. 1," SWHA, Minneapolis, Minn.

38. William T. Kirk to Reverend Eugene Carson Blake.

39. Dorothy M. Frost to Susan T. Pettis, memorandum, November 25, 1958, ISS-USA Papers, Box 10, File "Independent Adoption Schemes, Harry Holt, 1958–1959, Vol. 2," SWHA, Minneapolis, Minn.

40. "Harry Holt, Who Found Parents for 3,000 Korean Orphans, Dies," newspaper clipping, April 29, 1964, ISS-USA Papers, Box 10, File "Children—Independent Adoption Schemes, Harry Holt, 1960–1963, Vol. 3," SWHA, Minneapolis, Minn.

41. Dorothy M. Frost to Susan T. Pettis.

42. Director of ISS (American Branch), "Report of Visit to Korea, June 18–July 13, 1962," 14.

43. Paul R. Cherney, "Visit to Korea—June 23 to July 9, 1965," July 20, 1965, 16, ISS-USA Papers, Box 35, File "Reports and Visits to Korea, 1956–," SWHA, Minneapolis, Minn.

44. Ursula M. Gallagher, "Field Trip to Korea," November 15–19, 1965, 3, ISS-USA Papers, Box 35, File "Reports and Visits to Korea, 1956–," SWHA, Minneapolis, Minn.

These figures come from the Ministry of Health and Social Affairs in South Korea. Unfortunately, we cannot be sure that these figures are accurate because of the rampant practice of orphanages padding their figures to gain larger government subsidies. It is estimated that 10,000 to 15,000 orphans were actually ghost children.

45. Eleana Kim, *Adopted Territory,* 24–25.

46. Gallagher, "Field Trip to Korea," 3.

47. Cherney, "Visit to Korea—June 23 to July 9, 1965," 16.

48. Ibid., 17.

49. Nye, "Report on Visit to Korea, March 23–26, 1976," 2.

50. Ibid., 3.

51. Holt Adoption Program Inc., "Newsletter May–June 1965," 1, ISS-USA Papers, Box 10, File "Children—Independent Adoption Schemes, Harry Holt, 1960–1963, Vol. 3," SWHA, Minneapolis, Minn.

52. Holt Adoption Program Inc., "1963 New Years Greetings," 2–3, ISS-USA Papers, Box 10, File "Children—Independent Adoption Schemes, Harry Holt, 1960–1963, Vol. 3," SWHA, Minneapolis, Minn.

53. "Harry Holt, Who Found Parents for 3,000 Korean Orphans, Dies."

54. Foucault, *Discipline and Punish,* 137.

55. Ibid, 136.

56. Foucault, *Birth of the Clinic: An Archaeology of Medical Perception* (New York: Vintage Books, 1994), 34.

57. Ibid, 34, 35. Medical knowledge and health also constructs race and produces normative ideals of gender and sexuality. See Foucault, *History of Sexuality;* Nayan Shah, *Contagious Divides: Epidemics and Race in San Francisco Chinatown* (Berkeley: University of California Press, 2001); and Warwick Anderson, *Colonial Pathologies: American Tropical Medicine, Race, and Hygiene in the Philippines* (Durham, N.C.: Duke University Press, 2006).

58. The United States has had a long history of shaping their immigration policies based on norms created about the healthy body. See Shah's *Contagious Divides* and Douglas C. Baynton, "Disability and the Justification of Inequality in American History," in *The New Disability History: American Perspectives,* ed. Paul K. Longmore and Lauri Umanski (New York: New York University Press, 2001), 33–57.

59. Shah, *Contagious Divides,* 186. Shah states that politicians and immigration authorities increasingly relied on medical doctors and medical knowledge to create immigration policy.

60. Holt Adoption Program Inc., "1965 Annual Report," March 11, 1966, 6, ISS-USA Papers, Box 10, File "Children—Independent Adoption Schemes, Harry Holt, 1960–1963, Vol. 3," SWHA, Minneapolis, Minn. The fear underlying this emphasis on physical health is that persons immigrating to the United States will become public charges if they are unable to take care of themselves. See Baynton, "Disability," 45.

61. Holt Adoption Program Inc., "1960 New Years Greetings," 2, ISS-USA Papers, Box 10, File "Children—Independent Adoption Schemes, Harry Holt, 1960–1963, Vol. 3," SWHA, Minneapolis, Minn.

62. Ibid.

63. The process in which Korean orphans would be matched with PAPs took a variety of forms. One way included PAPs designating the age and sex of the child they desired. HAP would then match a child with the PAPs, send the PAPs a description of a child along with a picture, and the PAPs would "phone back [their] approval or disapproval" (Holt, "Dear Friends," December 27, 1956, 2). Another way involved flying a planeload of PAPs to the Il San orphanage and having them choose which children they wanted. Although the HAP was criticized for this practice (which highlighted the commodified aspects of Korean adoption), it was a common practice among adoption agencies. It is within these two contexts that Holt witnessed PAPs choosing the more physically attractive child over the less attractive one. See Gallagher, "Field Trip to Korea," 8.

64. Holt Adoption Program Inc., "1960 New Years Greetings," 4.

65. Ibid., 2.

66. Ibid, 4.

67. Letitia DiVirgilio, "Adjustment of Foreign Children in Their Adoptive Homes," *Child Welfare* 35 (November 1956): 15. ISS-USA Papers, Box 10, File "Children: Adjustment of Foreign Children," SWHA, Minneapolis, Minn.

68. Valk, "Adjustment of Korean-American Children," 3.

69. Holt Adoption Program Inc., "1960 New Years Greetings," 1.

70. Bertha Holt, *Bring My Sons from Afar* (Eugene, Ore.: Holt International Children's Services, 1986), 191.

71. Ibid., 137.

72. Ibid., 166.

73. Ibid., 143.

74. Ibid.

75. Ibid., 146.

76. Ibid.

77. Foucault, *Discipline and Punish*, 183.

78. Holt Adoption Program Inc., "Newsletter May–June 1965," 6, ISS-USA Papers, Box 10, File "Children—Independent Adoption Schemes, Harry Holt, 1960–1963, Vol. 3," SWHA, Minneapolis, Minn.

79. Baynton, "Disability," 36.

80. Holt Adoption Program Inc., "Newsletter May–June 1965," 6.

81. Baynton, "Disability," 49.

82. Susan Wendell, *The Rejected Body: Feminist Philosophical Reflections on Disability* (New York: Routledge, 1996), 13.

83. Holt Adoption Program Inc., "1965 Annual Report," 3.

84. David Serlin, *Replaceable You: Engineering the Body in Postwar America* (Chicago: University of Chicago Press, 2004), 3.

85. Ibid., 17.

86. Holt Adoption Program Inc., "Newsletter May–June 1965," 11.

87. Serlin, *Replaceable You*, 2.

88. Ibid., 78, 59.

89. Ibid., 62.

90. Quoted in Serlin, *Replaceable You*, 62.

91. Holt Adoption Program to Mr. Vasey, November 30, 1967, ISS-USA Papers, Box 10, File "Children—Independent Adoption Schemes, Harry Holt, 1960–1963, Vol. 3," SWHA, Minneapolis, Minn.

92. Matthew Rothschild, "Babies for Sale: South Koreans Make Them, Americans Buy Them," *Progressive,* January 1988, reprinted in Transracial Abductees, www.trans racialabductees.org.

93. Eleana Kim, *Adopted Territory,* 33.

94. Holt Adoption Program Inc., "1965 Annual Report," 4.

95. Holt, *Bring My Sons from Afar,* 199.

96. Holt Adoption Program Inc., "1965 Annual Report," 4.

97. John Adams, "Dear Friends," May 18, 1967, ISS-USA Papers, Box 10, File "Children—Independent Adoption Schemes, Harry Holt, 1960–1963, Vol. 3," SWHA, Minneapolis, Minn.

98. Holt Adoption Program Inc., "1965 Annual Report," 4.

99. Holt Adoption Program Inc., "Newsletter May–June 1965," 6.

100. Holt Adoption Program Inc., "Newsletter October and November 1962," 5.

101. Ibid.

102. Ibid.

103. Holt Adoption Program Inc., "Newsletter May–June 1965," 6. I use the terms *Korean Negro* and *Negro* here because this is what the adoption administrators used to refer to African Americans. Although the term *Negro* is now considered derogatory and offensive, I replicate its use here to stay true to the language used in the newsletters.

104. Harry Holt, "Dear Friends," December 27, 1956, 1–4.

105. Kori A. Graves, "'No future in their country': African-American Families and the International Adoption of 'Negro-Korean' Children" (working paper, Andersen Library Research Forum and the Social Welfare History Archives, University of Minnesota, Minneapolis, November 7, 2007).

106. Ibid.

107. Eleanor Linse to Lorraine Carroll, March 11, 1957, 1–2, ISS-USA Papers, Box 10, File "Children—Independent Adoption Schemes, Harry Holt, 1955–1957, Vol. 1," SWHA, Minneapolis, Minn. Again, the descriptor *Korean Caucasian* is not my own; it is the terminology used in the newsletters.

108. Harry Holt, "Dear Friends," n.d.

109. Bongsoo Park contends that Japanese colonialism also affected the racialization of mixed-race orphans. She explains that the Allied Powers worked in collaboration with Japan in constructing a notion of Koreanness that placed them below whites and the Japanese on the racial hierarchy. This, along with the implementation of the U.S. racial order in camptowns, "ultimately shaped racial thinking in Korea, through which the GI [mixed-race] babies were excluded from national polity and community in Korea, and differential treatments of half-white and half-back GI babies ensued in the United States" (15–16). For more information about how processes of racialization in South Korea and the United States shaped the racialization of mixed-race or GI babies, see Park, "Intimate Encounters, Racial Frontiers: Stateless GI Babies in South Korea and the United States, 1953–1965" (Ph.D. diss., University of Minnesota, 2010).

110. ELH to WCK.

111. Holt Adoption Program Inc., "Newsletter October and November, 1962," 4.

112. Ibid., 1–2.

113. Ibid., 8. See also Holt, *Bring My Sons from Afar*, 140.

114. Homi Bhabha, *The Location of Culture* (London: Routledge, 1994), 86.

115. Holt Adoption Program Inc., "Newsletter October and November 1962," 1.

116. Bhabha, *Location of Culture*, 85–92. Bhabha states that "colonial mimicry is the desire for a reformed, recognizable Other . . . that the discourse of mimicry must continually produce its slippage, its excess, its difference" (86). In other words, the project of mimicry is not to create an exact replication. Not only is this an impossible task, but it would also defeat the purpose of colonial discourse, as mimicry relies on a reformation that assures that the Other remains recognizable. This demand for recognition (to be recognized as different) is what feeds mimicry, as the recognizable difference of the Other justifies the continued reformation and discipline of the Other.

117. Mi Ok Song Bruining, "A Few Words from Another Left-Handed Adopted Korean Lesbian," in *Seeds from a Silent Tree: An Anthology by Korean Adoptees*, ed. Tonya Bishoff and Jo Rankin (San Diego: Pandal Press, 1997), 66.

118. Jane Jeong Trenka, *The Language of Blood: A Memoir* (St. Paul, Minn.: Borealis, 2003), 207.

119. Bhabha, *Location of Culture*, 86.

120. Holt Adoption Program Inc., "Dear Adoptive Applicants," n.d., p. 2, ISS-USA Papers, Box 10, File "Independent Adoptions, 1968–1972, Vol. 4," SWHA, Minneapolis, Minn.

121. Foucault, *Discipline and Punish*, 139, 140.

122. J. Calvitt Clarke to Harry Holt, April 30, 1959, ISS-USA Papers, Box 10, File "Children—Independent Adoption Schemes, Harry Holt, 1958–1959, Vol. 2," SWHA, Minneapolis, Minn.

123. *Preplacement care* is a phrase used by ISS. ISS procedures varied significantly from HAP. For example, after the birth mother signed the release form, the child remained with his or her birth mother until the final stages of processing. During this final stage, the child left the birth mother and was placed in an institution for preplacement care. Preplacement care involved the last-minute preparations that equipped the child for the journey and a new life overseas. It lasted about two weeks.

124. Cherney, "Visit to Korea—June 23–July 9, 1965," 17.

125. Ibid.

126. Traditionally, the Korean style of eating consists of sitting on the floor and eating with chopsticks and a spoon.

127. Cho, *Haunting the Korean Diaspora*, 140.

128. Holt Adoption Program Inc., "Newsletter May–June 1965," 5.

129. Holt Adoption Program Inc., "1963 New Years Greetings," 10. In Christian discourse, the soul and body reflect each other. Indeed, Richard Dyer points out that Christianity is a "religion whose sensibility is focused on the body." The body attains significance because it functions as the vessel in which the spirit, or soul, resides. Therefore, the meticulous regulation of the body is congruent with the meticulous governance over the orphan's soul. See Richard Dyer, *White* (London: Routledge, 1997), 15, 16.

130. Since the beginning of his program, HAP's policy was "to place as many children as we can in truly Christian homes." See "Newsletter May–June 1965," 2. In order to ensure that only Christian parents adopted, HAP required prospective families to fill out a form entitled "Family Information." At the bottom of the form, it reads, "If you are Christians, please give a brief statement of personal faith on back of card." See Holt Adoption Program Inc., "Family Information," ISS-USA Papers, Box 10, File "Children—Independent Adoption Schemes, Harry Holt, 1955–1957, Vol.1," SWHA, Minneapolis, Minn. This strict policy of placing orphans in only born-again Christian homes became more lax as the years went by. See John Adams, "From Mr. Adams" in "Newsletter July–August 1967," 8, ISS-USA Papers, Box 10, File "Children—Independent Adoption Schemes, Harry Holt, 1960–1963, Vol. 3," SWHA, Minneapolis, Minn.

131. Holt Adoption Program Inc., "1965 Annual Report," 3.

132. Louis O'Conner Jr., "From the Director's Desk," in "1966 New Year's Greetings," 2.

133. Ibid.

134. "6122nd Wing Revisits Korea Orphanage," *Pacific Stars and Stripes,* December 16, 1951, reprinted in Korean War National Museum, www.koreanchildren.org.

135. "Letter Home Helps Warm Tots," *Pacific Stars and Stripes,* November 18, 1952, reprinted in Korean War National Museum, www.koreanchildren.org.

136. "Color TV Used to Aid ROK Waifs," *Pacific Stars and Stripes,* November 3, 1953, reprinted in Korean War National Museum, www.koreanchildren.org.

137. "Epidemic Control Unit (USN), Ullong-Do Korea," July 13, 1952, Department of Defense, U.S. Army Audiovisual Center, Motion Picture, Sound, and Video Records, Record Group 111, National Archives at College Park. After some of the boys distribute Bibles, they sit on the ground, two rows deep and in the shape of a large rectangle. They bow their heads in prayer. Later on, we see the boys stand up as they take turns quoting scripture. Although this film is silent, the context of the scene and the brevity in which each child stands to talk suggest that they are probably reciting a short verse of scripture they memorized.

138. "First Faith, Then Food for Waifs," *Pacific Stars and Stripes,* December 4, 1953, reprinted in Korean War National Museum, www.koreanchildren.org.

139. Oh, "New Kind of Missionary Work," 162.

140. Ibid., 168.

5. "I Wanted My Head to Be Removed"

1. Trenka, *Language of Blood,* 118.

2. David Eng, "Transnational Adoption and Queer Diasporas," *Social Text* 21, no. 3 (2003): 3–4.

3. Ibid., 3–4, 33.

4. I draw on Janet Jakobsen to articulate the distinctions between norms, normativity, and the normal: "Normativity is a field of power, a set of relations that can be thought of as a network of norms, that forms the possibilities for and limits of action. Norms are the imperatives that materialize particular bodies and actions. . . . The normal

could be simply the average, the everyday, or the commonsensical, but norms and the normal can also become hooked together so as to make the average not only normal but normative" (517). Normativity acts as a rubric in which norms and the normal have become infused with power. Put another way, norms are actions, behaviors, practices, and so on that have been codified as normal (taken for granted, obvious, natural). The regime of power that sanctions all this is called normativity. See Janet Jakobsen, "Queer Is? Queer Does? Normativity and the Problem of Resistance," *GLQ* 4, no. 4 (1998): 517–18.

5. It is precisely the successful history in which Korean adoption has been able to emulate the white heterobiological nuclear family that has allowed nonnormative couples to achieve a semblance of a normal family through Asian transnational adoption. Indeed, Eng, in "Transnational Adoption," points out that Asian transnational adoption has enabled white lesbians and gays access to normative structures of family and kinship through the Asian child, thus allowing them to engage fully in robust citizenship.

6. Ibid., 33.

7. Michael Warner, ed., *Fear of a Queer Planet: Queer Politics and Social Theory* (Minneapolis: University of Minnesota Press, 1993), xxvi. According to Warner, this is why *queer* in *queer theory* gains its "critical edge" because it "defin[es] itself against the normal rather than the heterosexual" (xxvi).

8. I define white normativity as a field of power that sanctions whiteness as the norm, making whiteness the standard upon which everything else is judged. See Jakobsen, "Queer Is?," 517.

9. I would like to thank Grace Hong for helping me clarify and articulate this definition of *queer*.

10. Cathy J. Cohen, "Punks, Bulldaggers, and Welfare Queens: The Radical Potential of Queer Politics?" *GLQ* 3 (1997): 453–57.

11. I use "Jane" when I refer to the protagonist in *The Language of Blood*. I use "Trenka" when referring to the author, Jane Jeong Trenka.

12. The primary readership of this newsletter included adoptive parents, prospective adoptive parents, and religious and social organizations that were on their mailing list.

13. Dong Soo Kim, "Intercountry Adoptions: A Study of Self-Concept of Adolescent Korean Children Who Were Adopted by American Families" (Ph.D. diss., University of Chicago, 1976), 62.

14. Although some adoption agencies now allow gay and lesbian couples, and in some circumstances single parents, to adopt children from overseas, the prevailing standard for nearly the entire history of Asian transnational adoption has been that only heterosexual married couples could adopt. HAP, as the agency that founded Korean adoption, was adamant about this point and set the example for other agencies to follow. At present, Korean adoption continues to require heterosexual married couples to adopt. See Kristi Brian, "Choosing Korea: Marketing 'Multiculturalism' to Choosy Adopters," in *International Korean Adoption: A Fifty-Year History of Policy and Practice,* ed. Kathleen Ja Sook Bergquist et al. (New York: Haworth Press, 2007), 67.

15. Holt Adoption Program Inc., "Newsletter May–June 1965," 10, ISS-USA Papers, Box 10, File "Children—Independent Adoption Schemes: Vol. 3 (1960–1963)," SWHA, Minneapolis, Minn.

16. Ibid, 11.

17. Holt Adoption Program Inc., "Newsletter October and November 1962," 1, ISS-USA Papers, Box 10, File "Children—Independent Adoption Schemes: Vol. 3 (1960–1963)," SWHA, Minneapolis, Minn.

18. The strategic placement of photos is powerfully illustrated in Bertha Holt's *Bring My Sons from Afar*. On one page, we see Harry Holt holding an emaciated baby who looks to be near death. The caption alongside this photo reads, "Harry with the Gibb's baby" (38). On the next page is a photo of an attractive married woman (the wedding band on the left hand is clearly visible) with a healthy, beaming little girl in her arms. The caption alongside this photo reads, "Now the Gibb's baby has one of her own" (39). The success of Korean adoption seems undeniable here with this pairing of before-and-after shots. To refer to this mother as "the Gibb's baby" helps to preserve the aura of the miraculous, making her transformation from emaciated infant into a beautiful mother all the more astounding. The markers of success are evident: the adoption of the Gibb's baby has paved the path to marriage and motherhood. See Holt, *Bring My Sons from Afar*, 191.

19. As Grandma Holt explains, this section draws from the numerous photos and letters that their office receives from adoptive parents. As a result, it becomes a "picture gallery of smiling faces from far and near" that reveals "the straight A students, the basketball, swimming, and track champions, music and art talents, the first tooth, the date at the prom, the Eagle Scouts, and the summer jobs. We are delighted with each detail and recall the history that brought about these happy results." See Holt Adoption Program Inc., "Holt Adoption Program Newsletter," 15, no. 1 (January–February 1972), 8, ISS-USA Papers, Box 10, File "Independent Adoptions: Vol. 4 (1968–1972), SWHA, Minneapolis, Minn.

20. *Flower Drum Song* (Universal City, Calif.: Universal Pictures, 1961), VHS.

21. Holt Adoption Program Inc., "Holt Adoption Program Newsletter," 15, no. 7 (January–February 1973), 3, ISS-USA Papers, Box 10, File "Independent Adoptions: Vol. 4 (1968–1972), SWHA, Minneapolis, Minn.

22. Ibid.

23. See, for example, the following issues: "Holt Adoption Program Newsletter," 15, no. 5 (September–October 1972), 3, and "Holt Adoption Program Newsletter," 15, no. 6 (November–December 1972), 2, in ISS-USA Papers, Box 10, File "Independent Adoptions: Vol. 4 (1968–1972), SWHA, Minneapolis, Minn. I was unable to read every newsletter from this period; however, from the newsletters available to me, this was the trend. I contacted the offices of Holt Adoption Program, which is now Holt International Children's Services in Eugene, Oregon, to examine the newsletters missing from the Social Welfare History Archives collection. They refused my request for a research visit. Because a staff member would have to be present with me at all times during my research, they said they didn't have the manpower to escort me. In addition, they would have to find "someone we can trust" to get the materials and make copies. These two things, along with the fact that the newsletters were stored in a secured vault in a separate, climate-controlled building, made it "time-consuming" and inconvenient for them to have me conduct research at their facilities.

24. For more information about militarized sexuality in South Korea, see Cho, *Haunting the Korean Diaspora;* Yuh, *Beyond the Shadow of Camptown;* and Moon, *Sex among Allies.*

25. The musical *Flower Drum Song* illustrates this point nicely. Linda Low proclaims "I Enjoy Being a Girl" at the exact same moment when white feminists are demanding gender equality. The lyrics in this song not only advocate and celebrate traditional gender roles and conventional notions of femininity, but also invite men to see Asian American women as merely bodies to be sexually desired.

26. Trenka, *Language of Blood,* 24.

27. Brian, "Choosing Korea," 67.

28. The practice of delegitimizing nonwhite mothers in favor of reproducing white motherhood has its roots in colonial projects. Beginning with the forced removal of native children from their indigenous communities, race, gender, class, sexuality, and nation have intersected to perpetuate the construction of nonwhite mothers as unfit—not only for reproduction but also for mothering. See Margaret Jacobs, *White Mother to a Dark Race: Settler Colonialism, Maternalism, and the Removal of Indigenous Children in the American West and Australia* (Lincoln: University of Nebraska Press, 2009); Trenka, Oparah, and Shin, *Outsiders Within;* Twila Perry, "Transracial and International Adoption: Mothers, Hierarchy, Race, and Feminist Legal Theory," *Yale Journal of Law and Feminism* 10 (1998): 101–64; and Marre and Briggs, *International Adoption.*

29. The infertile white couple is nonnormative because their inability to reproduce puts them outside the established gender norms; however, unlike the figure of the Korean birth mother, focusing on their nonnormativity would not strengthen the case of Korean adoption as a normative kinship structure.

30. This narrative that situates single Korean mothers as unfit to raise their babies is also used to persuade Korean birth mothers to give up their children. Indeed, Trenka of TRACK (Truth and Reconciliation for the Adoption Community of Korea) notes that the Korean government makes transnational adoption the easiest choice for unwed Korean birth mothers to make. Of the twenty-seven unwed mothers' facilities (hospitals) that exist in South Korea today, thirteen are run by international adoption agencies. This direct line between hospitals and adoption agencies has produced what Trenka calls baby farms, as these facilities directly supply adoptive agencies with babies from unwed Korean mothers. See Jane Jeong Trenka, "A Million Living Ghosts: Truth and Reconciliation for the Adoption Community of Korea (TRACK)" (lecture, University of Minnesota, Minneapolis, February 11, 2010).

31. Bongsoo Park, "Intimate Encounters, Racial Frontiers: Stateless GI Babies in South Korea and the United States, 1953–1965," (Ph.D. diss., University of Minnesota, 2010), 132–33.

32. John Adams, "Annual Report for 1971," February 1972, 3, ISS-USA Papers, Box 10, File "Independent Adoptions: Vol. 4 (1968–1972), SWHA, Minneapolis, Minn.

33. Trenka, *Language of Blood,* 198. Ironically, it is precisely the ways in which the Asian female body has been figured as a prostitute that made Jane susceptible to racialized sexual violence in the United States. For example, Jane describes being propositioned by an Asiaphile at the grocery store in the canned goods section. She even discusses at length the semester in which she was stalked by a fellow college student. During their first encounter, he tells her, "You're nothing but a Korean in a white man's society. You're a gook, you're a chink" (73). Several months later, he was caught with a "Rape and Murder

Kit" (80) and confessed that "he purchased video camera equipment so that he could record his exploits of raping and killing the intended victim so that he could further enjoy the experience again and again later on" (76). According to Eun Kyung Min, "This was a terrifying riposte to her adoptive parents' failure to acknowledge her racial difference" (128). See Eun Kyung Min, "The Daughter's Exchange in Jane Jeong Trenka's *The Language of Blood*," *Social Text* 26, no. 1 (2008): 115–33.

34. Tammy Tolle, dir., *Searching for Go-Hyang* (New York: Women Make Movies, 1998), VHS.

35. Trenka, *Language of Blood*, 121, 198.

36. Ibid., 121–22.

37. Ibid., 121.

38. Ibid., 121, 122.

39. In spite of her adoptive mother's paranoia, Carol turned out to be the picture of proper sexual behavior. In high school, Carol dated just one boy: a son of the carpenter who built the Brauers' house and who was preapproved by her parents. After college graduation, she married a coworker, moved to the suburbs, and had a baby.

40. Adams, "Annual Report for 1971," 3.

41. Yellow desire is precisely what makes this a viable project. Historically, this erasing process has been seemingly more successful for Korean children than, say, for African Americans or American Indians. To be sure, the popularity of Korean adoption hinges on this fantasy that Asian bodies are more assimilable into the body politic than these other bodies. The racial hierarchy in the United States has worked to naturalize the racial order wherein East Asian bodies are perceived as more readily able to achieve honorary whiteness than, say, black Americans. This is why Korean children, and now Chinese children, are considered more suitable for this project.

42. Trenka, *Language of Blood*, 16.

43. Ibid., 17.

44. Louis Althusser, "Ideology and Ideological State Apparatuses (Notes towards an Investigation)," in *Lenin and Philosophy, and Other Essays*, trans. Ben Brewster (New York: Monthly Review Press, 1972). Althusser defines interpellation, or "hailing," as an operation of subject formation: "Ideology 'acts' or 'functions' in such a way that it 'recruits' subjects among the individuals (it recruits them all), or 'transforms' the individuals into subjects (it transforms them all) by that very precise operation which I have called *interpellation* or hailing" (174). He goes on to construct a "theoretical theatre" that reveals the process of hailing: a person (usually behind someone) yells out, "Hey, you there!" Inevitably, an individual turns around, knowing that the hail was for him or her, recognizing that "Hey, you!" was directed toward him or her. In recognizing and answering the hail, the subject is formed (174–75).

45. Ibid., 174.

46. Ibid., 176.

47. Ibid.

48. Ibid., 175.

49. For more examples on how projects of normalization and assimilation have enacted and justified all sorts of violence on nonwhite communities, see Brenda Child,

Boarding School Seasons (Lincoln: University of Nebraska, 2000); Anne Anlin Cheng, *The Melancholy of Race: Psychoanalysis, Assimilation, and Hidden Grief* (New York: Oxford University Press, 2001); Gloria Anzaldúa, *Borderlands/La Frontera* (San Francisco: Aunt Lute Books, 1987); and *Rabbit Proof Fence* (Burbank, Calif.: Miramax Home Entertainment, 2003), DVD.

50. Trenka, *Language of Blood,* 207.

51. Ibid., 17.

52. Ibid.

53. Ibid., 27.

54. See, for example, Deann Borshay Liem, *First Person Plural* (San Francisco: National Asian American Telecommunications Association, 2000), DVD; Me-K Ahn, *Living in Halftones* (New York: Third World Newsreel, 1994), VHS; and Helen Lee, *Subrosa* (New York: Women Make Movies, 2000), VHS. In all three of these films, disjointed memories and images from the Korean adoptees' past life in South Korea, as well as Korean words, erupt in their dream world or subconscious.

55. Judith Butler, *The Psychic Life of Power: Theories in Subjection* (Stanford, Calif.: Stanford University Press, 1997), 88.

56. Quoted in ibid., 97.

57. Trenka, *Language of Blood,* 118.

58. Ibid., 113.

59. I say this because Korean children who are adopted by white adoptive parents are forced and expected to become white. A recent study by Evan B. Donaldson Adoption Institute concluded that nearly 80 percent of Korean adoptees have either identified as white or have wanted to be white at some point in their lives. See Ron Nixon, "Adopted from Korea and in Search of Identity," *New York Times,* November 8, 2009, www.nytimes.com. Despite the incorporation of multiculturalism in the 1990s, this recent study suggests the limits of multiculturalism in nurturing an adoptee identity that is not rooted in whiteness. Multiculturalism—through Korean cultural camps and roots tours— is not enough because this particular kind of multiculturalism preserves whiteness as the normative center. See Joyce M. Bell and Douglas Hartmann, "Diversity in Everyday Discourse: The Cultural Ambiguities and Consequences of 'Happy Talk,'" *American Sociological Review* 72 (December 2007): 895–914. In addition, Kristi Brian points out that adoption agencies practice a brand of multiculturalism where race becomes conflated with culture, which allows both adoptive agents and adoptive parents to evade racial politics and white privilege. See Brian, "Choosing Korea," 71.

60. Trenka, *Language of Blood,* 35.

61. Ibid. On the basis of their recent study, the Evan B. Donaldson Adoption Institute hopes that "their work would guide policymakers, parents and adoption agencies in helping the current generation of children adopted from Asian countries to form healthy identities" by exposing the dangers of treating these children "without regard for their native culture" (Nixon, "Adopted from Korea," 1–2).

62. Trenka, *Language of Blood,* 59.

63. Ibid., 59–60.

64. Ibid., 66.

65. Ibid., 190.

66. Queer of color theorists have repudiated the epistemology of the closet and its corresponding discourse of coming out by identifying the ways in which they privilege the experiences of the Western white gay male. For example, Martin Manalansan reveals how the closet narrative presupposes a Euro-American liberal subject whose identity formation is situated within a "Western-centered developmental teleology, with 'gay' as its culminating stage" (488). In addition, Gayatri Gopinath points out that because coming out relies on an economy of visibility, the closet narrative produces normative, Western, and imperialist understanding of queer identity. See Martin Manalansan, "In the Shadows of Stonewall: Examining Gay Transnational Politics and the Diasporic Dilemma," in *Politics of Culture in the Shadow of Capital,* ed. Lisa Lowe and David Lloyd (Durham, N.C.: Duke University Press, 1997), 485–505; and Gayatri Gopinath, "Homoeconomics: Queer Sexualities in a Transnational Frame," in *Burning Down the House: Recycling Domesticity,* ed. Rosemary Marangoly George (Boulder, Colo.: Westview Press, 1998), 102–24.

67. I want to thank Jigna Desai for suggesting the phrase "coming to" in theorizing Jane's response to the regulatory codes of Korean adoption.

68. Trenka, *Language of Blood,* 193.

69. Carol recounts to Jane that even though she was four and a half years old when she left South Korea for adoption, her visit back revived no memories: "I couldn't believe I didn't remember places or people or anything. You'd think I would; four-and-a-half-year-old kids have memories. . . . And our mother was so mad at me! She couldn't understand why I didn't speak Korean, she was mad because I didn't like the kimchi that she said I used [to] beg her to make . . . And I didn't know how to use chopsticks, so she took them and flung them across the room" (123–24). The search for origins and identity is never resolved, even in the more positive experience that Jane encountered.

70. Trenka, *Language of Blood,* 191.

71. Ibid., 201. A year and a half passes before they speak again; it is to tell them that she is getting married. Interestingly, the ultimate symbol of heteronormativity does the work of reuniting Jane with her adoptive parents. Also, her marrying a white man may have made her more acceptable in her parent's eyes, or perhaps signaled to them that Jane was reclaiming whiteness and therefore her adoptive family.

72. Ibid., 167.

73. Ibid.

74. The single word *say* is an abbreviation for the phrase, "Watch what you're saying." It is a popular and useful tactic used by parents in the Midwest to simultaneously shame and discipline the child speaker when he or she has overstepped the perceived line of respect between parent and child.

75. Trenka, *Language of Blood,* 167.

76. Ibid.

77. Ibid., 175.

78. I want to thank Grace Hong for elucidating this point to me.

79. Fifteen-year-old Korean adoptee Vicki Olds, who is vying for the title of Miss Teenage Sacramento, puts it this way: "Your real parent is one who loves you and takes

care of you." See Holt Adoption Program Inc., "Holt Adoption Program Newsletter," 15, no. 7 (January–February 1973), 3.

80. Borshay Liem, *First Person Plural*. See also Min, "Daughter's Exchange," 117–25, and Eng, "Transnational Adoption," 23–33, for a psychoanalytic explanation for why this is the case.

81. Trenka, *Language of Blood*, 180.

82. Ibid., 202.

83. Ibid., 181.

84. Ibid., 198.

85. Ibid., 204.

86. Ibid.

87. Ibid., 204–5.

88. Ibid., 203–4.

89. See José Esteban Muñoz, *Disidentifications: Queers of Color and the Performance of Politics* (Minneapolis: University of Minnesota Press, 1999). Muñoz defines disidentification as "a strategy that works on and against dominant ideology. Instead of buckling under the pressures of dominant ideology (identification, assimilation) or attempting to break free of its inescapable sphere (counteridentification, utopianism), this 'working on and against' is a strategy that tries to transform a cultural logic from within, always laboring to enact permanent structural change while at the same time valuing the importance of local or everyday struggles of resistance" (11–12). Disidentification is not about picking and choosing. It is not about identifying with the productive aspects of dominant ideology and counteridentifying against the harmful aspects of dominant ideology. Instead, it is about reworking and reinvesting new life into something that is already present. Thus, disidentification is about revision rather than rejection, recycling rather than disposing.

90. My use of the terms *recycle* and *reuse* is informed by Muñoz's theorization of disidentification.

91. Trenka, *Language of Blood*, 208.

92. Ibid.

93. Ibid.

Epilogue

1. Michel Foucault argues that rather than "restor[ing] an unbroken continuity," genealogy "fragments what was thought unified" in order to reveal the heterogeneous and contradictory conditions in which discourses are created (146–47). Foucault, "Nietzsche, Genealogy, and History," 139–64.

2. Ibid., 148.

3. Ibid., 146.

4. North Korean Refugee Adoption Act of 2012, HR 1464, 112th Cong., 2nd sess. (September 12, 2012): 2, reprinted in Library of Congress, "Bill Text Versions 112th Congress (2011–2012): H.R. 1464," www.gpo.gov.

5. Christine Hong and Jennifer Kwon Dobbs, *The Case Against the North Korean Refugee Adoption Act of 2011* (Los Angeles: Korean Policy Institute, 2012). This brief

was distributed to policy makers on August 6, 2012, one month before the House vote that took place on September 12, 2012. At the time of this writing, there are four versions of this bill. Hong and Kwon Dobbs are referring to the first version of the bill, which was entitled the North Korean Refugee Adoption Act of 2011 because the 2012 version had not come out by the time they wrote their policy brief.

6. Ibid.

7. Ibid.

8. Benjamin, "Theses on the Philosophy of History," 255, 257. The "state of emergency" is the persistence of Korean adoption after multiple attempts to end it and the ways in which U.S. military occupation and national division continue to affect the lives of Koreans all over the world. Although outside the scope of this book, the state of emergency could also include the increased trafficking of nonwhite children into American homes under the auspices of humanitarian rescue (e.g., Haiti and now possibly the Chinese–North Korean border) and the expansion of U.S. empire under the auspices of militarized humanitarian in Iraq, Afghanistan, and Haiti.

9. Ibid., 262.

10. Hillary Clinton, "America's Pacific Century," *Foreign Policy*, November 2011, 2, www.foreignpolicy.com.

11. Amy Kaplan, "Imperial Melancholy in America," *Raritan* 28, no. 3 (Winter 2009): 13–31.

12. Clinton, "America's Pacific Century," 1.

13. Ibid., 3, 11.

14. Kaplan, "Imperial Melancholy," 31.

15. Cho, *Haunting the Korean Diaspora*, 23.

16. Clinton, "America's Pacific Century," 10.

17. Dreamland Arts (www.dreamlandarts.com) is a family-owned and -operated theater in St. Paul, Minnesota. Zaraawar Mistry, who owns this theater, directed these two shows.

18. Adoption scholars have pointed out this relationship between adoption and human trafficking; see David M. Smolin, "Child Laundering and the Hague Convention on Intercountry Adoption: The Future and Past of Intercountry Adoption," *University of Louisville Law Review* 48, no. 3 (2010): 441–98, and "Child Laundering as Exploitation: Applying Anti-trafficking Norms to Intercountry Adoption under the Coming Hague Regime," *Vermont Law Review* 32, no. 1 (2007): 1–55.

INDEX

Adams, John E., 106–7. *See also* Holt
    International Children's Services/Holt
    Adoption Program (HAP)
"Adjustment of Foreign Children in
    Their Adoptive Homes," 6. *See also*
    child welfare; DiVirgilio, Letitia
"Adjustment of Korean-American Chil-
    dren in American Adoptive Homes,"
    6. *See also* Valk, Margaret A.
Adolfson, Nathan, 8, 9
"'Adopted' Korean Girl Loves Officer,
    Now Happy," 60. See also *Pacific Stars
    and Stripes*
"Adopted Territory: Transnational
    Korean Adoptees and the Politics of
    Belonging," 14. *See also* Kim, Eleana
adoptee/adoptive child, 2–3, 5, 7, 9–10,
    12–15; adjustment, 6–7; adolescent, 7;
    adult, 7–8, 10, 16, 133, 156, 159–60;
    art, 8–10, 12, 42, 47, 122, 138, 158–59;
    assimilation, 5, 10, 13, 18–19, 44, 87–
    88, 96, 117, 122, 125, 131, 134–38, 142,
    144–46, 151–52, 155; emergence of,
    10–11, 16, 45, 86–87; identity, 6, 8–13,
    127–28, 147; LGBTQ, 129; memoir, 9,
    122, 133–34, 147; militarizing of, 40;
    nonnormativity, 125, 128, 130–31, 136;
    normalizing of, 125, 127, 133, 142,
    146, 151, 155–56; subjectivity, 7, 9,
    11–12, 16–19, 101–2, 128, 131

adoption: agencies, 11, 17, 101, 107, 117,
    121, 144; alternative narrative, 9, 19,
    131; domestic, 30, 71; dominant narra-
    tive, 3, 9, 13, 19, 94, 152, 155–56, 161;
    emergence of, 10–11, 16, 19, 22, 30–
    31, 35, 42, 74, 78, 105; gendering of, 1,
    17, 45, 74, 87; genealogies of, 2–4, 6,
    10–11, 13, 15–17, 19, 21, 45, 131, 137,
    155–56, 160–61; history, 2, 6, 8–12;
    imperialism of, 1, 17; industry of, 5;
    militarizing of, 1, 14, 40; normativity,
    5, 18, 139, 141; origins of, 10–11;
    proxy, 88, 106, 108; queer formation
    of, 4–5, 18, 99, 128, 130, 133, 139,
    148–53, 155, 158; racializing of, 1, 17,
    45, 74, 87; sexualizing of, 1, 17, 45;
    studies, 6–9, 13–14; transnational,
    7–9, 13–15, 23, 40, 46, 71, 73, 75, 86,
    88, 94, 100, 103, 105, 108, 121, 128,
    130, 134–35, 138, 141, 146, 158,
    167n2; transracial, 8, 13. *See also*
    adoptee/adoptive child; orphan
adoptive agent, 13, 115, 128, 131–32, 140
adoptive parent, 3, 7–8, 13, 18, 44, 93,
    101, 106, 113, 128, 130–32, 134, 138,
    148–50, 152–53
Advisory Committee on Voluntary
    Foreign Aid, 33
Afghanistan, 161; war, 158
Agamben, Giorgio, 78

International Children's Services/Holt
Adoption Program (HAP)
"Holt Family Portrait," viii (image), 1–5,
12, 15, 71, 73, 100–101
Holt International Children's
Services/Holt Adoption Program
(HAP), viii, 7, 17–18, 86–88, 101, 102,
105–7, 112–15, 117–20, 122–23, 128,
132–34, 136–38, 140, 142, 145. See also
Holt, Harry; Il San orphanage
homo sacer, 78
Hong, Christine, 157. See also Dobbs,
Jennifer Kwon
Hope Inc. Orphans' Home of Korea, 63
Howell, Signe, 78
"How to Be a Korean Woman," 160–61
Hubinette, Tobias, 13–14, 30, 88, 170n34
humanism, militaristic, 34
humanitarianism, 33, 39–40, 156; aid,
27–29, 31–38, 41, 42, 61, 66, 74, 76,
94, 98, 101, 104; militarized, 22–23,
32–35, 38–45, 47, 70, 74, 79, 81, 84, 87,
94, 100, 155, 161. See also Grewell,
Inderpal; Žižek, Slavoj
human trafficking, 160

Il San, South Korea, 110
Il San orphanage, 18, 102, 108–12, 113–
14, 118–22, 124, 128, 156. See also
Holt International Children's
Services/Holt Adoption Program
immigration, 9, 111, 115, 188n58
Immigration Act (1924), 74, 88, 91,
183n35. See also Asian: exclusion
Immigration Act (1965), 88
Immigration and Nationality Act (1961),
88
imperialism, 1, 9, 13, 15, 17, 19, 155. See
also United States: imperialism
Incheon, South Korea, 52
Interdepartmental Committee on Korea
(ICK), 24, 25, 27–28, 171n3
International Social Services—United
States of America Branch Inc.

(ISS-USA), 6, 81, 86–87, 105–8, 113,
117–18, 168n9
Iowa, 135
Iraq, 161
Iraq War, 158
Isaac, Allan Punzalan, 53
Isaacs, Harold, 99

Ja, Park Song, 116, 135
Japan, 6, 23, 25, 27, 75, 91–92, 94, 158;
colonialism, 23, 26, 29
Japanese Doll Festival, 92
Japanese Imperial Army, 45
Japanese internment camps, 75. See also
Executive Order 9066
Jeffie, Lee, 113, 115
Johnny, Lee, 120
Joint Commission, 23, 26, 172n17. See
also Korean War; Soviet Union; United
States
Jones, H. R., 124
Joseon dynasty, 30, 77

Kaplan, Amy, 158
Kim, Dong Choon, 23
Kim, Dong Soo, 7, 133
Kim, Eleana, 9, 14, 170n34
Kim, Jodi, 12, 46, 77–78, 88
Kim, Jung-Woo, 30
Kimpo Airport, 145
Kincaid, James, 61, 62
Kirk, William T., 107
Klein, Christina, 4, 73, 76, 82, 84, 90, 96.
See also Cold War Orientalism
Korea/Korean: adoption studies, 6, 8,
11–12, 130; communism, 55, 83–84;
customs, 133; division of, 70; folk
songs, 57; government, 23, 28, 58, 89;
independence, 24–26, 30; language,
133, 146, 152; Republic of, 28;
women: exploitation of, 42–45;
women: gendering of, 42, 44; women:
racialization of, 42–44; women: sexu-
alizing of, 42–44; women: subjectivity,

SOOJIN PATE is visiting assistant professor in American studies at Macalester College.